POLICE ETHICS
A Matter of Character

SECOND EDITION

POLICE ETHICS
A Matter of Character

SECOND EDITION

Douglas W. Perez, Ph.D.
Plattsburgh State University

J. Alan Moore, Ph.D.
Lyndon State College

DELMAR
CENGAGE Learning·

Australia • Brazil • Japan • Korea • Mexico • Singapore • Spain • United Kingdom • United States

DELMAR
CENGAGE Learning®

**Police Ethics:
A Matter of Character,
Second Edition**
Douglas W. Perez and
J. Alan Moore

Vice President, Editorial:
Dave Garza

Director of Learning Solutions:
Sandy Clark

Senior Acquisitions Editor:
Shelley Esposito

Managing Editor: Larry Main

Senior Product Manager:
Anne Orgren

Editorial Assistant:
Diane Chrysler

Vice President, Marketing:
Jennifer Baker

Marketing Director:
Deborah Yarnell

Senior Marketing Manager:
Mark Linton

Marketing Coordinator:
Erin DeAngelo

Production Manager:
Mark Bernard

Senior Content Project
Manager: Kathryn B. Kucharek

Senior Art Director: Joy Kocsis

For product information and
technology assistance, contact us at **Cengage Learning
Customer & Sales Support, 1-800-354-9706**
For permission to use material from this text or product,
submit all requests online at **www.cengage.com/permissions.**
Further permissions questions can be e-mailed to
permissionrequest@cengage.com

Library of Congress Control Number: 2011935575

ISBN-13: 978-1-111-54451-5

ISBN-10: 1-111-54451-4

Delmar
5 Maxwell Drive
Clifton Park, NY 12065-2919
USA

Cengage Learning is a leading provider of customized learning
solutions with office locations around the globe, including
Singapore, the United Kingdom, Australia, Mexico, Brazil, and Japan.
Locate your local office at: **international.cengage.com/region**

Cengage Learning products are represented in Canada by
Nelson Education, Ltd.

To learn more about Delmar, visit **www.cengage.com/delmar**

Purchase any of our products at your local college store or at our
preferred online store **www.cengagebrain.com**

Printed in the United States of America
ACC LIBRARY SERVICES AUSTIN, TX

For our children,
Annie and Elizabeth

and

Dylan, Maria, and Michaéla

CONTENTS

· ·

PART II

PART IV

PREFACE

It has been nine years since we wrote the first edition of *Police Ethics: A Matter of Character*, and ongoing change continues in the world of policing. The movement toward genuine professionalism, spurred on by the development of community oriented policing (COP), has made tremendous strides. This new philosophy has become accepted by more and more police officers and leaders, and equally supported by increasing numbers of politicians. As a consequence, in a steadily expanding number of jurisdictions American police work is slowly morphing into something new. The previously accepted notion that the police could not do much about crime in a proactive fashion is giving way to the idea that the police can impact in a positive way upon the quality of life on the American street. Various strategies extrapolated from the initial ideas included in the COP concept have taken hold all over America. Driven by the ideas first set forth by James Q. Wilson and George Kelling in their now famous article "Broken Windows" (1982), COP is changing police work in the direction of joining the ranks of America's professions.

Everything about police work is in flux. Those candidates selected to be today's police officers continue to be better educated and trained than their predecessors. Two-year and even four-year college degrees are more and more often required at the entry level. College and university programs of study in criminal justice continue to expand and are moving in the direction of becoming more sociologically based. The criminal justice major is the fastest growing major on American college campuses and in many places has joined the ranks of those majors enjoying the greatest popularity. Rather than emphasizing the nuts and bolts of police work, such college programs have begun to more appropriately prepare police officers for a world where an understanding of psychology, sociology, politics, law, and forensics is considered to be an essential aspect of modern professionalism. Police administrators and leaders today are more often directed by scientific study of how the police should be organized, how all levels of training should proceed, and what the police should be expected to do. The process of instituting this new philosophy is expanding and gathering speed as time goes on.

Of course, change is slow because it involves changing police cultures around the country, something that police officers, police leaders, politicians, and knowledgeable citizens all understand takes time and patience. Especially in places where the history of police operations includes systematic corruption or a history of antagonism toward higher education, the process of transforming such a powerful and isolated subculture into something alien to the police officers of the past is an incremental, halting, inexact, and uneven undertaking. Nevertheless, COP's new philosophy is here to stay. It has thrust police work into a new era of understanding about what the job entails and how a modern, educated, sophisticated officer corps behaves and operates.

In the original book, we put forth the idea that ethics are not something to be considered independently of the process of becoming a competent police officer. We noted that an ethical frame of reference circumscribes the entire endeavor of policing. We presented the idea that training—academy training in particular—should proceed amid an ongoing, ever-present understanding of the importance of ethical conduct. We suggested that it was time for police ethics to be studied from the very beginning of the officer's career, and in a positive way. The traditional approach to police ethics had focused on teaching young officers how "not to screw up." In a real sense this developed an understanding of police behavior in a negative and backward way. And it was certainly not enough for today's professionalism.

Not being a bad officer (a "screw-up") is nowhere near a high enough standard of practice for today's police. Today's officers should instead be involved in an ongoing consideration of ethics from a positivist perspective. At the very outset of their street experience they should focus on being a good officer (and person), as this was and is of primary importance. Because the police are the point persons of the justice system, and therefore of the setting that makes a good life possible, the internal tie between an ethical point of view and professional competence is more fundamental to police work than to practically any other profession. This was the central theme of our discussion.

But there was something else. In setting up our entire discussion, we suggested that today's police officers constitute a new breed, a new blue line of sorts that is perfectly capable of reading about, reflecting upon, discussing, debating, and understanding the more esoteric nuances of philosophical debates about ethics that date back more than two millennia. Up until very recent times, it was considered to be a waste of time to engage in discussion of such ideas with police officers. But a once blue-collar occupation is morphing into a profession. Police officers with college educations behind them are taking the streets in greater numbers, and police training in the academy is moving inexorably away from the old-fashioned, military-like, "stress-related" experience and toward a more collegial and therefore educationally productive method of teaching and learning. As this happens, those young officers who are engaged in discussions about police ethics are increasingly prone to understand their subculture, professional milieu, and, indeed, themselves in an insightful, analytical, and sophisticated way.

NEW TO THIS EDITION

This second edition of *Police Ethics* includes several substantive changes and additions. First, it includes more boxes with both contemporary and historical examples used for the purposes of illustrating the various concepts that we discuss herein. The ethical questions and ethical dilemmas that face police officers every day on the street are always replete with frustrating paradoxes, difficult to discern subtlety, and troubling nuance. As time goes on and police professionalism expands, driven as it is by the requirements of COP, more often than in the past the contemporary world of policing is visited by a juxtaposition of its checkered past and its bright future. Thus, there is always a wealth of examples from which to choose when illustrating the ethical problems of the modern officer.

Second, we have placed a key terms list at the end of each chapter to aid the reader with his or her journey through the material. This expansion, combined with new topics for discussion, will further illuminate each chapter. The original idea of creating a book that would have a chapter for each of the 15 weeks of the standard police academy and/or the 15 weeks of the standard college semester is still our goal. This extra material is aimed at making each chapter a synoptic piece in and of itself, and thus a subject for a week's worth of reading, reflecting, and discussion.

Third, we have included an ethical scenario and writing exercise at the end of each chapter. These are included in an effort to expand the usefulness of the book for the individual as well as to provide some creative ideas for the instructor. Whether it be in the environment of the college classroom or as a part of the police academy experience, we hope these aids will further enhance the book's utility.

Finally, the overall organization has been compressed in some places and expanded in others, in an effort to shed further light upon the subject matter. We include a separate chapter (Chapter 3) on "The Nature of Police Work" to illustrate the paradoxes of police work in specific relief. Rather than just a couple of paragraphs in the introductory chapters, we have decided to feature this discussion in order to illuminate the field for the undergraduate student and the academy cadet and to remind the experienced practitioner of the troublesome dynamics around which the police experience revolves. It is our belief that we needed more in the way of coverage of the paradoxes of police work at the outset, lest we dive into discussion about ethics without properly considering what the job itself entails.

Chapters 5, 6, 7, 8, and 9 have been enhanced due to the positive feedback we obtained from the first work. These chapters outline classical discussions about character and philosophical treatments of ethical frameworks. As is the case immediately above, we have expanded them in an effort to create contiguous, weekly topical areas that draw the reader more deeply through the field of theoretical concerns before the book gets more practical. In constructing our "ethic to live by" in the first book, we created what numerous reviewers have considered to be the premier treatment of the professional ethic for the police. Due to this positive feedback, we have attempted to amplify and distill the concepts here so that the idea has further utility for the contemporary reader.

Chapter 11, too, is new. It includes a discussion about the causes of police deviance that was included briefly in several chapters in the initial work. We felt that this introductory consideration of causal factors was given too little emphasis originally. Equally, we have compressed several short chapters from the first work into Chapter 12 here, a discussion of our typological approach to police misconduct. Hopefully, these changes, when combined with further polish and the additional reflection that nine years brings, will enhance the usefulness of the work of pre-service professionals and experienced practitioners alike.

◉ A WORD ABOUT "PHILOSOPHY"

While our first edition received almost universally positive responses around the country, we did obtain one negative evaluation from an anonymous officer somewhere in America's heartland, and we want to take a moment to engage that piece of feedback as it informs our discussion here. This reviewer wrote that the original book was "full of platitudes" and, thus, that it was just "another example" of a book written about police work that was unrealistic. Well, a platitude is something that is trite, meaningless, or silly that is presented as if it is significant or original. If this is the meaning of our fair reviewer, then we take issue with it.

Because a moral principle is absolutely basic, it can sound like a platitude. But how it sounds is a function of how it is said and also of the frame of mind of the hearer. "Do unto others as you would have them do unto you" or "if you can't say something nice, don't say anything at all" are examples of the kinds of statements that can sound platitudinous. But this is merely because they are truisms that we have heard often (and have stood the test of time). They may very well sound trite, but they are most assuredly neither silly nor meaningless. Given this definition, we are *not* in fact filling this work with platitudes.

But if our anonymous reviewer meant to say that some of the statements of principle we used—such as "first, do no harm"—sound axiomatic or aphoristic or philosophical, then our response to that piece of criticism is that we are delighted to hear it. That is fine with us. Discussions about ethics are about how human beings ought to decide what to do when they are confronted with conflicting conceptualizations of right behavior or of their duty. They are about how the intelligent person approaches making such decisions. Ethical discussions and debates have been about wrestling with such problems for more than 2,000 years. And they are *indeed* axiomatic . . . and aphoristic . . . and philosophical. They include normative thinking in its highest form. They include the stuff that delineates human beings from the animals—to wit, the ability to exercise self-control over our natural drives and propensities in favor of behaving in ways that might not be easy or desirous, but that are morally defensible. Of all the species on planet earth, only human beings have this ability to analyze their own behavior and to act in ways that might be personally costly and difficult but that involve cleaving to the right thing to do. This constitutes the essence of what is involved in the interdependent human experience. Because this is so, it involves the essence of what police officers see and do every day on the street.

Our endeavor all along—from 2002 until now—has been to assume that the contemporary reader will not only be entertained by engaging in such analysis but will also understand how important it is to mull over our notions of right and wrong. And, so, to the reader we offer an admonition of sorts, one that we hope will not dissuade the modern police officer or student of police behavior: "Warning: This Book Contains Philosophy."

—*Doug Perez and Alan Moore*
September 2011
Burlington, Vermont

ACKNOWLEDGMENTS

First, we would like to thank the director of the Institute for Ethics in Public Life at Plattsburgh State University, Tom Moran, and the fellows at the Institute. The concepts included in the original, first edition of the work have been polished and enhanced by the ideas and reflections of everyone there. The appointment to the Institute allowed us a freedom to read, reflect, and write on these subjects that would not otherwise have been possible.

Second, we wish to acknowledge the many hours of editing and discussion that were contributed by our group of loyal reviewers. Tom Moran took time off from his busy schedule running the Institute to review preliminary drafts. Jim Godfrey, full-time police officer and coach, took many hours out of his days and nights to do the same. Jeanne Zimmerman's insight and careful eye for editing were immensely helpful. Betsy Zumwalt Perez, though a dilettante in our field, took time to edit numerous first drafts and to give us an "outsider's" perspective. And finally, Mary Borrelli worked diligently over the second edition's draft.

Rita Latour, the departmental secretary for Sociology and Criminal Justice at Plattsburgh, was our savior on many occasions. Her typing skills and dedication to helping the project reach fruition hastened the completion of the work by several months at least.

This book has been put together after several decades of working with police officers. Through their examples, many officers and police leaders have contributed to the work, albeit indirectly. That is, by being modern professionals, by exhibiting their competence and insight, and by courageously embracing the challenges of police work in an ethical way, they have influenced the work's substance profoundly. Michael Barkhurst, John Gackowski, Skip Stevens, and Dick Rainey of the Contra Costa County (California) Sheriff's Department come to mind. Jim Simonson and Nolan Darnell of the Oakland (California) Police Department and Al Salerno of the Berkeley (California) Police Department equally have made pronounced contributions to our understanding of ethical policing.

Finally, there are the police leaders it has been our privilege to know and to work with who have also driven this work by their examples. Chief John Hart of Oakland P.D., Chief Dashel Butler of Berkeley P.D., Chief Kevin Skully of Burlington (Vermont) P.D., and Chief John Terry of Essex Junction (Vermont) P.D. have been sources of inspiration and, at times, lights in the dark forest.

To all these people, we owe our thanks. If this work is effective in accomplishing its appointed task, in making a difference on the streets of America, it will be a testimony to all of them.

The authors and publisher would like to thank the following reviewers:

Megan Cole
Brown College

Robert Davis
Edgecombe Community College

Mary Beth Robbins Finn
Herzing University

Richard H. Martin
Auburn Montgomery

Christine L. Stymus
Bryant and Stratton College

CHAPTER 1

Introduction

Chapter Outline

"You treat everyone the same, kid. You're civil to everyone and cordial to no one . . . everyone deserves some amount of respect, but no one deserves courtesy. . . . That's 'Kilvinsky's Law.'"

—Veteran Officer Kilvinsky, speaking to a
rookie in the movie *The New Centurions*

This is a book about an area of police work that is in the process of rapid change. Only a few decades ago, the phrase "police ethics" was a joke to many Americans. Commonly held images of police officers and of the dynamics of their subculture involved viewing the police as a group of unintelligent, uneducated, and untrained incompetents. The police were considered to be governmental agents who regularly abused their power, who often operated *against* the very principles of justice for which they ostensibly stood, and who were not intelligent enough to grasp these realities. Police officers were considered to be of dubious character and incapable of behaving in an ethical manner. Largely, this is what the public believed.

Unfortunately, the phrase "police ethics" was also a joke to many police officers. Police academy discussions about ethics were given and received with a grain of salt. The tacit understanding in the police world was that while ethics had to be discussed, whatever was said about them was unrealistic and bound to be ignored. Furthermore, a sort of "good ol' boys" attitude operated on the street which underwrote subcultural values rationalizing corruption and incompetence. Only those few police leaders who took police accountability seriously treated the subject of ethical behavior by police officers with any degree of genuine concern.

Today, in an era of **community oriented policing (COP)** wherein the police officers of America are making rapid progress in the direction of becoming genuine professionals, the subject of police ethics has begun to take center stage. Ethics are beginning to be considered as an important subject for academy discussion as well as something upon which to focus in-service training. Police ethics have come out of the shadows and have begun to be included along with discussions about police competence. It will be our central argument here that these two topics—police ethics and police competence—are linked together in such a way as to make them one and the same. To be a competent police officer is to be an ethical police officer. It is impossible to achieve the former without achieving the latter.

Let us take a moment to consider why the topic of police ethics is so important.

1-1 ● THE POLICE *ARE* THE LAW

Our title for this section may appear to suggest an open invitation to police officers to be egocentric, to do whatever they feel is appropriate on duty, and to avoid taking the rule of law seriously. We appear to be saying that the rule of cop is what's important because, on the street, what police officers say goes.

We seem to be confirming a police locker-room idea that the police are the law and that to operate on this basis is both realistic and morally defensible.

Is that what we mean by our title? Because they make thousands of important, life-changing decisions every day, often alone and unsupervised, is it true that the police are the law? The answer is both yes and no. The police must apply the law fairly, evenhandedly, and with a view to promote justice. Laws are created by legislatures, and the police cannot think or act as if they are completely free, by themselves, to define legal and illegal, to decide who are inherently good people and who are inherently bad people, or to rule the streets as an **occupying army**. This is exactly what the police do in police states against which America has fought a number of wars. In such countries, the police have so much power that the law, as written, is largely irrelevant to the lives of millions of people. Citizens in these countries are at the whims of absolute police power.

Ours is a country of laws and of constitutional principles, the sole purpose of which is to create a society where everybody is free to pursue what he or she, individually, believes is **the good** in life—that is, in his or her own life. This is exactly what Thomas Jefferson meant by his reference to the "pursuit of happiness" in the Declaration of Independence. This ideal of our system rests on the understanding that there is no such thing as a single good or best way to live for all people.

The definition of what counts as "good" in life is highly divisive and highly individualized. It is a life that is personally satisfying and meaningful to the individual and is the driving motivation of everyone. The pursuit of things that make life good, or better, makes up a person's life story or "storyline." It is what makes a person's behavior understandable. In other words, what counts as good for a person (having a family, getting an education, making a lot of money), and the way one pursues that good (being loyal, going to college, getting a good job), form the basis that defines his or her individuality.

A. Justice: A Preliminary Discussion

Justice provides the environment within which the pursuit of the good (of happiness) is possible. We will talk more about justice later, but for now we will suggest two concepts to consider. First, let us consider justice to be "fairness" in the general sense of the term. When justice prevails, people are treated fairly relative to each other. Second, let us also consider justice to be the Greek notion that it is the kind of balance that exists when "each is given his or her due." That is, justice involves allocating resources and rights in a way that allows individuals to obtain what it is that they deserve, in a moral sense.

When the police act, they must understand this underlying concept, and they must behave in a way that does honor to it. Thus, the streets of America must be ruled by laws that are applied fairly. While the business of law is to deal with people regarding how they behave, it cannot (in an ethically or legally defensible way) treat people in different ways because of their personal characteristics (such as race, religion, manner of dress, political views, etc.).

The image of curbside justice.

Thus, from this basic tenet, the law is absolute.

On the other hand, to a great extent the actions of the police do, in fact, determine what the law really means. The police put practical application into the American legal system. If the laws the police uphold are the skeleton, the on-the-street discretionary decisions of the police put flesh and blood on that skeleton. The police make the written laws of the penal code come to life for the public. See Box 1.1 regarding the idea of **"curbside justice."**

We intend to confirm what a number of analysts and well informed, intuitive police officers have pointed out for a very long time—that no matter what the law states, no matter what police training teaches, and no matter what police leadership may want to tell us, the true meaning of the law on the streets is determined by police officers.

When officers decide on a day-to-day basis where to focus their attention, whom to arrest, and when to use force, they determine the effects the legal system will have on the lives of individual citizens. This means police officers bear a tremendous and unique responsibility. If they either overlook or overemphasize certain types of crimes, they can (effectively) change the criminal law. If, for example, in a college town the police look the other way when college kids are involved in underage drinking, then underage drinking has, in effect, been **decriminalized** in that town. If the police in one jurisdiction decide not to worry too much about local gambling rooms, then gambling has been (again, effectively) decriminalized there.

When the police make such decisions in response to local pressures ("leave the college kids alone, they pay the bills in this town"), they might be making perfectly rational public policy decisions. But by avoiding the dictates of the law in this and a thousand other ways, the police can create the impression that police practices are arbitrary, preferential, or biased. Such impressions promote cynicism among citizens and alienate them from the criminal justice system.

B. Discretionary Decision Making

These two examples—ignoring underage drinking and gambling—involve the police deciding not to invoke the law. But the police can also appear to be guilty of unfairness and arbitrariness by applying the law too rigorously. For example, if the police decide that, in an effort to thwart the growth of

BOX 1.1

CURBSIDE JUSTICE—
THE EXERCISE OF ABSOLUTE POLICE POWER

In 1966 in Spain, dictator Generalissimo Francisco Franco was in power. The police, specifically the national police (the *Guardia Civil*), exercised absolute power over individual citizens. One day that summer, at a bullfight in Madrid, a young, starving, peasant boy was detained for trying to steal the purse of an American tourist. Instead of taking the boy out of the arena and to jail, two officers—each weighing in excess of two hundred pounds— marched the boy (who weighed under one hundred pounds) around the arena, beating him with their nightsticks. The beating continued on for several minutes until the boy was covered in blood and unconscious. He was then dragged from the arena. All of this occurred in full view of over 10,000 people.

The American victim who first called for the police was in tears by the time the altercation was over. She felt that she had caused this small, poor boy to be killed. Being an American, she felt ashamed of herself for not understanding what the consequences would be of reporting such a petty theft to the police in totalitarian Spain. She later said that she would have *given* the boy her purse if she had known what was going to happen to him. The woman left Spain vowing never to return to "such a country."

The Spanish police were never questioned and never sanctioned. Indeed, the crowd at the bullring remained completely silent throughout the entire incident. Knowing the absolute power of the police, this crowd of Spaniards feared that other members of the *Guardia Civil* (clearly evident throughout the arena) would treat them to a dose of such curbside justice if they protested.

local gangs, they will stop every teenage driver to make records and warrants checks, ask for information, and generally make things uncomfortable for gang members, then the police have effectively created a new, separate set of unique laws that apply to one segment of the population. It is imperative that police officers understand they have this power and, in order to use it wisely, understand how critical it is that they possess a personal ethic that is morally and legally defensible. It is around this theme that we have built this book.

Individual police officers often make decisions without supervision and with no direction to follow other than their own judgment. For all practical purposes, no one is there to hold them accountable when they decide whether

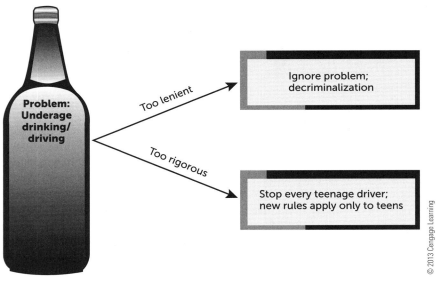

Discretionary decision making.

or not to stop a vehicle. No one can effectively monitor in real time how respectful, civil, and decent the individual officer is when dealing with citizens or—and this is especially important—how often the officer decides *not* to take action. **Discretionary decision making** is one of the unavoidable realities of police work.

The idea behind this book is to emphasize the full importance of police ethics. If an officer is corrupt, unfair, prejudiced, and/or driven by personal vendettas, then so is that officer's "law." If officers are honest, sufficiently educated, and controlled by a desire to apply the law in a fair way to all people, then the law will be a tool for the maintenance of justice. There is no way around this reality. How officers use discretion is of absolute importance to their communities, to the criminal justice system, and to America herself.

BOX 1.2

TWO DEFINITIONS OF JUSTICE

1. **Justice as process** Justice prevails when people under similar circumstances are treated in an equal and fair manner before the law.

2. **Justice as substance** Justice prevails when people receive from the law what they deserve to receive.

Put bluntly, the decisions of the police define justice, in both of the senses that we discussed above—justice as fairness (equal treatment) and justice in terms of the distribution of what people deserve.

So we are discussing the idea that a critical factor in police competence is ethical judgment. Police discretion is driven by the character of individual officers. To be a competent, professional police officer involves making wise judgments about people, situations, and the applicability of the law. Because police fix the limits of the law on the street, their ethical judgment, and thus their competence, is crucial to determining whether or not the legal system dispenses justice. Police ethics are not and cannot be considered something separate from police competence.

We will consider several classical theories of ethics and develop our own character-based ethic for police officers, "an ethic to live by," by combining the strengths of these theories. We will spend some time applying this ethic to the challenges and issues police officers face every day. Our intent is to bring to the reader an appreciation for the centrality of ethics in everyday police work. This will help not only to create an attitude about professionalism among police officers but also to generate a respect for law and for the police among citizens. Nothing could be more important for us all in contemporary American society.

1-2 ● THE NEED FOR ETHICS STUDY BY THE POLICE

Historically, police officers have been particularly prone to think that philosophy has nothing to do with real life on the street. The authors believe this is not only wrong, but that this impression severely limits the development of police competence and character. It is wrong because the idea of "philosophy" does not refer to specialized notions or terms. It simply means the idea of maintaining a critical frame of mind, a discerning judgment—what Socrates called "the examined life." He was talking about looking beyond the surface appearance of things to what they really mean, to what is really going on. This is a philosophic perspective, and this is what we mean. A philosophic perspective is the effort to see clearly, to see the reality of situations.

We stand on the shoulders of giants. We do well to acknowledge this fact and to learn from them. Why, then, is it so important for the police officer today to become involved in discussions about morality that have been discussed for more than two thousand years? The answer comes in several parts.

A. The Traditional Academy Approach

Police academies, even with today's sophisticated and broadly based curricula, include very little discussion about ethics. A nationwide survey found that state regulations require an average of only three and one-half hours of ethics training in an entire police academy experience. Thus, the amount of time spent debating, analyzing, and studying the sort of **ethical dilemmas** that are regularly encountered by police officers is very limited. Given the gravity of the problem of police misconduct and the opportunities to misbehave faced by officers on the street, this amount of discussion is woefully inadequate.

In addition to insufficient time, the *type* of discussion police cadets in academies experience with regard to ethics is also inadequate. In most places, police academy ethics discussions involve nothing more than lectures given by someone from internal affairs (IA) about what police officers should *not* do when they hit the street. These "lists of don'ts" are often disregarded by cadets who already possess some police subcultural cynicism about IA. Thus, discussions about how a cop can get into trouble tend to fall on deaf ears.

What is missing is an approach to the subject from the ground up. It is obviously worthwhile to teach recruits how to avoid getting into trouble. But such a negative approach cannot be taken alone. Police recruits are not hired in order *not* to do certain things. To focus exclusively on how to avoid getting into trouble implies that to be a good, competent police officer merely involves not making substantial mistakes. This idea is problematic because it distorts what is meant by police competence and the positive duties involved in being a professional officer—a person who possesses and exhibits good character.

Discussing examples of what police officers should not *do* ought to be an aspect of the larger issue of what competent, professional police officers should *be*. A systematic treatment of ethics, even if it is abbreviated, is necessary to make the connection between a police officer's duty and the common good of the community.

B. A Positive Approach

There is another reason to emphasize the study of ethics in the world of policing. An increasing number of police recruits have college experience behind them, and many major in criminal justice. Existing criminal justice ethics classes do tend to discuss ethics from the positive perspective that we are suggesting. They start with philosophical considerations of ethics in general and move through analyses of what it means to be a professional police officer. As opposed to the treatment accorded ethics in police academies, this is a much more appropriate way to deal with such a complex subject.

The problem is that many colleges don't offer criminal justice ethics classes at all. Also, most college programs don't require students who are pre–law enforcement to take a course in ethics. Thus, even though such programs offer good classes on the subject, college-educated officers today do not necessarily engage in the type of thoughtful analysis of personal character and police ethics that is necessary to be an officer in the twenty-first century.

C. The Intellectual Capabilities of Today's Officer

A third reason for today's police officers to study ethics seriously is because they can. It requires no argument to claim that it is an intrinsically good thing to develop one's abilities, especially those abilities directly related to one's profession. Why remain less rather than more proficient? That is, today we no longer presume police officers cannot understand discussions about the principles of philosophy, of good character, or of ethical conduct. This is not to say that the officers of yesterday weren't intelligent. But it is to say that today's officers can approach judgments about conduct from a more conceptually informed perspective. And it is critical they do so. As COP expands, the discretion of individual officers' personal ethical frames of reference is increasingly important.

So, there is no doubt that today's officers can engage in analytical discussions about police ethics. The question is, do they want to? Why should police officers want to debate the principles of being a good person that were outlined by Aristotle more than two thousand years ago? The answer is this: These principles are an integral part of what the modern, professional officer must become. A professional, knowledgeable, competent police officer must want to include in his or her body of knowledge about the world an understanding of the basis of right conduct or ethics. Everything the officer does hinges on this understanding.

We posit that to ask, "Why should I study ethics?" is to ask, "Why should I become a competent officer?" Embedded in the expectations of police competence is the central, grounding requirement that a police officer have a clear ethical understanding of the job and possess good moral character. A clear ethic anchors the officer in the good of the community. Without that ethic, the officer is rudderless and lacks personal direction. A police officer's general requirement—like that of other workers—is to do his or her job well. People expect this of each other. But with police officers, invested as they are as the state's instruments of power, the moral and legal ante is raised considerably. The public expects more. The only thing that both fosters and secures a competent frame of mind in the officer is a dominating interest in doing what is right for the public. It is the officer's ethical outlook, revolving around his or her personal character, that over time promotes respect for the police and trust in the police officer.

We are seeking to treat modern officers as the intelligent and knowledgeable people they are. Instead of talking about "what not to do" and attempting to intimidate police officers out of acting inappropriately, we seek to approach the entire subject from the opposite perspective. This work will discuss various schools of ethical thought and their integration with police practice in a way that, as we have said before, works from the ground up. We move from a general understanding toward practical applications. If we succeed, the reader will have a workable and yet theoretically based understanding of ethics that can be applied to the entire gamut of situations police officers encounter.

1-3 ● POLICE PROFESSIONALISM

It is no exaggeration to say that the central theme of modern policing, the north star that guides today's many changes in the field, is the drive to make police work into a profession. Later on, we will consider alternative modes

BOX 1.3

AN ETHICAL DILEMMA

Two police officers stop a motorist for speeding. The driver is somewhat cooperative but nevertheless is indignant about the stop and begins to tell the officers that they "should be out catching criminals." Officer A is not particularly upset by this talk, but Officer B is. Officer B bends over to the ground, drops two marijuana joints to the pavement, picks them up, and shows them to the driver, saying, "You dropped these." Officer B is now about to arrest the driver for possessing marijuana and take him to jail.

Officer A has seen what has happened and is outraged. But what can Officer A do? What *should* Officer A do? A concern for duty to the law makes Officer A understand that such behavior on the part of the police is unacceptable. But Officer A also feels another duty—to fellow officers and to the police as a group (to the police subculture).

How can an individual officer resolve such a dilemma between competing duties? Which duty is stronger? What duty does a police officer owe to himself or herself, to the law, and to the police subculture?

of explaining **professionalism,** but here in our initial chapter we will use the definition posited by sociologists.

A. A Preliminary Definition

The standard definition of a profession cited by sociologists is that it is an occupation that involves the practitioner in academic experience of substantial sophistication. The professional engages a college or university experience as the first step in becoming competent and eventually enfranchised to practice. This experience is then enhanced by a profession-specific type of training, either encompassing more academics (such as law school or medical school) or a more practical, internship-oriented seasoning (such as for the school teacher). This professional education provides a systematized body of knowledge that is unknown to the layperson.

Several other elements are endemic to the professions. They practice **self-regulation.** That is, professional organizations develop standards for the substantive content of the education obtained in academia, they delineate entry-level examinations and licensing requirements, and they create regulatory boards and commissions to monitor practice in their field. They also are **self-disciplining.** Boards of expert professionals are entrusted almost exclusively with the responsibility of reviewing allegations of misconduct and of sanctioning errant practitioners. While Americans often carp about the power possessed by doctors and lawyers, as two excellent examples, it is nevertheless true that in general society defers to their professional expertise almost universally. No one who is outside of the profession, and who therefore has not obtained the systematized body of knowledge possessed by practitioners, presumes to judge the competence of the professional. Doctors investigate allegations of medical misconduct, lawyers investigate allegations of legal misconduct, and so forth.

Professionals solve problems in a **collegial** way. Chains of command are universally eschewed in favor of a collective approach to dealing with roadblocks in the professions. Furthermore, the professional possesses an internalized professional ethic. This ethic is initially embraced during the academic training period and is thereafter maintained by professionals as individuals and in groups. Outsiders are kept at arm's length, outside of the operations of the profession's ethical canons.

B. Competence and Professionalism

The book is written with an eye toward making an impact upon police cadets in the midst of the academy experience and upon college students taking courses in criminal justice ethics. We hope it will constitute but one element in the ongoing development of an expanded concern for police ethics throughout the world of criminal justice practice and criminal justice studies.

Today the police academy experience and the college-level undergraduate education in the field of policing are both expanding to include topical areas that have heretofore never been engaged. It has long been understood that for police work to be done effectively the officer on the street needs to possess substantial knowledge in a multiplicity of subject matter areas. Studies now include the psychology of death and dying, gang theory, the psychology of domestic abuse, substance abuse analysis, the treatment of mental illness, and so forth. All of these subjects, and a dozen others, are studied by the cadet/college undergraduate. Under the auspices of COP, such non–law enforcement oriented topics have begun to enhance and amplify the systematized body of knowledge.

The idea that the competent police officer must be knowledgeable and experienced in more than a dozen fields of study has become accepted universally. The days of the old "dumb flatfoot" being long, long gone, today's police officer training includes such multiple subjects in an effort to expand the competence of the everyday officer. As substantive knowledge expands, as procedural problem-solving abilities are honed, and as a broad understanding of the knowledge base of the average officer improves across the

BOX 1.4

THE SYSTEMATIZED BODY OF KNOWLEDGE: WHAT THE POLICE PROFESSIONAL NEEDS TO KNOW

A PARTIAL LIST WOULD INCLUDE:

Adolescent psychology	Investigation techniques
Ballistics	Jail procedures
Case law	Juvenile hall procedures
Child psychology	Juvenile law
Crime scene searches	Local history
Criminal law	Local ordinances
Defensive tactics	Patrol procedures
Dept. general orders	Prisoner custody
Disciplinary systems	Public relations
Evidence custody	Riot control
First aid	S.W.A.T. practices
Forensics	Sociology of death and dying
Handling domestics	Sociology of gangs
Hostage situations	Theory of COP
Interrogation techniques	Weapons and marksmanship

American policing landscape, ethics, too, is a subject that is being included in this expanded coverage of academic and pragmatic topics. Clearly, if American policing is going to achieve genuine professionalism, ethics needs to be engaged by every member of the new blue line.

1-4 ● AN INTRODUCTORY NOTE ABOUT POLICE MISCONDUCT

Early on in this first chapter it is important to engage the idea of the **"Dirty Harry problem,"** as it can be considered to be the centrally most important element of police misconduct in today's world. Dirty Harry's problem involved the supposedly noble cause of attempting to get the job done. As such, the type of misconduct associated with this idea stills plagues American policing today, when other forms of corruption have (largely) become the exception rather than the rule.

A. Who Was Dirty Harry?

While the movie *Dirty Harry* is now quite dated, the point it made about the frustrations facing American police officers in the 1970s has been accepted by Hollywood as well as by many Americans. It is a constant, recurring theme on television, in the movies, and even in the contemporary news media. (Today, the idea that it is acceptable for police officers to become involved in Dirty Harry–like, vigilante justice has been labeled "the **CSI effect.**") The film depicted a hard-working detective (Harry Callahan, played by Clint Eastwood) who was frustrated by the machinations of the due process

Clint Eastwood (shown here in October 2010) was Dirty Harry.

system. Because of the exclusionary rule (about which at one point Harry indicates a profound ignorance), evidence obtained illegally by Harry is excluded at trial and the bad guy goes free. Harry becomes disgusted with the system's focus upon procedural guilt in lieu of focusing upon factual guilt. And this drives him to become corrupt.

If this movie had come and gone, fading into Hollywood history, it would not be the subject of discussion today. But because Hollywood, the media, and large numbers of the American populace accepted the premise of the film, today's police officers sometimes feel that they must break the law in order to "get the job done." The "Dirty Harry problem" has become the most difficult type of misconduct to deter in contemporary American policing.

B. Noble Cause Corruption

Entire books are written in today's criminal justice field about **"noble cause corruption,"** another way of labeling the Dirty Harry problem or CSI effect. This type of corruption comes with its own rationalization. The police officer who becomes involved in breaking procedural law in order to enforce substantive law is a hero, not only in public and in the imaginary world of entertainment, but in some circles on some occasions in the real world of policing.

In studying this phenomenon, numerous authors have come up with a laundry list of the classic actions taken by the Dirty Harrys of the police world in an effort to get the job done. "Testilying" refers to lying on the witness stand in an effort to secure a conviction. "Creative report writing"—or lying on paper—is another effort to obtain the same outcome. It is utilized to influence the decisions of public prosecutors. Planting evidence on suspects, usually drugs, is another tactic of the noble cause–driven miscreant. And finally, using force in order to obtain information is still another possibility. Taken together, this list of tactics underwrites what the Dirty Harry type of officer considers to be a morally defensible goal.

Because it comes with its own internalized rationalization (that of getting the job done), noble cause corruption finds support in the hearts and minds of many contemporary police officers. In an era where payoffs and organized graft have largely vanished, Dirty Harry still lives within the psyche of the police subculture.

C. Support for Harry

Unfortunately for those involved in pursuing ethics in the world of American policing, the Dirty Harry problem is amplified by support for Harry both within the police subculture and within American society as a whole. The noble cause is often sustained by police officers, citizens, and politicians, who consider themselves to be "tough on crime," pro-police, or good, patriotic Americans.

As we have noted, driven on by unrealistic media-created imagery that deifies Dirty Harry, Americans tend to consider him to be a hero of sorts. But there is also subcultural support for this type of misbehavior. In an era that has seen day-to-day corruption of the shake-down and/or payoff go by the wayside (almost everywhere, almost all of the time), Dirty Harry–type noble cause corruption is alive and well. While today's police officers will usually cooperate with investigations into old-style corruption, there will often be subcultural reluctance to aid in investigating Harry. That is, many, many contemporary American police officers who would never under any circumstance stand for others accepting, say, payoffs from drug dealers will nevertheless be loathe to help in investigating noble cause corruption.

BOX 1.5

NOBLE CAUSE CORRUPTION CAN INCLUDE

- Testilying
- Creative report writing
- Planting evidence
- Using force to obtain information

1-5 ● OUR ETHICAL PERSPECTIVE

In this book, we will suggest to the reader an ethical frame of reference that has been created specifically for the police professional. We call it "an ethic to live by." We will engage the set of ideas that encompass this ethic in some depth in Chapter 9. For now, let us merely outline the idea so the reader has it as a focal point for what is forthcoming.

A. Ethical Formalism

One of the most studied ethical frames of reference is ethical formalism. The origin of this line of thought is found in the biblical tradition, and the earliest example of it is the story of Abraham being commanded by God to offer up his son, Isaac, as a "burnt offering" (Genesis 22). In the biblical tradition, Abraham's readiness to sacrifice Isaac was a righteous thing not because Abraham understood why it was good or what God's purpose was but simply because God said so. Obedience to God made it good, the end. The moral authority of the sacrifice lay in Abraham's obedience, not in what it brought about. That is, the morality of the act (Abraham's readiness to sacrifice his son) lay in his *motive*, in the reason that lay behind the act. Abraham acted for a reason, and it was this reason that made his action moral. Abraham's good intentions made the act moral, not its possible consequences.

In the modern world, the father of this idea is the German philosopher Immanuel Kant, whose ethic, the *Categorical Imperative,* is a nonreligious version of the New Testament's "Golden Rule" (Jesus said, "Do unto others as you would have them do unto you.'). Kant's ethic is what philosophers call a **deontological** perspective, a term that indicates that a person has a *duty to be reasonable.* Kant maintains that the individual can only be held accountable for that over which he or she has immediate control, and in our conduct the only thing we absolutely control is our intention. When deciding what to do among several alternatives, a person should choose the alternative that he or she would choose if he or she were making a generalized rule for everyone, everywhere, at any time.

It is in the natural order of things that an animal act in the way it is best fitted by nature to act, that it does what it was born to do. Human beings are born with *minds*, their defining characteristic, hence they are born to reason their way through life. *Reason* is our defining trait—it is what makes us human. For Kant, and for Christianity

This marble panel depicts Abraham's trial by God.

© mountainpix/Shutterstock.com

generally, the "natural thing" sets the standard for the "right thing"—*nature* defines *rightness*. Therefore, human beings stand under a genetic or inborn obligation to live reasonably.

The idea is that what counts as reasonable connects us to everybody else and makes a shared, common human life possible. We live within the network of reason. This is our natural and only disposition. Consistency with reason is, then, the law that governs human thought *and* action. That the motives or purposes that lie behind what we do are just as applicable to others as they are to us is what makes our actions *moral*. This requirement of reason imposes an absolute, always-operational norm of conduct.

For Kant, arbitrariness is the chief enemy of morality. Motives that apply only to me or to my group are by their nature arbitrary and self-centered, since they disregard the dignity or the humanity of other people. In effect, such motives (those that are good just for me or mine) treat others as not as worthy as me. Morality is always other-regarding, not self-regarding, and Kant achieves this through the universalizability of motives. It is never enough that our actions simply conform to what is right: They must be done for the right reason. Only that action that would be applicable to everyone in a similar situation can be called reasonable, and not self-centered or arbitrary. This he called the "categorical imperative."

Kant was aware of the problem of making absolute rules. To say, for example, that a person should always tell the truth prompts the question, what should a person do if to tell the truth would cause harm? The answer, according to Kant, was that since no one can answer for the actions of others, since no one can definitively know what the logical outcome of any action might be, an ethical individual can only act according to such an imperative and ignore the consequences.

The ethic of Kant—his notion that morality consists in the universalizability of motives—is written in an entirely secular or nonreligious vein, but it is also the direct offspring of the ethic of the New Testament in the Bible. What differentiates it from the Christian ethic is that, for Christianity, conformity to God's will makes an act good, but for Kant nothing that is external to a person's reason—including God himself—can be a basis for right conduct. To say, for example, "I did it because it's God's will" or "Because it says so in the Bible" is, for Kant, not a morally defensible justification for conduct. In accordance with reason, a moral person is his own authority.

B. Utilitarianism

Ethical formalism is just one perspective from which the professional officer might choose. The Kantians of the world have trouble fielding criticisms that charge them with failing to promote good in the lives of people. As noted above, what should a person do if in cleaving to their absolute Kantian rules of ethical behavior they bring harm to others? What should you do when cleaving to the rule to always tell the truth if telling the truth would, say, cause hiding Jews to be found by the Nazis? Aren't the long-term consequences of our actions important? Should we not be expected to try to accomplish good things with our deeds? Is it not just making excuses when we say that what happens in the end is none of our concern?

The answer, of course, is that consequences of our actions *do* matter. And so, unlike with a deontological perspective, a person might very well utilize what is called a teleological perspective when deciding an ethical course of action. A **teleological** approach (the best known modern version of which is called utilitarianism) involves attempting to calculate the impact upon others of one's actions at any given moment. So utilitarianism is our second school of ethical thought.

C. An Ethic to Live By

After we consider the significance of these two schools of thought, our discussion will move on to present another ethical frame of reference to the contemporary police officer. Developed specifically for today's professional, our "ethic to live by" suggests that being a police officer involves managing *several* types of ethical perspectives on a regular basis. In other words, police officers will sometimes use a Kantian, deontological perspective and at other times will use a utilitarian or teleological point of reference. In managing the sorts of ethical questions involved in everyday policing, officers following our ethic will utilize a variety of perspectives depending upon what sorts of problems present themselves.

This ethic is the last of our several important, ongoing foci for the book. It is simply an extension of the initially outlined theme that *competence* and *ethics* are related, like a cart with a horse, where the horse gets us to where we want to go (ethic) and the cart delivers the goods (competence). Driven by what we call the principle of beneficence, we argue that police officers ought first to do no harm; and then, where possible, to prevent harm, remove harm, and to promote good, in that order of importance. Our book provides a frame of reference for the contemporary police professional that balances the concerns of promoting order (deontology) and promoting the good (utility).

1-6 ● THE ORGANIZATION OF THE BOOK

In Part I ("The Setting"), we set up several ideas that will echo through the entire book. Chapter 2 ("Police Professionalism") makes the case that ethics is a part of the drive to professionalize the police everywhere. Chapter 3 ("The Nature of Police Work") walks the reader through a basic primer on the experience engaged by the individual police officer and concludes with a discussion of the creation and maintenance of the police subculture. Chapter 4 ("Why Be Ethical?") is a discussion of why a person, any person, should consider ethics as an essential part of his or her life. It is critical that police officers begin their consideration of what might constitute ethical police conduct with this general question, rather than with police-specific discussions and examples. Beginning with the general ideal might better ground their understanding in a framework of thought that is deeper in its significance than an on-the-job type of perspective.

Part II ("Ethical Frameworks") develops an understanding of several different schools of thought about ethics. Chapter 5 ("What Is Character?") begins our treatment of these schools by discussing the idea of personal character and relating it to police officer ethics. Chapter 6 ("The Development of Character") engages the reader in a consideration of how character is determined, with an eye toward developing in himself or herself the most competent professional possible.

Chapter 7 ("Ethical Formalism") discusses the idea that there are absolute rules of morality (as mentioned above). Chapter 8 ("Utilitarianism") discusses a type of ethical thinking that relies exclusively on calculations of benefit and harm (consequences) brought about by action. Chapter 9 ("An Ethic to Live By") is our attempt to draw the previous chapters together into a concise set of principles that every officer can use as a guide on the street. Chapter 10 ("Judgment Calls") applies this ethic to some of the difficult problems presented to officers on the street. It discusses how a professional, competent officer of good character makes choices between different courses of action.

Part III ("On the Street") seeks to get the reader even closer to practical applications by relating the theory presented to the world of police work. Chapter 11 ("Types of Police Misconduct") discusses a rather dark side of police work, the various sorts of misbehavior into which officers sometimes fall. Chapter 12 ("The Causes of Police Misconduct") suggests individual, subcultural, and even society-wide forces and dynamics that tend to hasten the creation and support the ongoing maintenance of these several types of police deviance. Chapter 13 ("Practical Applications") engages in discussions about police review systems and disciplinary processes.

Part IV ("Implications") brings the reader back from these discussions of specific types of misconduct to engage the question of how an officer can work on his or her own integrated perspective of police ethics. Chapter 14 ("The Law Enforcement Code of Ethics") argues that the Code of Ethics, despite the criticism that it is unrealistic, is a good frame of reference to use as a basis for understanding ethics on the street. Finally, in Chapter 15 ("Being a Good Officer"), we put everything together, the theory and the practice, the ideal and the real, and reflect on what being a good officer means today and in the future.

1-7 ● A FINAL NOTE

Before we begin our systematic treatment of ethics, a word is in order about the limitations of such an enterprise. First, while the world is full of good, honest, competent police officers who have never studied ethics, our endeavor is to enhance the chances that recruits will enter the profession with the ideas and vocabulary of—and sense for reasoning about—ethical matters.

BOX 1.6

THE BOOK'S CENTRAL ARGUMENT

Police officers cannot be considered to be competent if they do not underwrite their behavior on the street with a personal ethic that is thoughtfully created and maintained. Ethics and competence are directly linked and inseparable. And they both are largely determined by the individual police officer's character.

Second, good ethical conduct is determined primarily by what a person already *is* before he or she enrolls in the police academy. It comes from a person's character and upbringing. That is, an "ethically disposed" personality trait is not likely to be created by simply reading a book or experiencing training. All we can hope to accomplish in these pages is to foster a sense of self-scrutiny about the relationship between ethics and police competence.

Let us begin by entering into the contemporary debate about what it means to be a professional police officer.

1-8 ☉ TOPICS FOR DISCUSSION

The authors suggest that the police give meaning to the law and make it come to life in the daily lives of citizens because of how they (the police) apply it. How is this done? Discuss examples of how the police use their discretionary powers to "make law."

1. The law discriminates among people. It treats some people one way and others another. There is nothing wrong with this—in fact, it is the job of the law to do so. Discuss the difference between treating people differently because of their *behavior* and treating people differently because of their *characteristics*.

2. This book attempts to deal with police ethics from a positivist approach. That is, the book spends little time talking about how police officers should avoid being guilty of misconduct and a lot of time talking about police officers having good character. Discuss the difference between "not making mistakes" and "doing the right thing."

3. The authors suggest that the central, dominant theme of the book is that police competence is inexorably linked to police ethics. What do they mean by this? How is it that, according to the authors, the two *cannot* be divorced from each other?

1-9 ◉ ETHICAL SCENARIO

An officer is testifying on the witness stand in a court trial. As her examination moves along, she realizes that the drug dealer that she arrested is likely to be found not guilty. This is because even though she obtained a verbal waiver of Fourth Amendment rights from the suspect, she had in fact searched the trunk of the suspect's car prematurely. She realizes that only if she lies ("testilies") will the suspect be found guilty. She also realizes that the suspect is confused about the entire process, and will not even be aware of her lie if she decides to tell it. Thus, the ethical dilemma is hers and hers alone.

What does she do? Does she "testilie" in the interests of justice? Why would she? What would her rationalization be? Would that, indeed, involve promoting justice? What would the ethical implications be if she *did* lie? Why do experts on police ethics consider that she is on a "slippery slope" if she lies? What is the long-term danger of police officers becoming criminals themselves by testilying? In other words, how would testilying impact upon justice from the opposite direction?

1-10 ◉ WRITING EXERCISE

Our text spends just a moment considering what elements might be part of the "systematized body of knowledge" that the professional police officer understands. Construct your own list of the necessary skills, knowledge bases, and types of expertise that might be possessed by the modern professional officer. Be synoptic—that is, make the list as long and inclusive as you possibly can. Consider any and every type of knowledge necessary. See if you can come up with 50 such elements (at least). [Instructors might have the class share their lists in an effort to construct a complete, synoptic list.]

1-11 ◉ KEY TERMS

collegial: As colleagues; refers to the problem-solving methods utilized among professionals.

community oriented policing (COP): Philosophy of modern, professional policing.

CSI effect: The idea that the media present unrealistic images to the public of the police, how they operate, and what they are capable of accomplishing.

curbside justice: Police-invoked justice on the streets, often involving the use of excessive force.

decriminalization: Making something that is a crime into a non-crime through the exercise of police discretion.

Dirty Harry problem: The idea that some police officers will break procedural law in order to enforce substantive law; done in the name of getting the job done.

discretionary decision making: Choosing between options, especially when deciding how to invoke the law.

deontology: Judgments of moral obligation; a term used for ethical systems that identify a person's intentions as the center of moral gravity.

ethical dilemma: A choice between incompatible courses of action, each of which is ethically defensible.

the good: That which makes a person's life worthwhile, happy, sustaining; defined uniquely by each individual for themselves; "the pursuit of happiness" as defined by Thomas Jefferson in the Declaration of Independence.

justice as process: Justice defined as equal treatment.

justice as substance: Justice as what a person deserves.

noble cause corruption: Dirty Harry–like behavior; involves police officers breaking procedural law in order to enforce substantive law.

occupying army: The police behaving as if they are foreigners, repressing American citizens.

professionalism: Defined variously, but in this context the police taking a place among doctors, lawyers, etc.

self-disciplining: The practice of professionals setting up standards of conduct for their own profession and then holding their peers accountable to same.

self-regulation: The practice of professionals developing and applying their own standards to their endeavor—standards involving minimum educational standards, licensing requirements, training practices, and so forth.

teleology: The position that design or ultimate purpose is a principle that organizes growth or development; the overall purpose of a thing or action that guides its development toward a particular end. For example, the oak tree is the telos (the natural end) of an acorn.

PART I

The Setting

In Part I, we will consider the importance of ethical judgment for modern-day police professionals, engage in discussion about living a moral life, and debate the nature of character. To begin with, we must discuss how today's police officers are involved in an exciting set of changes that affect every aspect of their careers. From who is selected to become police officers, to how they are trained, to the level of intellectual sophistication possessed by today's cops on the beat, things are different from what they used to be. It is toward a brief discussion of these dynamic changes and toward an understanding of what the new police professionalism means that we now turn.

CHAPTER 2

Police Professionalism

Chapter Outline

"Get a haircut. Shine your shoes. Polish your brass.
Take some pride in looking professional."

—Veteran Sergeant to a Rookie Officer

There has been a great deal of talk in recent years about something called "police professionalism" as if everyone is certain that he or she knows what it means. Police administrators, academics who teach college classes in criminal justice, and even politicians consistently call for the professionalization of the police. Some people argue that the police have been professionals since the end of the **political era** and the onset of the **reform era.** Others suggest that the police have yet to approach the elevated status of being professionals.

Unfortunately, many people, both inside and outside of police work, hold a concept of professionalism that is exactly the opposite of what those in the field should be working toward. This is largely because of the misconception that accompanied the changes of the reform era. (More on this in a moment.) This is troublesome because for professionalism to develop in American policing, everyone involved must understand the educational, sub-cultural, and ethical implications of what true professionalism means. Let us begin our discussion of police professionalism by briefly reviewing the history of its evolution.

2-1 ● THE HISTORY OF POLICE PROFESSIONALISM

Throughout the past century of organized policing, consistent reference has been made to the ideal of professionalism. But the definition of professionalism has changed markedly since the beginning of that history (see Box 2.1). We are therefore left with a problem when we attempt to understand it. There have been three distinct and contradictory definitions for this concept over time.

When **Sir Robert Peel** and the English Parliament created the first English police force in 1829 (the **Metropolitan Police of London**), they considered that they had created a "professional" police force. This was because they had replaced a semi-voluntary system of night watchmen and constables with an organization that employed people to be police officers on a full-time basis. These people were regarded as professionals because they were hired, trained, and paid to do the job. They were in uniform and stood apart from the public, unlike the night watchmen before them.

However, not everyone who is paid to do a job is a member of a profession. The idea of the professions emerged in the Middle Ages as a by-product of the development of the university. Initially, the professions included the clergy, lawyers, and physicians. At the time, these were the only people who could read and write. With the printing press yet to be invented, professionals were members of a small, elite group of people who had access to books, the world of ideas, and sophisticated learning.

BOX 2.1

THE HISTORICAL ERAS OF AMERICAN POLICING

- **Political era: 1837–1910** Police organizations are tied to machine politics. Officers are hired and retained due to their loyalty to local politicos. Corruption is rampant. Police training is nonexistent and, consequently, competence is limited.

- **Reform era: 1910–1980** One jurisdiction at a time, due to corruption scandals, paramilitaristic policing is developed. Civil service is created and controls hiring. Police academies are established. Police accountability begins to be taken seriously.

- **Professional era: 1980–present** Community oriented policing drives the creation of a new philosophy involving proactive policing, ongoing police–community networking, collegial problem solving, and the utilization of lower level expertise.

CAN THE LAW REACH HIM? ("BOSS" TWEED DEFYING THE LAW.)
(From a Cartoon in "Harper's Weekly" [1872].)

© Mary Evans Picture Library/Alamy

During the political era, the police were controlled by "political machines," as shown in this 19th-century "Boss Tweed" cartoon by Thomas Nast.

All sorts of people who are not considered to be professionals do jobs on a full-time basis. They are involved in occupations or careers that do not involve the education, training, experience, responsibilities, and ethical requirements that accompany the professions. While people may be butchers, bakers, or candlestick makers and are paid to be such, they are not professionals as are doctors, lawyers, teachers, or engineers. Despite the obvious skill involved in blue-collar occupations, the carpenters, electricians, plumbers (et al.) of the world are not members of the true professions.

Generations of police officers have been involved in an occupation that requires hard work, dedication, insight, and courage. Yet, until very recently, police work did not require of them the things that are required of genuine professionals. Making a distinction between the genuine professions on the one hand and occupations on the other is not an exercise in snobbery. As we shall see, this differentiation is critical to the development of an understanding of what modern police officers should be. It is about who should be hired and how they should be trained. It is about how police systems should be organized, how police supervisors should lead, and how police review systems should operate.

Eventually, the first era in the Anglo-American history of policing—the one begun by Peel's London police and usually referred to as the political era—was later replaced by the reform era. This happened in most American cities between 1910 and 1940. To fight the corruption and incompetence that existed in many police circles, strict controls were placed on police officers and police organizations. **Chains of command** were tightened. Uniforms and a more military look were sharpened up. **Internal affairs** sections, which investigated accusations of police misconduct, were created. The police academy was invented, and training was taken seriously for the first time. All of this was done in the name of professionalizing the police.

So a new, second-generation definition of professional was created. This new breed of officers had to pass background checks and civil service examinations. They were sent to training academies, investigated when accused of misconduct, and began to hear about competence as an important goal. Police officers began to hear, usually from their sergeants, that they should maintain a professional look and act professionally at all times. This meant that they should polish their brass, shine their shoes, cut their hair, and behave in a militaristic way.

Part of this era's idea of professionalism was that, like military men, policemen (all men at that time) would maintain a civil yet formal and distant relationship with the public. They would never play favorites in the performance of their tasks. They would be objective and legally precise in their application of the law. They would be taught to ignore the lure of payoffs and graft of all sorts and would thus be motivated to do their jobs as honest civil servants. They would be educated about the penal code and case law and would be aware of their roles as legal paraprofessionals. And they would follow the orders that came down from above as if they were in a military organization.

In most places, these changes were effective in doing away with old-style corruption and giving the police a new sense of honor,

Under the militaristic definition of police professionalism, police were expected to polish their brass, shine their shoes, cut their hair, and behave in a militaristic way.

power, effectiveness, and pride. Yet this second definition of professional was still inappropriate. It focused on the physical appearance of the police officer, on a military model of operations, and upon only a part of the knowledge (the law-related part) that the police should possess. It did not take into account the kind of academic experience and behavior that characterizes a true professional. Today's police are not professionals merely because they work full-time. They also are not professionals merely because they have training, standards of conduct, and uniforms. And they are definitely not professionals because they have chains of command.

Within the last few years, the American police have changed in the direction of becoming genuinely professional in every way. This set of changes, toward a third and more appropriate definition of professionalism, is still under way in some places.

2-2 ● TODAY'S PROFESSIONALISM

Sociologists who study the workplace have a distinct understanding of what separates the professions from what are called "jobs" or "occupations." Box 2.2 provides a summary of the elements that make up the true professions. It makes sense for us here to spend a moment discussing these elements so we will understand the critical nature of how personal ethics fit into the development of police work as a genuine profession.

Today's police officers, as a group, possess some of these characteristics. But because they do not possess them all, the label "professional" is not yet ascribed to the police in the way it is to others.

A. Systematized Knowledge

To begin, there is certainly a **systematized body of knowledge** that must be obtained from high school, college, the police academy, and in-service training experiences to operate as a modern-day police officer. The laypeople of the world, even other legal professionals such as lawyers and judges, are not familiar with the complexities of this body of knowledge. Lawyers know case law and codified law; judges also know the law; corrections officers know about dealing with prisoners; psychologists know about adolescent psychology and gang theory; social workers know about ongoing family problems and domestic abuse; criminologists know about the multiple causes of crime; military personnel know about guns and weapons tactics; and medical people know about drug abuse. But no group of people knows as much as an educated police officer about all of these things at once. One can thus make the argument that the police possess their own distinctive body of knowledge.

B. Education

The police are so very well trained today that this arguably gives them the type of academic experience that true professionals enjoy. A large number of officers have some college education, and many have earned degrees.

BOX 2.2

WHAT IS A PROFESSIONAL?

Professionals possess:

Knowledge A systematically organized body of knowledge that laypeople (nonprofessionals) do not possess.

Education An academic experience that involves studying and learning this systematically organized body of knowledge within a wider conceptual framework.

Regulation Self-regulation, standards of education, and licensing that are set by members of the profession themselves, normally controlled by professional organizations such as the American Medical Association (AMA) or American Bar Association (ABA).

Discipline Self-policing, investigation, and disciplining of members accused of misconduct by their peer professionals (again, normally done by professional organizations such as the AMA and the ABA).

Problem solving Done in a "collegial" manner; all licensed members of the profession are, in a sense, coequal partners in problem solving—using their expertise and insight to solve problems together (rather than operating in an authoritarian, command-driven structure).

Ethics An internalized code of conduct, engendered and supported by the entire profession that underwrites professional conduct.

Every officer goes to a police academy to obtain specific police-related knowledge. In addition, these academies, which lasted only a few weeks in earlier days, have become 15- and sometimes even 20-week experiences.

In most police organizations today, rookies are trained by **field training officers (FTOs)** on the street. Additionally, in-service training now takes the form of weekly and even daily videotapes, memos from training divisions, and line-up discussions about legal and forensic developments. These developments extend the educational and training experience well into the modern officer's career. In fact, the lifelong learning that is now a part of American police work involves just the kind of educational preparation and body of knowledge maintenance that is emblematic of the true profession. Doctors, lawyers, professors, and other professionals are involved in a lifelong updating of their knowledge base—and so are today's police officers.

While American policing is not known for being open to learning from policing as it is practiced elsewhere, the European model of police education might very well present an excellent model for the future of our policing. In many European countries, an apprenticeship must be experienced by a police cadet before he or she becomes fully accredited. This experience can take up to two years of probationary service time. During this time frame, the cadet takes college-level courses, and performs various police duties that are essential to operations but are not critical. In this way, the entry-level police officer gains experience and expertise, and at the same time the police organization accomplishes its multiple tasks. When fully certified, the police officer has an expansive level of experience unknown to the American rookie. Most important for the purposes of our discussion here, the police in many European countries have long ago achieved the sort of professional status that has eluded the American police for generations.

The European police supervisor comes into service from a different direction than that taken by the street officer corps. While in America it is assumed that every police leader must have experienced policing from the beat level, in Europe this is not the case. The supervisory structure is manned by individuals who have the equivalent of graduate school educations in what we might call police science. High-level commanders frequently possess the equivalent of a Ph.D. in criminology before they supervise police officers. Individuals can indeed make it up the charts from the on-the-street corps and into the ranks of the administration, but the majority of policy decisions are made by people with advanced degrees and not necessarily any street-level experience. If this sounds odd to the American reader, consider that most American corporations are operated along the same lines. That is, it is not considered necessary that those in supervisory and/or management positions be experienced in on-the-line productions.

It is clear that today's police possess a systematically organized body of knowledge and an academic experience that approaches being truly professional in its nature. Furthermore, today's police officer is beginning to experience a focus upon lifelong learning that is emblematic of the genuine professional.

C. Self-Regulation

With regard to **self-regulation**, in recent years experienced police administrators have been brought into positions where they have a great deal to say about hiring practices, testing procedures, and educational/academy standards. Most states have **Peace Officer Standards and Training (POST)** bodies that set standards for police work. These bodies listen to and follow the advice of police administrators. POST commissions determine the number of hours of which type of curricula must be covered in police academies, what types of training forensics officers need to obtain, how many hours of what type of training K-9 officers need, and so on. This is indeed self-regulation of the sort envisioned by the sociologists who have defined the professions historically. While the type of power to self-regulate enjoyed by the American Medical Association and the American Bar Association does not yet exist within police work, self-regulation of police is expanding. Thus, today's police also meet this criterion for professionalism.

D. Self-Disciplining

Regarding **self-discipline,** the story is different. It seems on the surface that the police regulate their own behavior. All police officers are subject to internal, police department–operated disciplinary systems. Most states require the police to have procedures in place for the reception and investigation of allegations of misconduct as a matter of law. In those few jurisdictions where civilian review operates, the internal system still works in parallel. Thus, all allegations of police misconduct are handled by police investigators.

But internal affairs (IA), as it is called almost everywhere, is operated by police administrators and by the city and county that hire and fire the police. IA is not run by police practitioners in the sense that accountability mechanisms are for the genuine professions. Investigators working for police chiefs and sheriffs investigate misconduct, but members of the police corps do not. Police unions and/or fraternal organizations do not take part in the self-disciplining of the police. In fact, police officer organizations of America often actively fight against IA organizations. When officers are accused of misconduct, it is the police officers' organization (the union) that provides a defense for the accused. Historically, unions tend to defend every officer ever accused of any form of misbehavior, no matter how egregious. Thus, rather than taking police accountability seriously as a part of the values of the profession, police unions tend to take the exact opposite tack.

When doctors or lawyers are accused of misconduct, their professional groups (the doctors' "union," the AMA; or the lawyers' "union," the ABA) have bodies that take an active role in the investigating and disciplining of their own members. Things operate in a similar manner in other professional fields, such as teaching and engineering. However, since police officer fraternal organizations have historically been averse to holding misbehaving officers accountable, true professional self-disciplining is not yet the standard method of operation in police field. The ethical implications of this reality are obvious. For the police to become genuine professionals, they must themselves, as a group, take seriously the disciplining of peers who are guilty of misconduct.

E. Problem Solving

The absence of **collegial problem solving** is also a problem that stands in the way of the development of professionalism. Command and control leadership involves an exactly opposite dynamic to that of the professions. Leadership develops strategies. Subordinates follow orders. Nothing is done collegially. This is definitely not the professional model.

BOX 2.3

COLLEGIAL PROBLEM SOLVING: AN EXAMPLE

Suppose there is a daylight burglary problem in one part of a city. In the days of paramilitary policing, a memorandum might have been generated from somewhere in the middle-management level of the local police department aimed at attacking this problem. A lieutenant or watch commander working within the administration building might very well have put together such a directive, which ordered officers to take certain steps (altering their patrol patterns and so on) to address the burglary problem.

Today, in many COP-oriented jurisdictions, developing a solution for such a problem would be collegially approached. Middle managers would get together with on-the-street supervisors and the beat officers who patrol the troubled area in an effort to come up with a solution—using everyone's input and expertise. Naturally, the middle managers would contribute a more veteran perspective, having the greatest amount of experience in police work. But the lower-level officers would be given credit for their expertise, too.

Beat officers, after all, work on the street, around the clock. They should be familiar not only with the general area's geography but also with the particular burglars who operate in the area, with their cars, and with their homes. Such knowledge should be, and in COP organizations is, treated with great respect. The solution developed this way would arguably be more logically based and effective than one that in the old days would have come down to the street in a memo written by someone who no longer patrols the beat.

Good news in this area is the development of the ideals of COP. This philosophy empowers individual line officers to make decisions on their own, using their steadily increasing expertise and education levels. Furthermore, instead of a top-down focus, COP requires a partnership within police organizations that uses the experience and overall view of middle and upper-level managers in coordination with the day-to-day, on-the-street expertise of the beat cop. When this is done effectively, the combined experience, education, and streetwise knowledge of both groups produce realistic, thoughtful, intelligent solutions to problems.

As COP expands, its idea of using the expertise of lower-level officers as the basis for police decision making is being taken more seriously. If this development continues, one of the roadblocks to police professionalism—that of being command-and-control driven and paramilitaristic—will be removed. For the purposes of our discussion of police ethics, this is again a critical element.

Here in Section 2-2 we have discussed how the classic sociological definition of professionalism does and does not apply to today's police officers. There is much good news here, and it is with pride that today's officers can look at the dynamic changes that are under way. But to finish our discussion of police professionalism, we must consider how all of this has been put together in a more practical and understandable set of principles. While the characteristics of the profession discussed above are important, they do not tell us much about the actual frame of reference that the professional officer should have as an individual.

2-3 • MUIR'S PROFESSIONAL

In one of the most important books ever written about the police, *Police: Streetcorner Politicians* (University of Chicago Press, 1977), political science professor William K. Muir, Jr., discusses police professionalism from a different perspective. Our discussion so far has involved a police subculture–wide consideration of the idea of professionalism. That is, we have suggested that doctors, lawyers, teachers, and police officers as groups are either professionals or they are not. But Muir's conceptualization is different. In fact, it is unique. Muir's analysis points out that no matter what labels may or may not be applied to police officers *in toto,* there are individual officers who behave as professionals and those who do not. Thus, his conceptualization brings us to consider the behavior of police officers as individuals.

BOX 2.4

MUIR'S PROFESSIONAL OFFICER

The Professional Officer possesses:

Passion The understanding that resorting to violence or threats—coercion, in essence—can be morally acceptable. This is true if and only if it is done in the interest of justice and in accordance with the welfare of the community. No guilt need be associated with the process of using or threatening to use force, as long as it is "principled bullying."

Perspective The development of an inner understanding of the motives of people, a sense of life's causes and effects, and knowledge of the tragedy of life—that all people suffer sometimes, that everyone yearns for some dignity, and that no individual is worthless.

Muir suggests that to operate as true professionals individual officers must possess "passion and perspective" when applying their considerable expertise to people's real-life problems. Let us look at Muir's two ideas and discuss how they create a model for professional policing that is understandable and practical.

A. Passion

Muir's first idea is that the professional police officer must possess what he calls an **"integrated passion"** to use coercive power. By this he means that police officers have to be comfortable using what amounts to extortion to achieve good, desirable ends. They have to have integrated it into their view of morality. Extortion involves obtaining desired behavior from others by using threats to harm something of value to them. Children may be told to behave themselves or they will be spanked. Countries tell one another to behave themselves or they will be invaded. Similarly, police officers will threaten to arrest people unless they do what they are told.

However, not all officers are comfortable doing this. Some police officers are reluctant to threaten others because they feel it involves bullying. Not being comfortable with such bullying, some officers prefer to use their powers of reason as often as possible to convince people to do the right thing because it is good or just or rational. There is nothing wrong with this idea. In fact, Muir takes great pains to point out that police officers should be experts at controlling behavior in just this way, using logic, intelligence, and their persuasive powers.

But police officers routinely encounter situations where appealing to people's better judgment, logic, religious ethics, or morality does not work. Under these circumstances, Muir writes that the professional officer should not be "conflicted" about intimidating people. Intimidation, when used in the best interest of justice, is an important tool in the police officer's arsenal. If officers are reluctant to use coercive power, they might avoid solving people's problems and thus not get their jobs done.

B. Perspective

There is a second characteristic endemic to the professional officer's personal makeup. Muir believes that professionals need to have a certain perspective on life that he calls the **"tragic perspective."** All people, he suggests, suffer at times from tragedy in their lives. Suffering from tragedy involves experiencing unfairness, calamity, or disaster. Muir does not suggest that when people suffer in this way their consequently deviant acts should be excused. But he does point out that one key to being a professional is the capacity to understand how tragedy explains a great deal about deviant human behavior.

This involves understanding that misbehavior, deviance, and crime are the products of many different dynamics and situations. Life is full of complex

CLASSIFICATION ACCORDING TO PROFESSIONAL POLITICAL MODEL

	MORALITY OF COERCION	
	INTEGRATED	CONFLICTED
Tragic perspective	Professional	Reciprocator
Cynical perspective	Enforcer	Avoider

patterns that cause deviance. The professional officer understands that unfortunate, unlucky, and un-controllable circumstances might affect any of us. Sometimes tragedy overwhelms people and produces deviance. Muir argues that the modern, professional officer's job involves not merely reacting to crime and violence but understanding the underlying causes for such behavior. While he never implies that the police shouldn't take action when they see crime occurring, he also points out that working for long-term solutions to these problems is the larger role of the professional officer. Especially in an era of COP, the police today are expected to attack enduring problems on their beats and not simply to react in moralistic ways to citizen misconduct.

So Muir's idea here is that the professional is a critical analyst of crime's causes and a student of its various solutions. But there is more. Because of this tragic reality

S.P./Shutterstock.com

Muir points out that all people experience tragedy in their lives, and that one key to being a professional is to understand how tragedy explains a great deal about deviant behavior.

of life, Muir argues that the world view of the police officer should not divide people into camps, into the "good people" and the "bad people," into "us" and "them." Thinking in this way involves embracing what he calls the "cynical perspective," which suggests that there are different sets of rules for different people: one set for them and another set for us. At a certain basic, human level, everyone is of equal value. This is the view of social reality expressed in the tragic perspective.

For the cynical perspective to be applied on the streets by the police, making citizens into the enemy in a real sense is to create a situation under which the people and the police are mutually suspicious of each other. Any good, competent police officer knows that policing cannot be done effectively without the help of the local community. The cynical perspective works against police–community cooperation and against the development of faith in the police.

2-4 • ANALYSIS

Putting together our various discussions about the definition of professionalism we will come up with an understanding of how far the "occupation" of policing has come in the direction of becoming a profession.

First, recall that the police of today already possess a systematized body of knowledge. This body of knowledge grows rapidly. As the knowledge base expands, so too must the educational experience of the modern police officer. Four years of college as a baseline is critical. In addition, college criminal justice programs need to expand in their content. What needs to increase is the amount of new research that is taught to tomorrow's police officers before they obtain their practical training in the academy. Furthermore, time spent in the police academy needs to continue to lengthen. Police leaders and those politicians who control the purse strings need to support this development.

Second, the acceptance of COP is necessary as an integral part of the development of police professionalism. As that occurs, several of the elements of professionalism will naturally follow. Important here is collegial problem solving. Led by collegial atmospheres in police academies, and expanded by a de-emphasis on paramilitarization, outdated command-and-control leadership should be ended. And as this occurs, the utilization of lower-level expertise, mentored and coordinated by today's middle managers, will expand in the direction of the long sought after goal of professionalism.

Third, the police officers of America need to take police misbehavior more seriously. Led by their union representatives, America's police need to understand that their status and, by translation, their salaries and benefits packages, will only increase and improve if they work together with police administrators in attempting to generate positive police behaviors. While this undoubtedly sounds absolutely "out of the box" to many people in the field, there is no particular reason why police unions cannot create partnerships with police administrations in pursuit of developing more positive police review systems and disciplinary mechanisms.

Fourth, let us recall Muir's tragic perspective. He wrote about how effective police officers would benefit from such an approach to life. Understanding the complexity of the causal patterns of deviant behavior and embracing the

BOX 2.5

 STEPS LEFT TO TAKE TOWARD PROFESSIONALISM

Aside from the critically important continued development of COP nationwide, here are some specifics that must be achieved:

- Extension of the academic experience
- Expansion of collegial problem solving
- Development of self-disciplining within the subculture
- Acceptance of the tragic perspective
- Internalization of a professional ethic

unitary nature of the human experience will inform the understanding that today's police officers have in a positive way. Through training and effective mentoring, all police leaders—whether they be immediate supervisors, administrators, union representatives, or just experienced veterans—can aid in the pursuit of this goal.

Finally, there is the focal point of our book here: the inculcation of a personal ethic into the operating principles and ethos of modern police officers. We of course will suggest that it be our ethic to live by. But whether or not this occurs, the police officers of America need to fashion and then apply such an ethic to every action they take. Thus, we have a sort of laundry list of important subgoals that potentially will feed the overall goal of the police achieving professional status in America in the way they have in Europe.

2-5 ◉ SUMMARY

Earlier in this chapter it was important for us to discuss the history of the development of definitions of professionalism. Everyone in police work needs to know what professionalism is and what it is not. It was then critical for us to consider the sociological definition of professionalism. While progress is being made in that direction, there are roadblocks inhibiting its final development. Both the good news and the bad news need to be analyzed with respect to developments in this area.

Finally, Muir gives us a more practical idea of what it means to be a professional police officer on a minute-to-minute basis. While it is by no means a "how to do it" list of specifics, Muir tells us that the professional officer needs to have integrated into his or her personal character both (1) the passion to use coercive power in the pursuit of just ends and (2) a tragic perspective on life that mitigates against cynicism and jadedness.

One final note is in order about the concept of professionalism. Professionalism is changing the way thousands of police officers view their jobs. The change is from seeing police work as an occupation that gives something to the police officer to seeing police work as a profession to which the police officer owes something. Over time, true professionals are embracing the idea that it is a privilege to be a police officer. This is not just because policing is a good job with great benefits and a dynamic workday experience. It is also because the amount of responsibility and power with which the individual officer is entrusted is unusually great.

2-6 ⊙ TOPICS FOR DISCUSSION

1. The text refers to several different historical definitions of police "professionalism." Why do the authors take time to point out that wearing uniforms, having grooming standards, and operating under chains of command do not make an occupation a profession?

2. Discuss the sociological definition of "professional." Are the police professionals from this perspective? If not, what would it take to make them such?

3. Applying Muir's tragic perspective, discuss why there is crime. That is, generate a discussion of the multiple causes of crime that is centered on the idea that tragedy, chance, social circumstances, opportunity, and necessity all drive some people to behave in criminal ways.

4. The cynical view of the world suggests that there is an "us" and a "them" that divides people. It is juxtaposed to Muir's tragic perspective. What would be the consequences if police officers applied one set of rules to those they felt were good people and another set of rules to those they felt were bad people? How would we know which was which? Would we look at ethnic characteristics or religion or gender? What's wrong with this?

2-7 ⊙ ETHICAL SCENARIO

In the wake of the events of September 11, 2001, police officers in Tennessee are confronted by a crowd that wants to burn down a Muslim place of worship. The most vociferous members of the crowd rave about how "Muslims have attacked the United States" and that, thus, vengeance is called for. What do these officers do? In addition to the obvious—keeping the crowd from committing arson—what can they do to calm things down and even teach the crowd some tolerance? How can a police officer explain the idea that *all* Muslims are not terrorists and, equally, that America has always stood for freedom of worship for all? In other words, how do police officers take a positive, mentoring approach to the crowd's desire to act in a cynical way? How might police officers couch the event in a way that educates the crowd about Muir's tragic perspective?

2-8 ◉ WRITING EXERCISE

Our discussion suggests that the sociological definition of "profession" includes self-disciplining as a critical element. Construct an essay that differentiates between the form of police officer discipline that occurs at the hands of internal affairs and the *genuine* self-disciplining that sociologists call for. (Hint: The difference hinges upon how police unions have traditionally fought against police accountability in lieu of working as a part of the system that enforces it.)

2-9 ◉ KEY TERMS

chains of command: Organizational system wherein orders are developed at upper levels and handed down the hierarchy to be followed by lower-level functionaries.

collegial problem solving: Professional mode of solving problems wherein peers come together and find solutions in an equitable and democratic fashion.

field training officers (FTOs): Experienced officers who train and mentor rookie officers out on the street after they have completed the academy experience.

integrated passion: Understanding that it is morally acceptable to use coercion in the name of accomplishing good ends.

internal affairs: Police internal sub-organization in charge of investigating allegations of misconduct.

Metropolitan Police of London: The first uniformed and organized police department in the Western world.

Peace Officer Standards and Training (POST): State-level commission that develops professional standards for police officer education and certification.

Sir Robert Peel: Prime minister of England who sponsored the legislation creating the Metropolitan Police in 1829.

political era: The first era of American policing, wherein the police were controlled directly by machine politics.

reform era: Time frame when the American police were reorganized and paramilitarism was exchanged for the older, politically controlled way organization.

self-discipline: Refers to professionals having the power to sanction the misconduct of their own peers.

self-regulation: Refers to professionals having the power to set standards for their own occupations.

systematized body of knowledge: The occupation-specific information gleaned by professionals in their academic experience.

tragic perspective: Muir's ideal for the professional police officer; includes the ideas of the unitary experience of humankind, complex causal patterns, and the necessity of human interdependence.

CHAPTER 3

The Nature of Police Work

Chapter Outline

> *"People talk all the time about the police being powerful individuals. That's ridiculous. The police don't have much power. Not really."*

—Joseph Wambaugh, novelist and
former LAPD sergeant

We begin with a cautionary note of sorts. In this brief rundown about the nature of the police officer experience, we are to some extent covering ground that the reader might have studied in a course on the sociology of the police or that the experienced police practitioner or leader understands. While the chapter might very well be a recapitulation, it is not a good idea to skip it altogether. It reminds the veteran officer as well as informs the novice student of the police about the critical, unique layering of frustrations that can inform the experience.

In particular, we will focus on just a few of the many paradoxes that are part of the experience of working a beat, supervising police officers, and of being a police administrator. The paradoxes of police work being legion as they are, it behooves anyone engaged in a discussion of police ethics to focus for a moment upon how the individual officer can feel at sea out on the street. And, concomitantly, it makes sense to reflect upon how the consequently formed police subculture is known both for its isolation from the citizenry and for its tremendous solidarity.

3-1   ●   THE NATURE OF PARADOXES

Everyone who experiences police work develops at least some level of frustration due to fact that the job is replete with **paradox.** Policing is not what people expect it will be when they enter into the endeavor. Programmed by media imagery that is unrealistic, driven by idealistic notions of what enforcing the law in a free society must be like, police recruits usually have some farfetched ideas concerning what they are about to experience. Perceiving that being a police officer regularly involves the application of force and the ongoing exercise of a tremendous amount of control over citizens, rookie officers believe that to be a police officer is to be a profoundly powerful individual. Of course, nothing could be further from the truth. The recruit soon discovers that police work is frustrating precisely because the police often *lack* the power to accomplish their basic charge. So frustration does not develop in the psyche of a young police officer because of stress brought about by exercising substantial power over others; it is brought about by possessing an *inadequate* amount of power over others.

The paradoxes of coercive power make up just one set in a larger set of paradoxes. Our discussion in this chapter will focus on these multiple paradoxes, and how young officers tend to deal with frustration in both individual and collective ways. But before we move toward these paradoxes, we must discuss a paradox so critical that it forms the entire discussion here.

3-2 ● AN INITIAL ADMINISTRATIVE PARADOX

The duties that police are supposed to accomplish and the roles they are supposed to play are **multiple, conflicting, and vague.** There is no single thing the police are supposed to do and no single role they are supposed to play. On the street, there is a constant struggle to get multiple jobs done using many varied tools while at the same time playing numerous roles. This can confuse police officer and leader alike.

The police have three basic sets of functions and roles, those of law enforcement, order maintenance, and service. An ongoing reality of police work—and a frustrating one at that—is that these functions often conflict with each other. For example, the police will sometimes observe drug use at a huge, orderly rock concert, or they will deal with a large group of underage drinkers at an otherwise calm and controlled fraternity party. To enforce the letter of the law on such occasions might very well involve creating major crowd control problems. Under such circumstances law enforcement is in direct conflict with order maintenance.

Such details are not unusual in police work. Thus, the multiple, conflicting, and vague nature of what the police do sometimes creates confusion for the police, distrust of the police, and difficulties that directly impact our discussion of what ethical conduct is. This is the baseline paradox of police work.

3-3 ● PARADOXES ON THE BEAT

A number of other central paradoxes face all police officers working on the beat (see *The Paradoxes of Police Work,* 2nd Ed., by Perez, 2010). In fact, one of the most cogent reasons for the police subculture is that officers cleave together to form a tightly knit group precisely because only other officers understand this paradox-driven experience.

A. Due Process

The police are the most visible representatives of the legal system. In theory, they should be the proud representatives of the American due process system.

BOX 3.1

MULTIPLE, CONFLICTING, AND VAGUE FUNCTIONS

The three major functions of the police, which are admittedly vague and often in conflict with each other, are to:

- Enforce the law
- Maintain order
- Provide services to the community

But often they are not. Because of how the criminal justice system operates, the police can be at odds with its due process principles. Some police officers are so inexorably opposed to the system's exclusionary processes that they are prone to break procedural law in order to accomplish what they believe to be their most important mission: protecting the citizenry by getting the bad guys off the street.

On the street, the police must focus on substantive guilt. But the system does not. It focuses upon procedural guilt. Thus, the legal system can appear to be lost in a wilderness of **legal technicalities.** The rules of the system seem to get in the way of finding the truth and making just decisions about citizen deviance.

This focus can frustrate police officers in a very personal way. When officers take the witness stand, the job of the defense is to impeach their credibility. Whether it be by implying that an officer is lying, incompetent, bigoted, or unintelligent, the system can make the police officer on the stand feel as if it is attacking him or her. In an effort to reach what the legal system considers to be the truth, the system seems disrespectful to the individual officer. And so, a profoundly important paradox of the experience of police officers is that the due process system is rejected by significant numbers of police officers because it seems to be against them. They become Dirty Harry, which we have discussed earlier.

B. Stereotyping

When we hear the word **stereotyping,** we tend to interpret it in a negative way. Most of us are opposed to racial, religious, or sexual orientation stereotypes that are misused to discriminate unfairly against groups of people. But stereotyping in and of itself is an operational principle of life. Everyone uses it as a way to cope with life's complexities. It is natural and logical. Psychologists tell us that everything we know is made up of nothing more than stereotyped notions of people, things, events, and language that are dropped into **"diagnostic packages"** stored in our brains. The label we attach to anything is nothing more than a stereotyped package stored as part of the grand scheme of information that makes up who we are and what we think we know.

But while all people stereotype, police officers tend to stereotype more readily than others. They live in a world driven, like all bureaucracies, by statistics and numbers. Police officers think in terms of penal code sections, vehicle code sections, and so on. They take the numbers associated with certain types of deviance and crime, and weave it into their on-the-street lexicon. A murderer becomes "a 187." An armed robber becomes "a 211 man." Police also stereotype by using organizational shortcuts such as radio codes for minute-by-minute communication. This phenomenon is labeled by psychologists as **"perceptual shorthand."**

Second, police officers, like others in the criminal justice system, tend to **"normalize crime"**). Officers must file all deviant behavior into diagnostic packages because of the dictates of *habeas corpus.* No matter how bizarre, disgusting, dishonest, horrific, or despicable human behavior might become, the police are driven to normalize it by attaching a number to it. The police are forever asking themselves, "This behavior is disgusting . . . but what type of crime does it involve?" It is not possible to arrest a person for *any* type of abnormal behavior unless there is a code number attached to it.

Third, part of the craft of police work on the streets involves "working the beat." Officers normalize how a beat looks, who belongs where, what the flow of traffic looks like, when, where, and how daily life operates in a standard way. In doing so, the police learn who belongs and, most importantly, who does *not* belong on their beats. It is part of the job of the police to engage in finding out what is "wrong" on their beats. Again, this requires the police to stereotype.

Finally, dealing with the constant possibility of violence, the police look for **"symbolic assailants"** (see Box 3.2). Concerned with potential violence, police officers are taught to consider the possible danger posed to them by every person they see on the street. In the academy setting, cadets are shown videotapes of incidents where police officers have come under fire and even been murdered. Usually taken from cameras in cruisers, these tapes are meant to instill in the young officer an understanding of the danger involved in working on the street, especially with automobile stops.

But the problem is that traffic stops rarely end up in violent confrontations, and they almost never end in injury or death. There are millions of traffic stops each year, and only a couple dozen end up developing into lethal confrontations. Attempting to prepare themselves for the worst, the police

BOX 3.2

ENCOURAGING PARANOIA

Jerome Skolnick, a leading American scholar on policing, wrote that the police are forever looking for "symbolic assailants," or people who might pose a threat. Cadets are taught from day one in the academy to watch people's hands, never stand in front of a doorway, stand at arm's distance from any civilian, keep their own hands free and ready, and any number of other axioms aimed at protecting the officer from assault. But in dealing with the public this way, the police are almost always wrong. What we mean is that citizens *almost never* pose any threat to the police. In a million daily interactions with the public, the police are confronted with citizens who may be upset and angry, but who are generally peaceful. By instilling a consistent, ongoing concern for their own safety, police training creates an artificially negative perception in the minds of citizens that the police are paranoid, authoritarian, and irrational individuals.

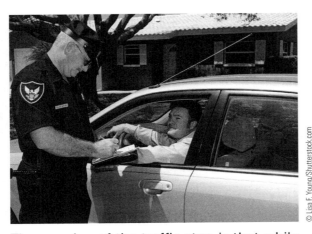

© Lisa F. Young/Shutterstock.com

The paradox of the traffic stop is that while the police are taught to treat such incidents as being potentially dangerous, millions of them occur each year without incident.

will treat a vehicle stop as being potentially dangerous. This is perfectly logical. But the behavior of the police under such circumstances *appears* to citizens to involve a sort of illogical paranoia aimed at perfectly harmless, ordinary people.

There are several additional dynamics associated with police stereotyping. Police officers tend to see people as "cases," as do other professionals who deal with the public. Social workers, doctors, and public administrators are sometimes accused of losing their humanity because of this propensity. Paradoxically enough, keeping some distance from the population that they police, nurture, and administer is an absolute necessity in the world of professionals who deal with the public. Becoming too involved in individual lives and tragedies can cloud one's judgment. But it can also make the delivery of public services appear callous and uncaring. When people cease to be human beings in the minds of professionals and become cases, this is always true. While police officers normalize crime for perfectly understandable reasons, citizens resent this stereotypification for equally understandable reasons. But the stereotyping involved in the police–community relationship goes both ways, for the overwhelming majority of people hold stereotypes about the police. This seems logical to the public. Most people only know one or two police officers; many know none. Almost always extrapolating from a very few, isolated experiences with the police, under the direst of circumstances, most people create stereotypes about the police that appear to be true. It is human nature for people to behave this way.

But such stereotypes are most definitely *not* true. Police officers come in all shapes and sizes, with different life experiences, different levels of education and understanding, different political beliefs and opinions, and different strengths and weaknesses. When police officers are faced with such unfair stereotypes, they feel affronted and can rebel. The more inexperienced the police officer, the stronger the propensity to be angry about such perceived unfairness.

C. Discretion

For several hundred years of American history we have fancied that we want to live in a world ruled by "laws and not men." We cleave to the rule of law as a guiding principle for our system of government. The rule of law, and not

BOX 3.3

STEREOTYPED IMAGES OF THE POLICE

Police officers are:

- Overly aggressive, authoritarian types
- Racial and religious bigots
- Anti-gay and lesbian homophobes
- Not particularly intelligent or well educated
- Intolerant, rigid, and unresponsive to logic
- Uncaring and aloof from human suffering
- Politically archconservative

"the rule of cop," should be administered out on the street. We Americans want those who exercise the law's powers over others to cleave to the spirit of the law, not some personalized or subculturally created principles.

On the other hand, the police are confronted every day by questions about whether they should intervene, whether they should arrest, whether they should use force, and what amount of force to use. Police work is all about such decisions. By applying their individual understandings of justice, the police put life into the law. But the law is often of marginal utility to the police. This is because no codified set of rules can definitively determine how the police should act under all circumstances, in all situations. Sometimes an arrest would not be in the best interests of justice. Sometimes a lecture, a trip home, or a discussion with Mom and Dad makes more sense. In other word, holding back on the application of the law can be the best tack to take.

Concomitantly, there are times when the law doesn't dictate any specific course of action when the police *want* to take action. This might mean taking non-legal or semi-legal steps. By getting a would-be abusive husband to "take a walk and calm down," urging a drunk at a bar to "go home and sober up," or dispersing a group of teenagers with "if we have to come back, you won't like it," the police are doing their job and being of service to the community. In these examples and countless others, they are clearly not involved in doing what is legally possible, but they are taking a common sense approach.

When citizens see the police making discretionary decisions and "making up their own minds what to do" they can be outraged. Citizens can become upset at the mere *implication* that individual police officer decision making determines how citizens are treated. Even though today's police officers are, on average, more educated and better trained than their predecessors, that does not matter to the public. They see the police deciding to arrest someone and they can conclude that the police are unfairly empowered.

BOX 3.4

SUPERVISORY MONITORING OF DISCRETION

The police leader occupies an awkward, paradoxical position vis-à-vis the exercise of officer discretion. Discretion not only exists as a practical dynamic, it *has* to exist as an important element of the justice system. The police *must* use their minds (and hearts) to infuse reasonableness and fairness into the system. But discretion can be abused. In fact, the abuse of discretionary latitude is perhaps the single most important minute-by-minute form of misconduct in police work. The police leader must find a way to encourage the right kind of discretion and discourage the wrong kind. This is a tough proposition, given that police supervision is done in fits and starts, and from a distance.

So the paradox associated with discretion that is that while it is absolutely essential that the police infuse the law with their intelligence and empathy, the public will naturally be driven to resent it.

D. Coercive Power

In *Police: Streetcorner Politicians*, William K. Muir, Jr. (see Chapter 2) engaged in an in-depth analysis of the paradoxes of **coercive power:** situations when the apparently powerful have trouble coercing the apparently powerless. In creating a profound understanding of how these paradoxes work, he shed light on the idea often expressed by police officers that they sometimes feel powerless.

Muir began by pointing out that the police occupy a unique position in society because they are empowered to use force and the threat of force (coercion). Coercion involves obtaining desired behavior from another by threatening to harm something of value to them, or what Muir calls a **hostage.** Examples of coercion could include phrases such as "Calm down or you're going to jail," or "if you come back here again, we're going to have a problem," or "shut up and listen, or you'll get a citation."

But coercing others can be difficult or impossible due to what Muir labeled the four paradoxes of coercive power. First, it can be difficult to coerce those who are so disenfranchised that they have no hostages—nothing of value to threaten. This is known as the **paradox of dispossession.** This paradox states that the less one has, the less one has to lose. Muir discusses dealing with the homeless in this regard. In solving details that involve the homeless, police officers are confronted with people who have nothing; they have no jobs, no status in society, no homes, and no reputation. They are dispossessed in a way that frustrates attempts to control them through coercion.

BOX 3.5

DETACHMENT AND TERRORISM

Understanding Muir's paradox of detachment is of particular importance to everyday Americans today because it informs our understanding of how difficult it is to fight a war on terrorism. Suicide bombers, such as those who flew planes into the Twin Towers on 9/11, have detached themselves from valuing what is arguably their most dear possession: their own lives. When terrorists do this, there is nothing that a potential coercer can threaten to do that will dissuade them from their suicide missions.

What if the police are confronted with people who *do* have hostages that can be threatened—jobs, families, homes, or social status—but who detach themselves from caring about them? This is the second paradox Muir discusses, known as the **paradox of detachment.** Muir uses the example of domestic disturbance to make the point that people who can consciously detach themselves from valuing their freedom can be difficult to coerce. As any experienced police officer knows, a wife can respond to the suggestion that if she doesn't calm down her husband is going to be arrested by saying, "Go ahead, and arrest the S.O.B." When this happens, the police are powerless to control the situation through coercion. The paradox of detachment suggests the less one values a hostage, the less effective is the coercer's threat.

The third paradox discussed by Muir has to do with the importance of making believable threats. Muir points out that if the police have a reputation for being able to follow through on their threats (to arrest or to use force) they can be extremely effective in coercing others. Especially when dealing with crowds, the police must show a tough face to the public. The **paradox of face** states that the nastier one's reputation, the less nasty one has to be. Police officers know this intuitively; they are not often challenged if they carry a "badass rep." Of course, if someone calls their bluff, a coercer must *always* follow through on their threats. Muir points out that in dealing with crowds, the police must walk a fine line and take care not to make threats that are hollow ("you're all going to jail") since their bluff might be called. But if the police carefully manipulate their individual and collective reputations, then coercing even large groups can be done effectively and without often having to actually follow through on their threats.

Muir's final paradox of coercive power has two sides to it. The **paradox of irrationality** suggests that the crazier the victim of coercion, the less effective the threat. For example, juveniles often don't understand the situation that's presented to them; Muir says that anyone who "doesn't get it" can be difficult to coerce. Of course, juveniles are not the only citizens who,

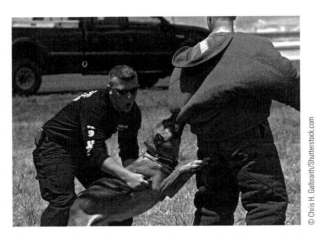

© Chris H. Galbraith/Shutterstock.com

The paradox of irrationality is aptly illustrated by the coercive power of K-9 units.

for one reason or another, don't understand what's being threatened, or that the police truly mean to go through with their threats. Drunk, stoned, frightened, old, mentally unbalanced, or non-native-speaking citizens form a long list of people "who don't get it." This group can be difficult to control.

The second half of this paradox suggests that the crazier the co-ercer, the *more* effective the threat. In police work, this principle is best illustrated by the behavior control exhibited by K-9 units. People are more afraid of dogs than police officers because dogs, in the mind of the public, are irrational. No matter how much a citizen thinks they understand how well police dogs are trained and how effectively the police can control them, they are afraid of the threat of harm presented by a dog, an irrational, nonhuman antagonist. A dog is a nasty, angry, vicious animal who presents a profound threat.

One of Muir's central points is that this list of people who can be difficult to coerce is a list of citizens with whom the police most often interact. The paradoxes suggest that it can be difficult for the police to coerce the homeless, people engaged in family disturbances, crowds, juveniles, the elderly, the drunk, the stoned, the frightened, and the insane. This is a veritable "who's who" of the people the police are expected to control. And so quite often the police feel constrained by the paradoxes of coercive power.

But there is more to Muir's discussion of paradoxes. For not only do police officers suffer from the paradoxes of coercive power in the sense that they have trouble coercing others, but the opposite is also the case; the police can *be coerced* by citizens. Police officers have many hostages for citizens to threaten to harm, such as clean uniforms, professional reputations, and future advancement. Some citizens understand the complaint process and they know that the average police officer doesn't want to be the recipient of a citizen's complaint. Some homeless people learn that the police don't want to arrest them and don't even want to put them in their police cars. Some people understand that police officers tend to avoid making questionable arrests because they are concerned about moving up the chain of command (e.g., making sergeant) in the future. Because of these realities, Muir suggests that the police can actually be coerced out of taking actions that might otherwise be appropriate.

BOX 3.6

MUIR'S PARADOXES OF COERCIVE POWER

- The paradox of dispossession: The less one has, the less one has to lose.
- The paradox of detachment: The less one values a hostage, the less coercible one is.
- The paradox of face: The nastier one's reputation, the less nasty one has to be.
- The paradox of irrationality: The crazier the victim, the less effective the threat. The crazier the coercer, the more effective the threat.

E. Paramilitarism

It is said that the police are organized along paramilitary (or semi-militaristic) lines, because they have chains of command, uniforms, and ranks that are analogous to those used by the military. There are numerous reasons for this military focus. First, it makes the police visible. Citizens who desire the protection and support of the police can readily identify them. Second, it makes the police feel more accountable. That is, operating within a paramilitary organization makes officers *believe* that they are under regular, intense scrutiny. (This is true in all organizations run along paramilitaristic lines, not just police departments.)

Third, **paramilitarism** instills a sense of duty in the individual—a duty to "the corps" of police officers. As is true in the military, the corps of officers exerts a pressure on individuals that motivates them to do their duty, even when they are outnumbered and in danger. Furthermore, this sense of duty makes the police behave in a more legally defensible way, making good, rational, and "correct" decisions in a legalistic sense. It generates a desire to look sharp and to present a more no-nonsense carriage toward the public. It can motivate the individual officer to handle a hot detail without cover, if necessary, despite their fear of doing so.

These examples illustrate the positive side of taking a paramilitaristic focus. But there is a downside to paramilitarism. Analyzed a generation ago by Tony Jefferson in *The Case Against Paramilitary Policing* (London: Open University, 1990), there are tremendous drawbacks to this way of organizing the police, giving pause to anyone who is open-minded about the issue. Four important points can be drawn from Jefferson's work that illuminate the issue of paramilitary organization in police work.

First, going out into the world each day as a military force, to fight a "war on crime" or a "war on drugs," necessitates that the police must struggle against an enemy. Who is the enemy in such wars? Criminals, of course.

And who are the criminals out there? Everyone who has broken the law, to be sure. And who is that? Well, everyone who has drunk alcohol under the age of 21, driven a vehicle under the influence, smoked marijuana or used any other illegal drug (estimates place this number at about 70 million American citizens), or broken any other law is a member of the enemy camp. So under a paramilitaristic focus the police are going to "war" every day against a huge population of American citizens. Millions of Americans are members of some sort of enemy camp in a war on crime.

What's the problem here? All militaries, throughout history, spend time **dehumanizing the enemy.** If the enemy can be couched in less-than-human terms in the hearts and minds of soldiers, sailors, and marines, then it is easier to do violence to them. Military basic training has always included this type of dehumanization as a part of its indoctrination of young recruits. Unfortunately, a paramilitaristic focus tends to do the same for police officers; it dehumanizes the citizenry, and works on a regular basis to create an "us versus them" focus. And nothing good comes from having the police consider themselves to be fighting *against* the citizenry. It is bad for the citizenry, the police, and the interests of justice.

Second, living and working within a command and control structure tends to work against individual problem solving. The stronger the chain-of-command feeling is in any organization, the less prone its individuals are to think for themselves or try new ideas. They might develop a propensity to believe that there is only one way to do things and not participate in the sort of "thinking outside of the box" that we want to encourage in the modern, professional police officer. Under COP, our contemporary police officer corps is encouraged to become involved in the lives of citizens as agents of change, independent problem solvers, and "criminologists in uniform." That is how it should be. Paramilitaristic organization works directly *against* the development of these relatively new dynamics within our modern police officer corps.

Third, the American public began railing against police "fascism" during the tumultuous era of the 1960s. At that time, we heard a great deal about how the police sometimes operate "like the Gestapo." People did not like the "occupying army" feel of inner-city policing in particular. Part of the call for the new philosophy of COP came as a result of these feelings on the part of the citizenry. After the reform era came along, behaving in an aloof, detached, impersonal, paramilitaristic manner somehow made citizens, especially those in the inner cities, distrust the police even more than they would otherwise.

Fourth, paramilitarism seems to have a fixation with police officer facades. "Haircuts and shoe shines" are a big part of this. While there is certainly nothing wrong with police officers looking smart out on the street, having sergeants and lieutenants deal with officers like children trivializes police work in a strange way. Telling grown men and women, who are armed and licensed to use force against the public, to "get a haircut" or "shine your shoes" demeans the police endeavor. Focusing upon such trivialities is odd at best and debilitating at worst.

BOX 3.7

THE DRAWBACKS OF PARAMILITARISM

A list of Jefferson's drawbacks of paramilitaristic policing include:

- It creates an "us against them" feeling among both the police and the citizenry.
- It necessitates making citizens into "the enemy" in a warlike battle.
- It intimidates people unnecessarily.
- It focuses upon such trivialities as haircuts and shoe shines.
- It works contrary to several of the principles of COP, especially those of collegial problem solving.

So, paramilitarism presents us this paradox: while paramilitary organization has a number of rational reasons for its implementation, it has an equally long list of arguments against it. But in an odd way, this first paradox of paramilitarism is accompanied by still another paradox. For paramilitarism is absolutely necessary under certain unusual circumstances. During riots, hostage situations, sniper-related events, and other circumstances where the police are involved in the degeneration of social norms and/or gun-related, life-threatening events, the police *must* behave like a military organization. When weapons are drawn and gunfire erupts, there must be a chain of command that fixes responsibility specifically.

While paramilitarism might very well be deleterious to the development of good police–community relations 99 percent of the time, it is a necessary part of the organization that the police must "morph into" at a moment's notice when such extraordinary events present themselves.

Today's police are involved in creating and maintaining two organizations at once: a community-oriented system of problem-solving agents of change, and a

© arindambanerjee/Shutterstock.com

The paradox of police paramilitarism is that while almost everything about it is bad for police-community relations, under certain, limited circumstances—such as riots—it is necessary.

militaristic system of people who do precisely what they are ordered to do. These are the COP style and the paramilitaristic, crisis-oriented style.

F. Media Imagery

In contemporary America, the media enjoy a rather strange, and sometimes strained, relationship with the police. With regard to the news media, there is an ongoing symbiotic relationship that affords police news coverage that is generally favorable. Owned and operated by major corporations, and driven (in terms of content control) by advertising dollars that come from other major corporations, the news media, particularly television news, tend to be rather conservative and pro-police. Of course, if scandal surfaces the media will turn on the police and cover it with an almost maniacal interest. But on a day-to-day basis, the news media in America report exactly what the police say about virtually anything related to crime. Stories about criminals, gangs, drugs, and crime trends are reported verbatim from police updates.

With regard to the entertainment media, another set of dynamics is operable. Several totally unrealistic ideas are packaged and sold to the American public in movies and on television screens. These images tend to convince the average citizen that while the police on television or on the silver screen are competent and even heroic, their local police are the exact opposite—incompetent and ineffective. The *pretend* police are effective crime fighters, but the *real* police are somehow unable to live up to normal police standards.

There are several sets of these unrealistic images. First, there is the **"RCMP Syndrome."** Named after the Royal Canadian Mounted Police, because "the Mountie always gets his man," media-created images drive people to expect the police to solve every crime—a preposterous idea that, again, tends to convince American citizens that their local police are incompetent. Second, and as previously discussed, there is the Dirty Harry problem. Hollywood sells Harry as a hero who must break the law (procedural law) in order to enforce the law (substantive law). In essence, this suggests that the police must become involved in vigilante justice if they are to be effective. Third, there is the media packaging of **"cosmetized violence."** Coined by the ex-LAPD-sergeant turned novelist Joseph Wambaugh, this term refers to making violence appear sexy and cool while, at the same time, transforming police officers into Superman-like heroes. As with RCMP Syndrome, cosmetized violence makes local police seem incompetent to citizens who believe the images they see on the screen.

Fourth, there is an almost universal problem in America with *Miranda* warnings. On television and in the movies viewers see that arrestees are *always* Mirandized at the moment of arrest. This, of course, is incorrect. Again, this makes the local police appear to be incompetent. Even worse, it seems ethically inappropriate. Each year in this country, thousands of Americans believe they have observed police misconduct when they witness arrests that are not accompanied by *Miranda* warnings.

BOX 3.8

HOLLYWOOD'S UNREALISTIC POLICE IMAGERY

- The RCMP syndrome
- The Dirty Harry problem
- Cosmetized violence
- Miranda inaccuracies

So another paradox is that while the media tend to be very pro-police normally, unrealistic images tend to work against good police–community relations.

3-4 • IMPACT

What are the consequences for the police when all of these paradoxes work in concert with each other and come together to influence the attitudes and behavior of police officers? For individual officers, great frustration may develop. For leaders, the job of supervising the police is made doubly problematic: They must deal with some of these dynamics themselves, and must work with their charges in an effort to mollify the multiple frustrations they bring on.

A. Officer Anomie

As individuals, police officers can often suffer from what the great sociologist Emile Durkheim labeled **anomie.** This was Durkheim's term for the feeling of "normlessness" that many suicidal people experience. Such people feel that there is a disconnect between themselves and society. Their personal views of the world, how things function, and norms/values are out of sync with the feelings of the majority of people. The individual police officer who experiences citizen–police enmity out on the street, and feels the multiple frustrations of the job created by the paradoxes, can suffer from anomie on a regular basis. In fact, one can argue that police officers are the group of American professionals most often prone to suffer from anomic feelings and a consequent isolation from the public.

So often do police officers suffer from anomic feelings that it is perhaps the single most important reason for the creation of the police subculture. The feeling that "nobody gets it" is a perfectly logical one. And cleaving to others who understand one's lot in life is a normal reaction for any person. This is not to say that police officers in general are "in trouble." But it does mean that the individual police officer and the effective police leader must be aware of the counterproductive dynamics and behaviors that might develop due to anomic feelings.

B. Subcultural Power and Solidarity

Sociologists tell us that a subculture is a "culture within a culture." It is comprised of people who, because of their unique work, hobby, or ethnic experiences, develop values that are at odds with those possessed by the dominant society. Members of a subculture tend to develop a perspective on life that is to some extent deviant as viewed from the perspectives of the average person and the larger social order.

The police subculture is known for its solidarity. This is perfectly understandable given the frustrations and paradoxes of the policing experience. The police tend to cleave to each other in order to protect their physical safety. But they also do so for the purpose of obtaining psychological sustenance. Only surrounded by those who "get it" can the average officer maintain a sense of personal worth and feel safe in his or her professional world.

In being isolated from society at large and interacting almost exclusively with other officers, the police tend to develop norms that are driven by this experience. Some of these norms operate in a way that is counterproductive to the interests of justice. First, the police tend to believe in an "overkill" principle with regard to the use of force. Because they are always outnumbered and they understand Muir's paradox of face, officers tend to believe that developing a "badass rep" is necessary for their survival. In order to develop and maintain such a reputation, the police tend to be driven by the idea that when physical violence erupts they have to "win and win big." In the police locker room, this norm presents itself with comments like "If one of us gets assaulted, the a__hole should end up in jail. If one of us gets *hurt*, the a__hole should end up in the hospital." In this way, the subculture tends to support the use of excessive force.

Second, in former times, the police subculture supported the **"blue code of silence,"** meaning that no police officer would (or should) aid in any investigation into the misconduct of other officers. Today, driven by modern notions of professionalism, this idea is not as powerful and controlling as it used to be. Contemporary police officers will often aid investigations into police corruption that involve taking payoffs and graft. Officer cooperation into misconduct investigations of this sort is no longer unheard of.

But when investigations enter into the arena of noble cause corruption, even officers who would never consider becoming involved in such behavior tend to protect those who are. Police officers tend to believe that if some criminal is going to be let out of jail and a police officer is going to go to jail—because an officer lied on the witness stand, for example—they should not participate in helping that happen. Even otherwise honest police officers will resist (and work to thwart) investigations into noble cause corruption.

Third, there is a subcultural norm that works directly against the development of COP. It has to do with the idea that "real" police work involves

BOX 3.9

POLICE SUBCULTURAL DYNAMICS

- Solidarity within the group
- Police socializing: parties, vacations, and celebrations
- "Overkill" (support for excessive force)
- "The blue code of silence" (especially a tolerance for grass eating)
- Anti-COP diffidence (in some areas)

enforcing the law and enforcing the law only. Officers who are committed to developing an ongoing relationship with the public, providing non–law enforcement type services to their community, mentoring teenagers, taking care of the elderly when possible, and acting (as COP demands) as agents of change can often be labeled "social workers," still an epithet among many members of the subculture.

The paradox here is that while the development of the police subculture is completely rational and understandable in many ways, it tends to create a set of problems that are bad for the public, for police–community relations, and for the interests of justice. Although we have mentioned only a few examples, the isolated subculture of the police can generate operational norms that work contrary to the mission of the police.

3-5　SUMMARY

In these and a dozen other ways, the experience of being on the streets of America today can work to frustrate the individual officer, who may feel alone and isolated. Police officers tend to feel that only other officers understand their predicament. Replete with paradox, the individual police officer's experience can work to develop norms that operate directly at odds with what the police are supposed to accomplish.

Experienced officers, politicos, and police leaders must understand these challenging paradoxes, and develop methods of leadership and discipline that take them into account. Nothing good can come from attempting to ignore the power of the police subculture and its norms, the frustrations experienced by the individual police officer, and the fact that creativity is required to control, motivate, manage, discipline, and mentor police officers engaged with the extraordinary experience of working a beat. And nothing can mollify the critical importance that an understanding of the paradoxes brings to the drive to create a professional ethic for the modern officer.

3-6 🔘 TOPICS FOR DISCUSSION

1. Our discussion about stereotyping suggests that the police appear to the public to be "paranoid" much of the time. Why is this? What types of actions do the police take in the name of self-preservation that seem to be unrealistically worrisome? Is there anything the police can do about this appearance?

2. What is the paradox of detachment? Why is it so important for American citizens to understand it in an era when we are fighting a war on terrorism? What are other examples of people who make themselves uncoercible (other than terrorists)?

3. What is the RCMP syndrome? What are examples of other unrealistic images that are sent out to the public via the media? Why/how can this be frustrating for police officers?

4. What is anomie? Do you know people who suffer from it? Do you think it is true that an inordinate number of police officers suffer anomic feelings? Do you agree with the authors about this? Why or why not?

3-7 🔘 ETHICAL SCENARIO

Two officers are sent to the house of a family of "regulars" with whom the police interact on an almost nightly basis. Mom and Dad are drunk. Two of the teenaged boys are stoned. The teenaged girl—the only reasonably sane person in the house—is in charge of the family's 4-year-old child. Nobody else can accept the responsibility. In front of the officers, the man gets so mad at his wife, who is herself raving at her husband at the top of her voice, that he kicks over the family television set and it explodes into oblivion. The officers are worried about the safety of the little child and the teenaged girl, but no laws have been broken. The law, in this case, does not give the police the "proper" or "necessary" tools with which to handle the situation. While they sense that *something* ought to be done, there are no legal steps for the officers to take.

What do they do? Do they leave because no laws have been broken? Do they act in a semi-legal manner and attempt to intimidate the father into leaving, going out, and sobering up? Do they act in an illegal manner by asking the husband and/or wife to go out with them onto the porch and then arrest them for being drunk in a public place? How would an ethical officer solve this type of paradoxical situation wherein the multiple functions of the police (order maintenance and law enforcement) conflict with each other?

3-8 🔘 WRITING EXERCISE

Construct an essay that utilizes both the kamikaze pilot and the 9/11 terrorist as examples of people who are largely impossible to coerce. Make specific reference to Muir's paradox of detachment, and how the dynamics associated with this paradox are important for all American citizens to understand in today's war on terrorism–driven world.

3-9 ◉ KEY TERMS

anomie: Emile Durkheim's concept of normlessness; when people feel out of sync with their society.

blue code of silence: The propensity for police officers to keep quiet about the misdeeds of others.

coercive power: Obtaining desired behavior through using threats to harm.

cosmetized violence: The idea that the media make violence appear to be sexy and cool.

dehumanizing the enemy: The military propensity to make enemies less than human; aids in creating a killing atmosphere.

diagnostic packages: The sorts of "boxes" within our minds where we store information.

*habeas corpus***:** The judicial concept requiring a charge to be brought before a person can be kept behind bars.

hostages: Valuable possessions of a person that may be threatened for the purposes of coercion.

legal technicalities: Refers to procedural laws of the criminal justice system that are often considered to operate against efforts to hold the factually guilty accountable for their misdeeds.

multiple, conflicting, and vague: Applied to the functions of the police, the idea that what the police are expected to prioritize is complicated rather than easy to discern.

normalize crime: The idea that criminal justice practitioners must take all deviant behavior and codify it.

paradox: Something that operates contrary to normal expectation or to common sense, or contrary to the thing's apparent purpose.

paradox of detachment: The less a person values a hostage, the less coercible that person is.

paradox of dispossession: The less a person has, the less they have to lose.

paradox of face: The nastier a person's reputation, the less often they are required to prove it.

paradox of irrationality: A two-part paradox—the crazier the victim of coercion, the less effective the threat; the crazier the coercer, the more effective the threat.

paramilitarism: Semi-military or quasi-military way of organizing the police.

perceptual shorthand: Process by which people make quick decisions in life.

RCMP Syndrome: The idea that the police will solve all crimes all of the time.

stereotyping: The normal human propensity to categorize data and utilize it later for the purpose of making life simpler and more manageable.

symbolic assailants: Citizens about whom officers should be concerned because they might assault the police.

CHAPTER 4

Why Be Ethical?

Chapter Outline

"All I want is to enter my house justified."

—From the movie *Ride the High Country*

Why should a person be concerned with ethics? What is so important about doing the right thing? Isn't the world full of people who bend the rules, cheat the edges, and work the system in their favor? Don't we worship achievement so much that at times it seems it doesn't matter how you played the game, it only matters whether you won or lost? A survey of Americans once found that a majority would take an illegal drug if they thought it would guarantee they would win an Olympic medal. In such an ends-oriented society, why bother trying to be ethical, moral, and right?

A police officer would never ask, "Why should I care about being a good cop?" or "Why should I care about doing my job well?" Yet, in effect this is what is being asked if a cop should wonder, "Why should I be moral?" This question raises one of those issues that is so obvious it makes one wince just to hear it. But in the case of police officers, this is an especially relevant question because the way officers answer it frames the way they understand the job more conspicuously than is the case for almost any other profession. Since a person's conduct is the product of what he or she understands, it is always relevant for the cop to think through the implications of the question, "Why be moral?"

More than is the case for the great majority of professions, competence in police work necessarily involves far more than just intelligence, skill, and education. It involves a basic and daily concern for moral conduct. Now, this does not mean that it is the job of the law to make people *good*, because it is not—that's the job of the citizen himself or herself, and of his or her family, community, and religion. But it *is* the job of the police to ensure that people act correctly, and in that way work to make society better. The police do this by maintaining justice—as the old saying goes, "Your rights stop where my nose begins." Generally speaking, the duty of the police is comprised of three distinct functions: service, order maintenance, and law enforcement. Every activity that falls into these areas involves issues of justice. In their various duties, then, the police are the point-persons of justice, and justice is the only context within which morality in society becomes a realistic possibility.

There are many answers to this question, "Why should I care about ethics?" and some of them make up part of the ethical frames of reference that we will discuss later. But in the grand scheme of things, there is an overarching reason why all people should be concerned with values, norms of conduct, ethics, morals, and character. These are the very things that make us human. In other words, at the most basic level, to be concerned about ethics is to be a human being.

4-1 • ETHICS MAKE US HUMAN

What differentiates humans from other members of the animal kingdom? We are animals, of course, mammals in fact, who have all of the basic needs that other animals possess. We need water, food, rest, and warmth (clothing and

BOX 4.1

THE HUMAN EXPERIENCE

In nature, there is no good or evil. There is no morality. There are no good gazelles and no bad gazelles. There are no good lions and no bad lions. When the lioness hunts for her cubs and kills the gazelle, it is not a bad thing. It might very well be unfortunate for the one gazelle out of the herd that is killed. But in the grand scheme of things there is only the creation of a meal for hungry young lions. There is no more morality involved in the lion's kill than there is when the gazelle eats some grass.

In nature, there is only action and consequence. Unless an animal suffers from some sort of illness, its behavior is driven by the need for food and the desire to survive and to procreate. Some animals are food for others. Many are hunted and a few are the hunters. There is only survival of the fittest. As they say in several Eastern religions, nature just is.

shelter) to survive on a daily basis. And so we have the same drives to obtain these things as do other animals. Like the animals, we need to procreate. So we also have sex drives that are animalistic in their basic nature.

Nature—that is, biological evolution—has not fitted human beings to any specific environment. On the contrary, by comparison with other animals humans have a rather crude survival kit; and yet, and this is the paradox of the human condition, one that fits human beings to all environments. Among the multitude of animals that scamper, fly, burrow, and swim around us, man is the only one that is not locked into his environment. Human imagination, emotional subtlety, and toughness make it possible for humankind not to accept the environment but to change it. And that series of inventions, by which humankind from age to age has remade their environment, is a different kind of evolution—not biological, but cultural evolution.

Every human action goes back in some part to our animal origins. Nevertheless, it is right to ask for a distinction: What are the physical gifts that make us different? The fossil record shows that in prehistory the larger brain of the ancestors of human beings made two major inventions. First, they made the fundamental invention of the tool, the purposeful act that prepares and stores a stone for later use. By that lunge of skill and foresight, a symbolic act of discovery of the future, they had released the brake that the environment imposes on all other creatures.

The other invention was social. From the fossil record, archeologists know that the ancestors of humans lived to a ripe old age of eighteen or so. This means there were many orphans, for like all the primates they had a long childhood. Therefore there must have been a social organization in which

There are no *bad* lions. There are no *good* wildebeests. Animals just *are*.

children were made part of the group and in some general way trained. That is the great step toward cultural evolution.

Language is unique to human beings, outside the range of anything an animal can do. And it derives from the same human faculty: the ability to visualize the future, to foresee what may happen and plan to anticipate it, and to represent it to ourselves in images that we project and move about inside our head or in a square of light on a TV screen.

We look through the imagination, a telescope in time, and look back at our experiences in the past. To speak, to write something down, to make a drawing, to build a wall is to anticipate a future as only people can do, inferring what is to come from what is here. There are many gifts that are unique to humankind, but at the center of them all, the root from which all knowledge grows, lies the ability to draw conclusions from what we see to what we do not see, to move our minds through space and time.

With language we create a world of meaning. This is a human world that is just as natural to us as the physical world. Language enables us to think, and the images and references and connections of thought are *abstractions*. That is, our thoughts are not reality itself, they are about reality. Thought calls reality to mind. The meanings created by language are a lens through which we understand the world. Animals are locked into the immediacy of the present physical environment where sensory input is their only source of information. Of course, humans are also physically rooted in the world, but, unlike the animals, we live in a world of meaning, a world we are constantly trying to understand. The world of meaning is the human world, our natural life.

In putting together our society, we are the only species that has created rules of conduct, norms, laws, and morals that require each of us to (at times) overcome our animal instincts and control ourselves in ways that are in a real sense "not natural." We are thus the only animals that put together codes of conduct that seek to control our animalistic or **hedonistic impulses.** Civilization is all about these rules and this attempt to discipline ourselves. As people interact in society, they need to define their own personal space and they need to determine how much of the world belongs to which people. This can be done in a very egalitarian fashion, with every person obtaining the same amount of individual, personal freedom of action and free space. Or it can be done in some hierarchical way, with people obtaining differing amounts of freedom and space. However it is done, the formula that is eventually used is applied and protected by the police. This is true everywhere and at all times. And it has always been so.

For example, humans created the institution of marriage apparently to organize society in a way that is (or at least historically seemed to be) best suited to raising children and to maintaining the long-term social order. It takes longer to raise and to educate human children than it does to raise offspring of virtually any other species. To ensure that parents are committed to their young for this extended period of time (about eighteen years or so) and thus to ensure that human children learn all they need to know to reach the independence and maturity of adulthood, marriage creates and maintains a certain long-term commitment. It requires sexual fidelity, financial responsibility, legal obligations to support children, and so on. It requires sacrifices of the parents. For example, married couples must eschew the natural desire to have sex whenever and with whomever they wish. This is, presumably, in the best interests of their children and therefore of society as a whole.

A. Norms, Values, Rules, and Laws

This is just one example of how we humans use our rational minds to decide upon norms of conduct, to create rules and obligations, and to maintain order in society. We even utilize one form of political decision making or another to decide upon codified laws. Those rules of behavior that are deemed to be the most important are written down and made into laws. All sorts of norms exist that are not important enough to be codified. It is considered by most people to be disgusting to, say, fart or pick one's nose in public. In some sense, these forms of behavior are considered to be abnormal. But while they might be informally sanctioned, such forms of behavior are not important enough to turn into laws. One constant public policy debate in this and other societies is what to do about victimless crimes such as prostitution, gambling, drug use, and possession and sale of pornography. These are types of abnormal behavior that some people consider to be matters of personal choice and, thus, not the collective business of all citizens all of the time.

All norms, rules, and laws are supposed to be in the best interest of society. Informal norms are created, maintained, and abusers are sanctioned in a rather casual way. The form of sanction used for them is merely social ostracism. When rules take the form of laws, of course, they apply to everyone, everywhere, and all of the time. They are administered by governmental agents. And for penal code and vehicle code (and so forth) laws those agents, of course, are the police.

Our norms, rules, and laws—our ethics—are what make us different from all other species. The job of our social institutions—families, schools, religions, economic systems, laws, and so forth—is to instill these principles in people and maintain adherence to these principles. The job of police officers, among others, is to apply such norms, rules, and laws in a way that encourages order and civility among people.

While it is obviously important for all people to concern themselves with ethics, it is of absolutely critical importance that police officers do so. Anyone who wishes to be a police officer but who thinks that such concerns about ethics are irrelevant to his or her job has misunderstood what it is that police do. Such an individual is not a good candidate to be a police officer as he or she doesn't possess the most basic understanding of what makes us human and what police are supposed to be doing on the street.

B. Why Be Ethical?

As we will see in Part II, and as is briefly indicated in Box 4.2, the reasons for being ethical have been further divided by analysts and philosophers into several sets of ideas, each with a different perspective. How far society's agents or police should go in applying such norms, rules, and laws varies according to philosophy and type of more. But these perspectives all include as their most basic principle the idea that ethics are the central thing that makes us human. (We, too, will develop our own, separate ethical perspective later on in Chapter 9.)

Thus, to the followers of ethical formalism (Immanuel Kant's philosophy, see Chapter 7), being ethical is something that everyone should do because reason requires it of us. Human beings owe a duty to society, to each other, and to themselves to be ethical as part of the requirement to behave as rational beings. This duty is absolute. No amount of rationalization can (or should) be attempted to avoid the unqualified nature of duty. Our duty is consistent over time, under all circumstances, in all places. And the police, from this perspective, are in the business of being absolutist themselves.

BOX 4.2

WHY BE ETHICAL?

Our study will consider several different perspectives on ethical thought, each of which has a somewhat different answer to this question.

Ethical formalism Reason is our natural and governing disposition; to fulfill our human nature we must fulfill our duty to be rational.

Utilitarianism An ethic that rests on the principle that it is always good to maximize benefit; in the words of J. S. Mill, we ought always to do "the greatest good for the greatest number."

Religion Created in God's image, we are endowed by Him with a conscience, the spark of the Divine in us; God's will is the ultimate moral authority in a religious life.

From a different perspective, utilitarians (John Stuart Mill's philosophy, see Chapter 8) believe that being ethical, as they define it, is something that people ought to do because it involves behaving in the interests of the majority of society's members. Utilitarian principles suggest that behaving ethically involves caring for and nurturing others. They suggest that their approach comes from a natural drive that helps (again) society to proceed in the most fair and equitable manner. When analyzing what to do in any circumstance that requires deciding what is ethical, rules are not absolute. Instead, the individual calculates as best he or she can what action would create the greatest good for the greatest number of people. In this way, a utilitarian might act one way one day and another way the next.

All religions take the approach that conscience, or the moral sense, is the "spark" of the divine in human nature. The Bible tells us that we are created in His image, which theologians and philosophers take to mean that we can communicate with God and that, like Him, we are equipped with a moral sense, a sense of good and evil. This is of course different from the other two **humanistic perspectives** (ethical formalism and utilitarianism). But religion is similar to these other schools in that it clearly prescribes the idea that behaving in an ethical manner is central to one's humanity, that morality defines our humanity so that if we lose our morality we cease being fully human. Again, sensitivity to moral or ethical requirements differentiates humans from the animal kingdom.

While these perspectives take different views of ethics and give us different general guidelines for approaching ethical dilemmas, they all focus on the fact that ethical behavior defines us, not just as intelligent and civilized, but as human beings.

4-2 ● POLICE MORALIZING

When they make discretionary decisions on the street, the police are moralizing for, or about, people. This is of course not true with respect to felonies, where there is little discretion *not* to take action. But with regard to misdemeanors and infractions (the stuff of which most police decision making is made), in effect the police possess absolute discretion. When they decide that someone should be arrested, the police are in fact deciding that this person or that one *deserves* to go to jail (or to be cited). When they decide not to arrest, they are deciding that no arrest is deserved. In doing so, they are applying some ethical frame of reference. And, thus, it is imperative that police officers possess an internalized, well-thought-out ethic in the first place.

A. The Ethical Basis for Discretion

Our discussion thus far has pointed out why it is important for all people to be ethical and why ethics are an important component of the drive to professionalize the police. But it is critical at this point for us to engage in a discussion of the practical reasons why police officers are particularly prone to be confronted with **ethical questions** and **ethical dilemmas** in their professional lives. The reasons are several.

First, police work is all about making critical decisions about other people's lives. The discretionary decision-making power the law gives to the police involves deciding when to make (and when not to make) arrests. It involves when to use (and when not to use) force. It involves what level of force to use in dealing with deviant citizens. In making decisions about arrest and force in particular, the individual police officer makes decisions that affect people's lives profoundly. On occasions, these are life-changing and even life-threatening decisions.

Such discretion must be exercised in a logical, intelligent, educated manner with an eye toward what is in the best interests of justice. And in focusing on the ideal of justice, each officer must consider what justice means for the individual citizen, for other closely related citizens, and for society in general. So, to begin with, the police make discretionary decisions that must take into consideration the meaning of justice, of community, and of morality. Ethics, then, are at the very center of the police function.

For example, the individual police officer is empowered to treat a shoplifter in several very different ways. A first-time shoplifter with no record of criminal behavior may be given simply a warning or a lecture. This decision, in essence to do nothing or to take no action, occurs often. In fact, it happens more often than people outside of police work might think. Or alternatively, perhaps in the case of a child or a teenager, the police may take the deviant, misbehaving citizen (child/teen) home to Mom and Dad to be dealt with by the institution of the family. When they have the time, and when they believe that this is the best, most effective, and indeed most ethical course of action, the police will do so. On the other hand, a shoplifter may be cited or arrested and taken to jail or juvenile hall. The decision with respect to such minor offenses is clearly left in the hands of the police. No form of post-decision accountability is in place to suggest after the fact that the police might have acted otherwise. So the police possess a profound amount of discretionary decision-making power, because they have the power to do nothing.

When confronted with a minor offense of the misdemeanor or infraction sort, what will they do, what should they do, in the interest of justice? The answer is that "it depends." It depends on the circumstances, what was stolen, the attitude of the suspect, the attitude of parents, the (perceived) interests of the shop owner, and so on. The criminal justice system not only wants, it also expects the police to use their judgment in such cases, and it is totally appropriate that it does so. As the California Penal Code section in Box 4.3 indicates, the police are not supposed to apply the law arbitrarily but with "an eye toward justice."

Second, police officers are often faced with conflicting interests. On a regular basis, the cop on the beat must judge the relative merits of conflicting claims from citizens with different perspectives. This is even more difficult than simply exercising the discretionary power discussed above because quite

BOX 4.3

CALIFORNIA PENAL CODE, PRELIMINARY PROVISIONS, SECTION 4

The rule of the Common Law that penal statutes are to be strictly construed has no application to this code. All of its provisions are to be construed according to the fair import of their terms with view to effect its objects and to promote justice.

often both parties in a dispute have legitimate claims. Thus, the individual officer on the street is often presented with two (or even more) sides to a story that are correct from the perspectives of the citizens involved.

What should police officers do about a Saturday night complaint regarding a loud party in a college town? Certainly the peace and quiet of any neighborhood should be respected. And people must be listened to when they wish to be protected from what they consider obnoxious music. Yet partygoers, especially on a Saturday night, have their rights too. If not on a Saturday night after a victorious football game, when *can* a large group of young people have a party? What about the rights of 150 people to celebrate their football team's victory?

Again, the answer to the question, "What should the police do?" about such a complaint is, "It depends." It depends on how late at night it is, how many people are partying, how many complainants there are, how often this has been a problem in the past, and so on. There is no "how to do it" manual for deciding among such legitimate claims between citizens who each want the law to respond to their legitimate demands.

Sometimes in police work such balancing of interests is not required. It is clear that an arrest for a violent, felonious crime (armed robbery, for example) should be made irrespective of what anyone in a neighborhood believes should be done. Under such circumstances, the duty of the police to the people is clear. If the elements of the crime are present and there is probable cause to believe that a suspect is responsible, then the arrest for a violent felony should be made.

But such incidents are rare in police work. For as much as police officers, inexperienced police officers in particular, focus on dealing with violent felonies as a central part of the role they perform, such arrests make up only a small part of what the police do on a day-to-day basis. Any number of studies indicate that 90 percent of what the police do is service and order-maintenance oriented. Thus, more often than not, the police are handling the sort of minor details discussed in the loud party example. Calls about quarreling lovers, loud parties, drunks in a bar, juveniles on a street corner, homeless people in business districts, and so on are what make up the overwhelming majority of police calls. And in all of these commonplace examples, the police are required to face ethical dilemmas and conflicting claims and make moral judgments about people and events.

For quite some time now, sociologists and psychologists have discussed the effects of today's modern world upon the human psyche and upon the social fabric of America. We live in a world replete with ongoing, constant, ever-present change. Technology changes and even social norms and values change. And they do so in contemporary America with a rapidity unprecedented in human history. Given how profoundly important this change is to the average citizen and to society in general, those who administer the laws—laws which ostensibly represent communally determined norms and values—will have an increasingly difficult time of it as professionals on the street.

B. Anomie

About a century ago, the great sociologist Emile Durkheim conducted a study of suicide. He sought to determine what drives people to this ultimate act. His conclusion was that a substantial number of those who took their own lives suffered from a sort of disconnect between themselves and their society. Durkheim was able to determine through studying suicide notes and interviewing loved ones left behind that people who commit suicide almost invariably believe that they do not hold values that are held by their peers. This feeling leads the individual to suffer from a profound identity crisis. He labeled this problem to be *anomie* or a feeling of normlessness.

Of course, when an individual feels that they are out of synchronization with their own society, they can react in several ways. Those who commit suicide react in a negative, self-deprecating way. In the end, they are driven to take their own lives in an effort to escape the pain visited upon them by their feelings. On the other hand, people suffering from anomie can react with outrage and in a positive (for them) way by denying their own problems and proclaiming that it is society that is lost and confused. This is, from the perspective of the potentiality of suicide, a more healthy reaction.

Those individuals who suffer anomic feelings but possess an ego-sustaining stability that allows them to reject suicide as an option can still have difficulties in life. They can be without personal support systems. They can lack relationships with other humans upon which to depend for sustenance of the psychological sort. This reality can be devastating to a person no matter how much internal fortitude they possess. Many of the people in our society who are deviants and who act out in antisocial ways suffer from anomie. And they behave as they do as a consequence.

But there is another, perfectly logical, dynamic associated with anomie. The anomic individual might be able to develop and sustain relationships with people who are similarly situated in life. If there are enough others who are equally at odds with societal values, and if an individual can develop ties with such others, then the anomic person can sustain himself or herself in a positive way. This dynamic suggests the number one reason for the existence of the police subculture. Many police officers feel that society is "going to hell in a

BOX 4.4

FORT APACHE

The "Fort Apache syndrome" refers to the propensity of police officers to get into an "us against them" mode vis-à-vis the public. The label refers to two movies. One was a black and white John Wayne movie from 1948 entitled *Fort Apache*, wherein the soldiers were inside the fort and surrounded by hostile savages. The other movie was a 1981 Paul Newman movie entitled *Fort Apache, the Bronx*, which was the true story of a precinct in New York that was notorious for being the highest crime area in all of America. The officers there nicknamed the station "Fort Apache."

Associated Press

Paul Newman walks out the front door of the 41st Police Precinct while filming the 1981 movie *Fort Apache, The Bronx.*

hand basket" and that only the police officers of the world "get it." That is, they have a world view that suggests an "us versus them" or **Fort Apache** approach to life on the street. The Fort Apache metaphor symbolizes the idea that the police operate in an isolated reality, surround by the hostile "savages" of society.

Interacting with other anomic police officers, such men and women can live, work, and even flourish despite these feelings of normlessness because the police subculture is there to sustain them. Even though there are negative dynamics and values associated with the police subculture (as we have seen), its ongoing existence is forever ensured because it provides the sort of positive support that sustains individual anomic officers. We have seen in Chapter 3 that a number of different frustrations can be laid upon the individual police officer, creating a feeling of distance from the public. The paradoxes of coercive power, the negative dynamics associated with police stereotyping, the frustrations of the due process system, the drawbacks of paramilitarism, and the unrealistic imagery sold by the media all tend in this direction. Durkheim's idea of anomie explains cogently how this all comes together to create and to sustain the subculture in a way that makes it one of the most solid and isolated subcultures in the world.

C. Future Shock

But there is more. As noted briefly above, every society has a number of people within it who experience feelings of anomie. This has undoubtedly been true throughout history. But in today's American society there are an inordinate number of people who are anomic. The argument can be made that this number is perhaps greater than ever before in human history. This is because in today's ever-evolving society, rapid, almost wild changes occur to the social fabric on a regular basis. Social historians (e.g., Daniel Bell, Alvin Toffler) tell us that there has been more change in human affairs since World War II than in the previous five thousand years. Frequent technological change, in combination with the morphing of the social fabric into a new and different reality every few years, creates anomic feelings of epidemic proportions because people naturally react this way to instability.

The greater the number of people in a society who develop anomic feelings, the more unstable is that society's social fabric. For revolution to be successful, the desire for change must be substantial. And it is anomie that drives such movements, created by change of both the technological and sociological sort. Led by an explosion in technology, change develops more rapidly than ever before. Since the onset of the industrial revolution, people have begun to experience a different reality than that of the past. Throughout human history, change had always been a slow and incremental process. Within a person's lifetime, an important invention or two might come along. But people's lives were pretty much like those of their parents and even those of their grandparents. Until a couple hundred years ago, almost everybody would grow up to live the same life as that of their grandparents. In their lifetimes, few people traveled farther than five miles from the bed they were born in. For centuries, life was so stable that people grew up learning in a very straightforward fashion who they were, what norms and values were, how to behave themselves, and so forth. Change was easy to deal with, as it was always greeted as a positive development.

About two centuries ago, science began to change life rapidly. Along with technological change came social change. People first moved into the cities by the millions. And that experience provided much in the way of required adaptation. Lifestyles changed, as cities grew crime increased, work morphed into something new and different, raising children became a different endeavor, and living conditions necessitated new forms of human interaction. A century later, schooling became universal, communications began to be electronic, travel was expanded first with the locomotive then with the automobile and then with the airplane. The cities adapted, the idea of the suburb was born, and a majority of people no longer lived on farms. And as a consequence of all of this, people changed because they had to. Norms and values and even laws morphed into new and different forms.

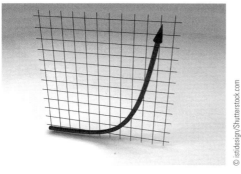

Toffler suggested that the recent exponential changes in society have produced mass anomie in the United States today.

All of this change happened at a geometric rate. Quickly the world would morph into a new reality that people had to face. And then, just as quickly, it would change again. Change begat change which begat more change. Social change was wedded to technological change. People began to live a life that was transformational instead of stable. Four decades ago Alvin Toffler noted in his book *Future Shock* that change had become so rapid in contemporary society that the human experience was morphing into something unprecedented. A new "tomorrow" was something that had always existed off in the mists of the distant future. Now it arrived almost daily. And it shocked people into an anomic state. Toffler suggested that these developments had created a new sort of mass anomie in America.

Now, the police are forever moralizing for others, applying norms, values, and laws to human behavior, and deciding who deserves to be sanctioned and who does not. In doing so, they must make decisions based on . . . what? The answer is that they make decisions based on their own ethics and view of justice in the world—based on their character. Thus, it is unavoidable that the police, more than average citizens, be in close contact with solidly based, well-thought-out sets of ethical principles. For in today's stress filled, ever changing, anomic world the police will be on the cutting edge of seeing and having to deal with the realities of future shock. Arguably, because the individual police officer cannot retreat from this anomie he or she is even more prone to develop a confused and confusing world view than are citizens.

4-3 ● THE USE OF POWER

The police are licensed to use force on citizens in a way that no other agents of the state are. Yet it is important to acknowledge that there are different ways to do the job of controlling people's behavior. Power is the ability to exercise control over others. And there are three different types of power that the police can use (see Box 4.5).

Because the power of the police to use force is so apparent, and because people so often object to this type of power, most people focus on coercive power as *the* way that police obtain cooperation from citizens. Any time police are around, the implied threat of arrest is present. The uniforms, badges, weapons, and carriage of the police also imply that they are ready to use violence. None of these threats is unrealistic. They are substantial.

BOX 4.5

THE THREE TYPES OF POWER

Exhortation Convincing people, through the appeal to logic or reason or morals, to do the right thing, the logical thing, the honest thing, the ethical thing.

Reciprocity Exchanging something to obtain the desired behavior from another.

Coercion Obtaining desired behavior using threats to harm something of value to the person being coerced.

But focusing on the use of violence suggests that threats to arrest or use force are the only means at the disposal of the police, that these are the only tools the police use in controlling people's behavior. Nothing could be further from the truth. The police can also use their powers of logic and intellectual persuasion to convince people to behave themselves (using exhortative power) or they can exchange something to obtain desired behavior (using reciprocal power).

Consider the following examples. Because of their authority, intelligence, and civility, the police regularly convince people to behave themselves using exhortative power. Police officers convince drunks to go home and sleep it off. They convince teenagers to "straighten up and fly right." They convince quarreling spouses to calm down in the interest of their children. They convince teenagers not to join gangs. In these and a hundred other ways, the police use their powers of persuasion to accomplish the job of controlling people's behavior.

Similarly, the police use reciprocal power (exchange) on many occasions. They obtain cooperation by promising to look into the arrest of a friend or relative. They obtain information by going easy on someone. They handle a detail involving homeless people by getting them to a shelter and so on. In this way, the police exchange something of value with citizens to obtain what they (the police) want.

Coercive power is also available, but the intelligent, professional police officer uses it only as a last resort. That is, instead of threatening people, the officer tries the other forms of behavior control first. If it is at all possible, the police use their authority, education, training, substantial resources, good will, and moral standing either in exchange for desired behavior or to convince people how to behave. This involves **power prioritization,** or utilizing the several forms of power in their appropriate order. When the police use these other forms of power, they are most effective in doing their jobs because people do not react to exhortation and reciprocity the way they do to coercion. Coercion sets up an animosity toward the police that can come back to haunt officers in the future.

BOX 4.6

AVOIDING THE USE OF COERCIVE POWER

At the Berkeley Police Department in the 1980s, officers were consistently frustrated by attempting to control homeless people using only coercive power ("move along or you'll go to jail"). Berkeley had an extremely large homeless population, and the limitations of threatening people on a regular basis were made apparent daily. The people didn't like being coerced, and the police didn't particularly like to do it.

In cooperation with several local businesses, the police developed a program wherein people could be given coupons by the police. These coupons were redeemable for free coffee, for example, at several local stores. When the police wanted to achieve some level of cooperation from homeless people in particular, such coupons could be given to cooperating citizens in exchange or as a reward for behaving themselves.

Citizens, and the police too, felt better about such an exchange-related type of interaction than they did about being coerced or using coercion. In this way, coercive power was changed into reciprocal power.

Of course, it is not always possible to go the easier route and use the two more gentle types of persuasion. When that is the case, police officers, as Muir tells us, must feel perfectly at home with coercing people. As the educated, well-trained, intelligent people they are, the modern police must always attempt to exhort people to do the right thing. When they can accomplish this, the police have operated effectively and have left people with the feeling that they did the right thing on their own. This makes people feel good about themselves and (even) about the police. Such positive feelings reap rewards in the future in terms of citizen–police cooperation that benefits everyone: the beat officer, the detective, the individual citizen, and the community. The ethical police officer must be driven by the realization that coercion is a last resort.

4-4 • CHARACTER AS A FOCAL POINT

When we think about police work, we naturally think in terms of training, experience, and professional competence. But everything we see about the police shines a light on what kind of person each officer is. The "cops and robbers" TV programs we watch seem to center on the savvy and the toughness and personality traits of very practical, no-nonsense cops. But invariably the issue that turns these programs into dramas are the moral qualities these people exhibit. That is, the *character* of these people creates the problems and possibilities and relationships that make the programs lifelike and worth watching.

What we see in the motivations and habitual responses of police officers are the traits that make them morally good or blameworthy, responsible or rogue, decent or despicable, stand-up or weak. The way they treat people is not just matter of intelligence or training. All the traits that shape the way we care about the welfare of other people (i.e., about what is good and bad in their lives) and of ourselves are traits of character. It is these traits that explain how people evaluate others, how they deal with them. As permanent dispositional features, traits of character explain not merely why someone acted this way now, but why someone can be counted on to act in certain ways. In this sense, character gives a special sort of accountability and pattern to action.

The police regularly decide what type of power to exercise over citizens. We have argued here that the professional officer should use exhortative and reciprocal power as often as is practical. There is an ethical component to these types of decisions. The character of individual police officers is of critical importance, for example, when attempting to control people. The competent, professional officer will avoid using coercive power whenever possible, even though in the police world there is a great deal of romantic, macho-driven support for acting like a **"cowboy."** It might seem like fun and feel like a more appropriate method of operation (given police norms regarding toughness), but coercing people has long-term drawbacks that need to be avoided if possible. The officer who possesses a clear ethical frame of reference will understand this and will take the less troublesome routes to obtaining citizen cooperation. But it takes strength of will and character to do so.

Sometimes there is confusion regarding how to make judgments on the street and what considerations to take into account. As we shall see in Part II, such decisions can be made based on different ethical grounds depending on the circumstances of a given detail. Sometimes absolute principles seem to be called for. An arrest for a violent felony must be made irrespective of circumstances and the identities of participants. This involves invoking ethical formalism.

At other times, circumstances such as the age of citizens, the location of events, the intentions of suspects, the previous records of those involved, and so on will play a major role in arrest decisions. When making calculations that relate to the greater good of the community regarding minor crimes, for example, police officers use a less absolutist and more relativistic or context-bound set of principles. Philosophers point out that what something means is created by the context in which it occurs. Meaning is situational, always. When attempting to use non-coercive power, the police are adapting themselves to the nature of the situation in order to obtain their desired ends. In such cases, we can say that they using utilitarianism. They are treating different situations in different ways, taking into account the good of the community and the interests of individual citizens. In other words, when the police give citizens the chance to decide to do the right thing for themselves, they are acting in an utilitarian manner.

When and how these different perspectives should be used is often not clear, and that is why character is the driving issue for us. It is for this reason that we have created our "ethic to live by" for police officers. But it is clear that with so many diverse roles to play, with so many conflicting demands being made by citizens, with so many types of crimes to consider and options available to them, the police are confronted with a confusing reality. And rather than try to sort this reality out in a piecemeal way, our effort here will attempt to focus on one central idea that links all ethical schools of thought together—police officer character.

4-5 ⊙ SUMMARY

In this chapter, we have considered the importance of ethics in the lives of all human beings, the nature of the moralizing that police in particular must do every day, the nature of the power they possess, and the importance of understanding various types of behavior control. In doing so, we have outlined the importance of the ethical point of view and stressed the ethical foundation upon which police officer decision making must rest.

In Chapter 5, we will consider the personal character dynamics involved in attempting to accomplish these tasks. As we have taken some trouble to point out here, the personal ethics of individual police officers are critical to the impact the entire criminal justice system has on life on the street. And within individual officers themselves, the character they possess forms the basis for the application of ethics to the everyday problems of people in America.

4-6 ⊙ TOPICS FOR DISCUSSION

1. Consider the idea that there are numerous reasons for being ethical. What are they? Which is the most convincing to you? Can you think of other reasons, either more specific or more general, for people to want to behave in an ethical manner? How about police officers?

2. Discuss why "ethics make us human." Why do philosophers and religious authorities agree that the single most important difference between the animal kingdom and human beings is this propensity to create moral codes and control natural instincts?

3. The authors suggest that police officers are regularly confronted with details wherein "both sides are right." Discuss examples of such ethical dilemmas or confrontations where the police have to "referee" between citizens (or groups of citizens), each of whom is, from his or her perspective, right.

4. Discuss examples of the three types of power. Use non-police examples first and then move to consider some police-related uses of exhortative,

reciprocal, and coercive power. Then discuss the idea of power prioritization and why Muir believes this is a critical idea for police officers.

4-7 ◉ ETHICAL SCENARIO

Two officers are confronted with an arrest/no-arrest decision for the misdemeanor crime of disturbing the peace. A fraternity party has gone on into the night—past midnight—and the frat boys have been warned about cutting down the noise several times. In making their decision, the officers are—as we have pointed out above—making moral judgments. They are deciding who "deserves" to go to jail and who does not. One officer suggests that because it is now after midnight, and because those responsible have been warned earlier, the party should have been shut down long ago. He believes that the fraternity leaders should be cited. The other officer suggests that "this is a college town" and that a party that "only" goes just past midnight is not something that should be sanctioned in such a town. Her logic is that "if people live in a college town, they should expect to endure such parties."

How should this dilemma be decided? What criteria should be utilized to determine whether or not party leaders "deserve" to be cited? In debating their decision, the two officers utilize their own personal notions of right and wrong and of morality. Is this right? Is it just? Is there any definitive way to make such a decision—some objective way of determining what the law should do about it—or is it just a case-by-case decision about which the two officers will/should/must argue?

4-8 ◉ WRITING EXERCISE

As an exercise in understanding the nature of Toffler's notions about "future shock," construct an essay that reflects upon what you thought the future would be like when you were young. When you were a kid, what did you think it would be like out there in the future? Did you expect that we would all have our own helicopters? That we would be able to travel in transporters (as on *Star Trek*)? Did you think that poverty or ignorance or war would be over forever? Have some fun with this; instructors should have the class share these ideas.

4-9 ◉ KEY TERMS

cowboy: A police term for officers who are cavalier about the use of force and about viewing citizens as the enemy in an "us against them" perspective.

ethical dilemmas: Situations wherein two or more alternative behavioral options present themselves and both are ethically defensible.

ethical questions: Situations wherein a person must choose between the ethical thing to do and the easier or more comfortable or less costly thing to do.

Fort Apache: A metaphor for the idea that the police are huddled together inside a stockade, surrounded outside by hostile savages.

future shock: Alvin Toffler's idea (from the book of the same name) that change occurs so abruptly in contemporary society that people are shocked by it.

hedonistic impulses: Human inclinations to behave like animals or in a natural, as opposed to civilized, way; when people are moved to do what feels good.

humanistic perspectives: A viewpoint that is based on the values, characteristics, and behavior that are believed to be best in human beings, rather than on any supernatural authority.

police moralizing: The propensity for police officers to make judgments about people when they make arrest/no arrest discretionary decisions.

power prioritization: The idea from Muir that the three types of power ought to be utilized in a specific order whenever possible; first exhortation, then reciprocity, and then (and only then) coercion.

PART II

Ethical Frameworks

In Part II, we will present our "ethic to live by" for the police officer, building it upon a two-chapter discussion about the nature of character. We will consider what it is, how we get it, and how it operates. Then we will present and analyze the ideas discussed by Kant and Mill. Only after juxtaposing these two classical perspectives on ethics will we be able to present our ethic to live by in a cogent and comprehensive way.

Part II provides the essential framework upon which we will construct our more practical discussions later on of police misconduct, its causes, and what to do about it. We begin by discussing character and why it is so critical to police officers and to the delivery of justice on the streets.

CHAPTER 5

What Is Character?

Chapter Outline

"Character is what you do when nobody's looking."

—Anonymous

Character is one of those elements of life that are assumed to be understood by everyone. Yet few people have ever thought much about its definition. For example, elections are driven by debates about the good or bad character of candidates for office. But when we analyze such political discussions, we find that the term "character" has no specific substance to it. Politicians have good character if we support them, they lack character if we do not. And that is just about all there is to it.

Character in the competent police officer is so important that we cannot proceed in this work without a solidly constructed definition. We need to have a good grasp of character because our central thesis is that character is the single most important determiner of police officer competence and effectiveness. Character is not just a part of what makes up police professionalism; it is the essential element in professionalism.

5-1 ● CHARACTER AND VIRTUE

Character traits are often called **virtues,** an old fashioned but still useful term, and include things like integrity, courage, loyalty, honesty. Unlike personality traits (e.g., sense of humor, intelligence, energy level, shyness, or optimism), virtues and vices are not innate; they are acquired through experience and learned from those people with whom we identify. We take on the ways of our people (clan, tribe, family). We are impregnated with their sympathies, inclinations, and speech patterns, their beliefs and tolerances.

A kid growing up in Arkansas can be identified by the rest of America as someone who grew up in Arkansas. He grows up in a Southern Baptist

BOX 5.1

TWO VIEWS OF CHARACTER

"We cannot judge . . . the character of men with perfect accuracy, from their actions or their appearance in public; it is from their careless conversation, their half-finished sentences, that we may hope with the greatest probability of success to discover their real character."

—Maria Edgeworth, Irish novelist

"What is character but the determination of incident? What is incident but the illustrations of character?"

—Henry James, American novelist

Church and for the rest of his life his musical tastes are inflected by all those church hymns he sang, as well as by the country music on the radio. He tends to view the Civil War as the War Between the States. He likes grits with his breakfast and he likes his fish Southern-fried. As with most Southerners, he has a playful, flexible sense of English that kids from Oregon and Nebraska do not have. Like water scouring rock, his Arkansas life leaves traces in him, and his character is etched by the circumstances in which he is becoming a man.

Now, a child in school or a police sergeant in a squad car may wonder whether something is the right thing to do. She may wonder how she feels about it. She may wonder what her responsibility is toward others in relation to the act in question. This activity of wondering is highly personal. The idea of "right" has a general, common meaning, of course. But as an individual she is making a specialized, personal use of the concept. This child or cop derives the concept of right initially from the language and culture she shares with everybody else. But she then takes it away into her private world. There, concepts of this sort—moral concepts—are functions of the child's or the cop's history. They are modified in relation to the life of the person: of *this* child or of *this* police sergeant in her squad car. Viewed through the lens of their personal history, moral concepts take on special, individualized meanings.

This active reassessing and redefining is the main characteristic of a person's living and growing personal history. So the ideas of right, or honesty, or loyalty, for example, may mean something different to an individual at different times in her life. She may very well have a different image of right in her home compared to what she has in her school or in a squad car. What the concept of right fully means to her is a part of her life and cannot be understood except in that context.

When we talk about the meaning of an idea or concept we must remember that words remain stable in a way that concepts do not. For example, the *word* "right" has a fixed dictionary definition, one that is known to the child and to the cop. But the *concept* of right varies for each of them according to changes in their two circumstances. For the child, the question of what is right when she's in her classroom is not exactly the same as when she's with her best friend, or with her mother, or with a bullying boy. With the cop, her understanding of what is right has changed over the course of her life, from when she was a little girl through when she was a teenager through when she went to college and now into her professional life. Furthermore, it now modifies according to whether she's dealing with a drunk driver, a lost child, or her husband.

These are two different senses of knowing what a word means, one connected with ordinary, conventional usage and the other very much less so. Knowledge of a value concept or a moral concept, such as honesty or courage, is something to be understood in depth. It cannot be known in terms of some impersonal network or group or code or set of rules. Besides, if morality is essentially connected with change and progress in a person's life, we cannot be as democratic about it as we might like to think. Contrary to Kant's position, for example, we do not simply *know* the meaning of all necessary moral words just because we are rational. We must recognize the contexts in which they apply, and how they apply. Meaning is always determined by context. We learn from our accumulated experience, we progress, we refine, and we develop. Our movement of understanding is onward, in the direction of the ideal of **Aristotle's** "Golden Mean" (more on the Golden Mean later in this chapter).

Character, our basic moral disposition, originates in childhood. This is where we first learn about friendship and meanness, deceit and honesty, suspiciousness and trust. These various traits become ingrained early on, absorbed in the atmosphere of our family life and through the effect worked on us by our life circumstances. Just as our early family life shapes and molds the personality traits we are born with, so, too, the family is where our basic moral temperament takes its form.

Two thousand four hundred years ago, Aristotle was the first person in the Western world to define and discuss "character."

© Panos Karapanagiotis/Shutterstock.com

While our character traits begin to form very early in childhood they are unlike personality traits and physical attributes. They are not set by genetic endowment. Our character is learned, not inherited, though we do seem to have a genetic or inherited pre-disposition for our character to develop in certain ways. Character is malleable, moldable, and forever subject to adjustment. Awareness is the key, for whatever character trait a person is aware of, she can change, if she wants. And herein lies all the good news, and all the bad news, about people and who they are.

Over the door to her office, a friend had a little sign that read, "Reality is your friend." In a quirky sort of way, the sign is a warning against self-delusion, rationalization, egotism, excuse making—it's a warning against what Socrates referred to as an "unexamined life." It's a reminder that any possibility of happiness depends on being realistic. The changeableness of a person's character is what we have referred to as the progressive, developing life of a person. The ongoing reassessing and redefining of ideas and values and beliefs is what character looks like, you might say. A person's character is the engine that drives the move to, or away from, being realistic. Aristotle argues that a human being's natural disposition is a realistic frame of mind. He says that any deviance from realism, from a realistic appraisal of situations and of oneself, is a vice to some degree. Those moral qualities he called the virtues are what bring about a realistic attitude. A person is in control of his life. In this way, he chooses the kind of person he will be.

So our lives are a never-ending project of deciding not just *what to do*, but, most importantly, *who to be*. (We say that deciding who to be is most important because knowing what to do is a function of the kind of person you are.) The formation of our character is not static, it's dynamic. At crucial moments of choice most of the business of choosing is already over. This does not imply that we are not free, certainly not. But it implies that the exercise of our freedom of choice occurs in small, piecemeal ways. The choices that define us go on all the time and are not grandiose leaps that only occur at important moments. The moral life, in this view, is something that goes on continually, not something that is switched off in between the occurrence of explicit moral choices. What happens in between such choices is crucial. It's a matter of character.

Aristotle's **ethics of virtue** do not focus on absolute rules of conduct applicable to everyone at all times but rather on the internalized character of the individual. This school of thought suggests that the individual of good character might behave in different ways at different times given different circumstances and different goals. Times change; people change; different people need and want different things; and no two situations are ever exactly the same.

Suppose that a police officer has a music store on his or her beat and is regularly presented with details where sales personnel have detained shoplifters. On one Christmas week workday, the officer is confronted with three such details. In one instance, the suspect is a 17-year-old gang member who has stolen some CDs to sell for cash. In another instance, the suspect is a 15-year-old welfare recipient who has stolen several CDs to give as Christmas presents. In still another instance, an upper-middle-class 16-year-old has stolen CDs for her own personal use.

The gang member, who has a long record of arrests, "knows the drill" and is reasonably cooperative and deferential to the police officer. The welfare recipient, who has no record whatsoever, is visibly upset. She is not only scared about being caught, but she is obviously embarrassed that due to her financial situation she is stealing Christmas presents. The upper-middle-class teenager is belligerent, telling the police officer that she is not a common criminal, is a very important person, and should not be "harassed" by the police.

What should the officer do? Several schools of ethical thought that believe in absolute rules of conduct (see Chapter 7) would say that, in the interests of equality, each of these suspects should be treated in exactly the same way. This is what the rule of law demands. To approach similar details in different ways, taking into consideration the individual circumstances, would be to ignore the requirement that the law be absolute in its application. Furthermore, to treat people differently due to their status and histories would be to ignore one of the principles of law: that the police officer is an agent of the state who merely applies the dictates of the law in an evenhanded manner on the street. Equality of treatment, and only equality of treatment, is important from such an absolutist perspective. Thus, arresting all three suspects and taking them all to jail would be the ethical thing to do.

The ethics of virtue, however, might suggest otherwise. Aristotle's conception of the wise or virtuous officer would have the greater, long-term interests of justice in mind. What is just can be different from what is equal. The virtuous police officer would focus on the long-term implications—for the community, for the music store, and for the individual suspects—of taking different types of action. It might be in the interests of justice and crime control to (1) arrest the gang member and deal with him firmly; (2) issue a stern warning to the welfare recipient and release her, and (3) take the upper-middle-class suspect home to her parents and explain the situation.

Each of these solutions is appropriately aimed at the accomplishment of the officer's duties to victims, suspects, and community. Yet each situation has been dealt with in a different, unequal way. The ethics of virtue, driven by the good character of the police officer, would accept these inequities and understand that there really wasn't any different treatment involved. The police officer was always acting in the best interest of each suspect and always in the best interest of the community. Justice and crime control (in the long run) were always the focus of these different actions. And thus, in treating each instance differently, the officer was doing the ethical and virtuous thing.

Aristotle came to define virtue as what he called the **Golden Mean.** This concept suggests that circumstances in life tend to trigger a natural range of response. This range is a continuum and it includes a mean between two extremes (see Table 5.1). A person's virtues and vices are his more or less habitual or accustomed ways of responding. They are his character traits. The individuals who are the most admirable are those who habitually or characteristically incline toward the virtue on the continuum between the two extreme responses. These individuals Aristotle considered to be **exemplars.**

For example, Aristotle argued that one indication of a person's character was how he or she dealt with money. If people were too possessive of their money, they would be guilty of stinginess. If they were too free with it, willing to give money away, they would be guilty of extravagance. The appropriate,

TABLE 5.1

ARISTOTLE'S LIST OF VIRTUES			
AREA	**VICE**	**VIRTUE**	**VICE**
fear	cowardice	courage	recklessness
pleasure	insensitivity	self-control	self-indulgence
possession	stinginess	generosity	extravagance
honor	small-mindedness	high-mindedness	vanity
anger	apathy	gentleness	short temper
truth	self-deprecation	honesty	boastfulness
shame	shamelessness	modesty	prudishness

healthy response, the Golden Mean, lies between the two extremes, namely, generosity. A generous nature is an element of good character.

This specific discussion of Aristotle's virtues will now be developed into a more general explanation of the elements of character as they have come to be defined through the ages. What makes up character? What are its elements?

5-2 ● MORAL JUDGMENT

Character must be differentiated from personality. **Personality** consists of the outermost indicators of an individual's makeup, those traits such as intelligence, wittiness, or charm that make an impression on others. Character, on the other hand, refers to one's inner makeup, those traits that indicate the person's habitual moral qualities or defects (the composite of virtues and vices). When we ask if people have good character, we are asking if they possess the moral strength to do the right thing, if they understand what constitutes the good in life, and whether they have integrity.

Integrity is a part of good character that is of particular importance in police officers. Integrity is that characteristic of wholeness, unity, and completeness that means a person is well rounded in his or her approach to life. It is critical that police officers have integrity because they must possess multiple sets of skills, areas of substantive knowledge, practical understandings of the real world, and physical/athletic abilities. Ethics and integrity thus play off of each other in a mutually dependent way. To draw together all the characteristics, knowledge, and skills that are necessary to make up a competent, professional police officer, one needs the interweaving "glue" of an ethical perspective. An intelligent and thoughtfully developed ethical perspective is essential to personal integrity. And integrity is a key ingredient in good character.

Good character, then, is absolutely essential to the development of police professionalism. Our thesis is that without a consciously thought-out commitment to living an ethical professional life, without good character, no amount of intelligence, training, skill, or physical ability will suffice. Put more bluntly, you cannot be a good police officer without having good

© Joshua Haviv/Shutterstock.com

Abraham Lincoln is generally considered to be America's greatest president because he stuck by his principles. Even when the going got toughest, his actions as president exemplified the concept of "integrity."

character. All of the rest is wasted if officers do not underwrite their traits, skills, and experiences with an understanding of the ethical implications of life.

We now turn to a consideration of the elements of character that will make more clear what it is and why it is so critical.

A. Judgments about Possibilities

The dominating, central fact about the intelligence of human life is that it is so open to possibility. Unlike animals, we see our lives reflectively. That is, we see our lives in terms of our memories and imagination, in terms of our plans, beliefs, and ideas. We daydream, we wonder, we plan, we fantasize, we assess possibilities, and we live accordingly. Animals adapt to their environments in a way that makes them part of it. The gazelle, for example, is exquisitely matched to its surroundings, but its lovely leap will never take it outside of the savanna. The biology of adaptation fixes the life of the animal through its instincts, and no other options are available to it.

Human beings adapt to their surroundings too, but by reflection, not biology. Unlike animals, people can live anywhere because they can change their environments to suit their needs—by cutting trees, irrigating fields, farming, or domesticating animals. Then, too, people can change their immediate surroundings by making clothing or building housing to adapt. A person's options are not determined in advance by the laws of nature. Instead, they are indeterminate. Only a person's imagination limits the range of options. The conduct of a person's life has all the characteristics of an unfolding plan. And our personal histories are part of that plan.

Our histories can be seen as including two sets of constantly converging possibilities: (1) those things that might or might not have happened to us (fate) and (2) those things we might or might not have done (our choices). On looking back at our lives, we may regret what might have been, seeing other possibilities in life for ourselves and regretting the sudden turns of fortune. Or we might equally regret choices we made, reflecting upon the other possible lives we might have made for ourselves. Or we may feel we were lucky things turned out as they did and that if we had it to do over again, we would do the same things.

In this self-reflection, we make moral judgments of different kinds about the past. People might think that they ought to have chosen differently at various junctures. Was it right to marry or not to marry, to have children or

BOX 5.2

THE TWO IMPACTS OF "POSSIBILITIES" ON OUR LIVES

Fate = Possible outcomes that happen to us

Choice = Possible outcomes that we control

not to have children, to pursue careers that involved doing work important to them or to pursue careers aimed at getting a lot of money, and so on. In such moral reflection, we are aware of our present desires and feelings and our present situations, and we link those to past good and bad fortune and good and bad choices.

We explain ourselves to ourselves by using our own history. Our recollections, however, are always colored with a sense of unrealized possibilities, by the things that might have been. And the things that could have happened are crucial parts of our lives. Our personal histories are thus filled with a sense of "what if" and "what I should have done." Our nature, the quality of our lives, and our character do not merely depend on events and actions that occurred, but also on possibilities (real possibilities) that we did not act upon for one reason or another. This consideration of possibility is the essence of moral reflection.

Moral judgments—that is, judgments about right and wrong, about good and evil—are best understood as a class of judgments about possibilities. The natural setting of such judgments is within personal deliberation where, either publicly or in the privacy of our own minds, we compare and evaluate possibilities. This deliberation happens in families, in offices, on job sites, or wherever people meet to discuss or argue about how to get along. We talk, we think, we listen, we respond, and together with those around us, we develop our understandings of ourselves, of the world, and of morality. At the interpersonal level, this is the way people create, maintain, and change the norms and values of entire cultures.

But people are not all the same. They have different points of view. This variation in points of view is the natural consequence of the fact that people do not live the same lives. When people are well matched, when they have a lot in common, their points of view will overlap. In the case of good friends or lovers, their views will quite often reflect each other's, depending on how long they have been together. Their two lives blend together because they have come to share similar values and, to some extent, they have each influenced the tolerances and expectations of the other. There remains, however, a difference between them, and they depend on it. They know themselves and each other by this difference. They enjoy and rely on each other because of the common place they have come to inhabit from the different courses of their two lives.

Thus, even in the case of close friends with a lot in common, we have different perspectives because of our different histories. We have experienced different possibilities, both in the sense that fate has presented us all with different experiences and in the sense that we have made different choices

©martan/Shutterstock.com

BOX 5.3

LEARNING ABOUT TRUTHFULNESS AND LYING

Is it wrong to tell a lie? Some would make this an absolute rule of life—a moral principle that should always govern interpersonal relationships. Others might say, "It depends." It might be acceptable to lie under certain circumstances and not under others.

For example, is it immoral to tell children "lies" about Santa Claus, the Easter Bunny, and the Tooth Fairy? When filling stockings in the middle of the night or hiding Easter eggs or taking a tooth from under a pillow, parents are, in fact, deceiving their children—lying to them. No amount of "little white lie" rationalizations can change this reality. The question is this: Is this kind of lie somehow acceptable because no harm is meant by it? Is it, in fact, the product of parental love and therefore something different from a lie?

In most families that play the Santa Claus game, for example, an interesting twist is made when older children grow out of believing in this myth. They—the older children—begin to help Mom and Dad "be Santa" by filling stockings and so on for those younger siblings who are still believers. Here is a good example of how children, in the home, learn the rules of interpersonal relationships—that telling such little white lies is not only acceptable, but it also helps to create an atmosphere of excitement and wonder around holiday time. It is not really lying, they learn, to talk of Santa Claus and flying reindeer and so on.

between possibilities. Differences present both the interesting commonalities that make for friendship, issues to which we must make adjustment, and areas wherein we must find ways to get along. They produce both the comfort of agreement and the predicament of disagreement. From this basic fact comes the core notion of procedural justice—that there are "rules of the game" for getting along and for deciding differences (see Box 5.3).

B. Justice

In our discussion of ethics, we will consider justice to be the requirement for fairness. It is a moral concept. It may be the most elementary and most prevalent moral aspect of how people get along with each other as well as the condition for the development of most other moral concepts. The concept of justice emerges from the common type of human interaction that is found everywhere. Justice is essential to the possibility of satisfactory relationships and to the possibility of the development of community between people.

The community into which children are born is a major shaping force in their lives. The language and religion of their people, the emotions of their family, the way they are cared for, what they learn to expect, the norms and values created and maintained by society's major institutions—children begin to assimilate all of this long before acquiring a clear sense of their independence and individuality. They are thus socialized from the earliest of their experiences and continually throughout their lives.

The child's original community, his or her family, provides the conditions for the development of his or her mental and social abilities. It is the original source of the development of the sense of individuality, of self. And the nature of this original community builds in a demand for some form of justice—that is, for fair treatment, for the chance to be taken seriously and to count in the estimation of others. Children will protest if they aren't given the same treatment as their brothers and sisters, whether it be in terms of food, clothing, and love; in terms of discipline; or even in terms of gifts at holiday time. Children will (naturally) protest if they are not listened to, if their ideas are not taken seriously, and so on. The voice of this protest is the voice that demands justice.

This natural demand for justice creates in children a sense of how relationships with other people, both friends and family, work—the rules of the relationship game. In learning what is and is not appropriate in relationships, they engage certain virtues such as truthfulness, kindness, trustworthiness, and loyalty, the basic qualities essential to a common life. They therefore learn how to care for others and for themselves.

We all bring this sense of justice with us into adult life. It is an underlying theme of all morality. Dealing with people justly and fairly is necessary to keep a balance between different ideas of what is good (differing views of life's possibilities) and to support procedures for deciding differences. Put another way, at the core of public morality is a concern for how people ought to interact, ought to get along, ought to argue (when they argue), and ought to solve problems when disagreements arise. Without agreement upon how this process for deciding differences works, any society would be in chaos.

Much of what police officers do deals with people in conflict. **Procedural justice** encompasses the rules of the game for regulating the inevitable conflict between different perspectives, expectations, and tolerances in people's lives. The police officer's job does not include attempting to make people's conflicting expectations come together and agree within some overarching conception of what is good (the good in life). Rather, the job involves, where possible, finding ways to enable people to coexist. Citizens don't have to agree, they don't have to reconcile their differences, and they don't have to find common ground. It is neither possible nor desirable that

BOX 5.4

TWO TYPES OF JUSTICE

Substantive justice Society's specific rules of conduct (examples include rape and murder laws in the penal code)

Procedural justice The "rules of the game" (for example, the *Miranda* decision, which requires that suspects be advised of their rights)

Concepts of **substantive justice** are derived from particular concepts of the good. Under what conditions is execution justified? Under what circumstances is it justifiable for an abused woman to shoot the abusing husband? When might abortion be justified? These are questions of substantive justice, and universal agreement cannot be expected.

However, universal agreement can be expected, in the name of rationality, on the methods of fair argument, of weighing claims and counterclaims, of arbitrating between the conflicting answers to these questions when an answer is needed for public purposes, and of—in the arena of the police officer—how a citizen ought to be treated, no matter what he or she is accused of having done.

their mutually hostile concepts of good should be combined to form a single and agreed-upon concept. The justice meted out by the police on the street can only clear the path to recognition of temporary compromises between incompatible desires and ideas of what is better.

Police officers cannot solve all the problems of the world that are created because of diverse opinions, experiences, and possibilities. But they can and must attempt to deal fairly with the conflict that arises. The police are umpires on the street. They referee the game of life, attempting, if they are competent professionals, to have as little impact as possible on the final score while making sure the game is played fairly. Continuing with the sports metaphor, some people will win and some will lose when the final score is counted. But it is neither possible nor a good idea to think that the police will influence people's views of the good (what type of formations to run, using a football analogy) or decide who is worthy of being treated fairly and who is not (directly influencing the game's score).

Thus, the basic human experience involves the demand for justice. It is a naturally occurring demand in all of us. The human experience also creates an individual idea of the good. We need a free society, and we need justice so that each person's individual idea of the good can flourish.

C. The Good

As is true with procedural justice, the moral notion of **the good** grows naturally out of a basic human experience and not out of a belief or theory that all people know and universally accept. People have very different ideas, for example, of how important education, financial security,

BOX 5.5

A PROBLEM WITH DIVERSE VIEWS ABOUT THE GOOD

America is a diverse society with more than 150 different ethnic and religious traditions coming together and seeking to exist in some sort of harmony. Our argument that there is no single universal concept of the good rests upon a central American theme: the freedom of the individual to hold, voice, and act upon his or her own opinions, views, and philosophy. But there is a problem with this idea that cannot be ignored.

Orthodox religion takes the opposite approach to understanding the good. That is, orthodox religions claim there is one universal good for all people. The Bible, the Koran, and the Torah in particular, the holy books of the three orthodox, "modern" religions, each take the perspective that to be a good person is to understand the one, true concept of the good and to behave in one particular way. Some believe the Ten Commandments, for example, are aimed at all people at all times with no qualifications or reservations. Everyone must accept them and cleave to them.

There is no room in such a view for the type of diversity we are discussing. While we certainly do not want to insist that police officers do not—or worse, cannot—cleave to their own religious faiths, it must be understood that in policing a diverse, free, tolerant society, police officers cannot foist their own religious views upon others, specifically with reference to the good. American legal and even religious tradition demands just the opposite—that tolerance for the ideas, philosophies, and world views of others be a central tenet in how society operates.

With specific reference to police work, American tradition demands that the police not behave in a way that attempts to underwrite any universal idea of the good. Police officers may hold their own views and behave accordingly in their private lives, but they may not police as if these views are supposed to be accepted by everyone.

exercise, or entertainment are to living a good life. They not only value these concepts to different extents, they also possess different definitions of them altogether.

For example, some people consider "getting an education" to entail learning about life in general (in the "school of hard knocks") and/or becoming educated about their professions or occupations. Others consider that truly educated people are those who go as far as they can in the academic world and learn as much as they can about every subject in which they engage. Similarly, some people are entertained by the opera or the symphony and others by tractor pulls and roller derby. Often, people who love one will detest the other. In a free society, we must acknowledge that these differences exist, are the right of every person to possess, and are, indeed, part of the fabric that makes life in our society interesting. Put another way, if everyone liked the same things and prioritized them equally, life would be pretty boring.

In a free society, ferociously held interests and passions are often reconcilable or compromised through rational calculations. But ferociously held concepts of the good and of right and wrong are not. No mechanism of rational choice can help in moral conflicts as they might with the conflicts over competing interests. The idea of justice, then, is embedded in an unavoidable predicament. It involves the necessity of agreement by discussion—without force or outright surrender—between antagonistic people who have clashed because one or both are not getting their way. This, in turn, is because of their different concepts of the good.

To review, people's different concepts of the good come from the human experience, from the tendency to praise, to blame, to want something better, to live guided by ideals, to focus on the important, to ignore the trivial, and so on. And the thread that links the human experience to the individual concept of the good is this idea of possibility—what might have been and what might be in our lives.

In this section we have discussed the general notion of moral judgment in terms of possibilities and the moral concepts of justice and the good. We have argued that our moment-by-moment experience is alive with possibility, charged with electricity about what can happen and with the feeling of responsibility that comes from knowing the possibilities are our possibilities. Making realistic judgments about our possibilities and the way we want to live requires fair dealing, that is, justice. This is the only condition under which people can pursue the good of their lives.

How do you define "the good"?

5-3 ● DISCRETIONARY DECISIONS AND THE IDEA OF CHARACTER

The idea that a police officer's character is critical to the integrity of the justice system turns on one central reality. Police officers possess a tremendous amount of discretionary decision-making power. In terms of the impact their decision can have on the lives of citizens, the police have more discretionary power than any other actors in the entire American legal and political system. The police have the power, right on the street, to completely ignore deviant behavior and not bring a person into the grips of the criminal justice system. No other actor in the process can have this impact on the lives of people, because once a public defender, prosecutor, judge, or probation officer focuses on a citizen's behavior, the citizen has already entered the system. Only the cop on the beat has the power to keep a person completely out of the system.

Police officers regularly make decisions to arrest or not to arrest, to use force or not to use force, to intervene in altercations or to leave people alone to solve their own problems. These decisions are made on the street, often alone and often at night without any witnesses. Particularly when the decision is to ignore deviance and leave people alone, police officer actions are not reviewed by others. Thus, this tremendous power is not accountable to anyone else. So, to whom (or what) is the police officer accountable?

The answer is that most of the time, under most circumstances, the discretionary decisions of police officers are accountable to the personal ethical standards of the individual police officer. Thus, the focus on police officer character is critical. Police officers, faced with arguments on both sides of an altercation between citizens, will make choices about what to do based on their understanding of what constitutes justice, the rule of law, the practically achievable, and most important, the good in life. There is no escaping this reality.

Police officer character molds and drives the life of the law. The character of individual officers gives a certain meaning to society's norms and values. Police officers who possess good character, who understand the difference between truth and distortion, and who have a firm fix on what it means to do good in life, are the guarantors of justice on the streets of America. Their discretionary decision-making power makes them the critical people in determining what the law truly means (what it looks like, what it feels like) in the lives of American citizens.

5-4 ● REVISITING THE IDEA THAT "THE POLICE ARE THE LAW"

We suggested in Chapter 1 that it is time for modern, intelligent, educated police officers to struggle to understand what the good life means, reflecting on what constitutes virtue and formulating specific ideas about what it means to have good character. This is not just an academic exercise that was of interest to the ancient Greeks. Such reflection directly targets what it means to be a good person and live a meaningful life today and always.

For police officers, people who exercise a great deal of power over the lives of others, such discussions and analyses are critical. As we said earlier, no amount of physical agility, intelligence, training, or street sense can make a person a good police officer. Only when he or she has integrated all of this talent, skill, and information into an individual, character-driven, working personality that resides within a solidly based professional ethic can true competence and professionalism develop.

Thus, we expand our idea that the police are the law. The law must have a conscience that keeps its operations consistent with American ideals of justice. The law must be a living entity that is not stagnant but that responds to the heartbeat of life on the street, to people's hopes and dreams. The law must be tempered with a feeling for life's circumstances that allows human empathy to modify its application. The law must be underwritten with an understanding of the practical, sometimes violent and ugly nature of the drama of real life. And the police officer whose character is formed with all of these ideals at its base is the person most likely to bring these dynamics into play. Judges, attorneys, probation officers, parole officers, and any number of other actors in the legal system can help to bring these ideals to life. But the cop on the beat is the state agent who is closest to the lives of all citizens.

5-5 ◉ SUMMARY

Chapter 5 brings several ideas together. The first is one of our central themes, the idea that in the lives of many if not most people, the decisions of the police define the law. The second is that because there are multiple, conflicting, and vague roles for the police to play, and because the police are so often faced with conflicting arguments and delicate balances of rights, those decisions are very often made with reference to the ethical perspectives of individual police officers. Third, such ethical perspectives are direct expressions of the character of those individuals who become police officers.

Thus, the integrity of the law is dependent upon the integrity of the individual police officer. The consistency of the law is the consistency of the police officer. The fairness, objectivity, and justice of the operations of the legal system are all dependent upon the good character of police officers.

5-6 ◉ TOPICS FOR DISCUSSION

1. In Aristotle's terms, who are your "exemplars"? Who in the contemporary world are your role models? Discuss where and how we get our heroes today.

2. A rather critical differentiation is made between "equality of treatment" and "justice." Create your own examples of how justice might not be served by equal treatment. How might injustice be created by treating people in exactly equal ways?

3. Police officers often think that they are constantly under scrutiny and being watched. But this is a myth. Discuss why police officers are taught to believe this myth—why it might be a good thing that many believe it and why it might be a bad thing. How does this discussion plug into our analysis of the importance of individual police officer character?

4. The Declaration of Independence states that we have the right to "life, liberty, and the pursuit of happiness." This idea of "happiness" is analogous to that of "the good," which we have been discussing here. We each define it for ourselves. What do you define as "the good" in your life? What are your long-term goals? What would you like your life to look like in the future?

5-7 ◉ ETHICAL SCENARIO

Think about the ethical implications of telling a lie. Is it always wrong? Can it be ethical "sometimes"? Are there circumstances wherein a police officer might lie to a citizen, and risk eventually being found guilty of some kind of misconduct, but be acting in the best interests of justice, of the community, and of the citizen herself? Consider these examples.

Is it ethical for an officer to tell a distraught mother that her injured child—being taken away in an ambulance—will be okay, even if the officer does not know this to be the case? Is it ethical for an officer to tell a hysterical husband that he is "going to jail if he does not calm down," even though the man has done nothing for which he can legally be arrested? Is it ethical for officers to tell one perpetrator that "The other guy turned you—you're going to the joint" in order to elicit information, even though it is a lie?

These and many, many other examples can be cited as circumstances under which police officers might lie and yet be acting in the best interests of justice. What do you think about the morality involved here? Do you see the paradoxical situation in which it places the police? Remember, it is a crime for citizens to lie to the police (in most jurisdictions). So should it be acceptable for the police to lie to citizens?

5-8 ◉ WRITING EXERCISE

Consider Aristotle's list of the virtues. Do you agree with his conceptualization? Would you add anything to this list? For example, he does not specifically discuss integrity, which many people have always believed is an additional, absolutely critical element of good character. To have integrity is to live one's life in agreement with one's philosophy. To be hypocritical is to lack integrity.

Or what about kindness? Isn't kindness toward others another critical element of good character?

Construct an essay that discusses what you might add to this ancient list. (Instructors: Have your class share and discuss their conceptualizations of this Aristotelian concept of the virtues and of what other ideas your students might wish to add to it.)

5-9 ◉ KEY TERMS

Aristotle: 384–322 BCE. Greek philosopher who was taught by Plato, tutored Alexander the Great, and established his own school, the Lyceum; created virtue-based ethics as well as the study of logic, politics, drama, and biology.

ethics of virtue: School of ethical thought suggesting that good character is determined by living a life that attempts to emulate role models or exemplars.

exemplars: Role models or heroes; people who live lives that others aim to emulate.

Golden Mean: Aristotle's idea that people should act with moderation, behaving in ways that seek a norm between defects and excesses in personal conduct.

the good: An individually developed understanding of what the pursuit of happiness should entail.

integrity: That characteristic of wholeness and of living a life consistent with one's principles.

personality: The outermost characteristics that determine a person's nature, such as intelligence, wit, charm, cordiality, and so on.

procedural justice: The rules of the game that must be observed by criminal justice practitioners when applying substantive law; for example, applying the *Miranda* decision.

substantive justice: The rules of conduct which people (citizens) must observe when dealing with each other in daily life; the idea of justice as what people deserve.

virtue: A particular moral excellence or moral quality that is perceived to be good.

CHAPTER 6

The Development of Character

Chapter Outline

"The truth is that the most brilliant exploits often tell us nothing of the virtues or vices of the men who performed them, while on the other hand a chance remark or a joke may reveal far more of a man's character than the mere feat of winning battles in which thousands fall, or of marshalling great armies or laying siege to cities."

—Plutarch

In the discussion about the critical importance of police officer character we made general reference to character as a concept. The police officer must have a perspective on life that is underwritten by an understanding of our moral disposition, the central element in character. But in a more practical, day-to-day sense, how do we refine our character? Let us remember that character is not necessarily a laudable thing, for there are vices as well as virtues. What can we do, as we pass through life's journey, to modify and improve our character? In particular, what can police officers do to transform their character, given the stress they are under and the powerful position they occupy in the lives of other people?

This chapter will delve more deeply into what character is, how we obtain it, and how it operates. This discussion will often seem unrelated to police work per se because we must amplify our considerations of police officer character and ethics with a more worldly understanding of these concepts as they relate to everyone—police officers and citizens alike. Then, and only then, can we move to focus directly on the police.

Throughout this work, we have stressed that character is the most critical aspect of ethical conduct. Since character is defined as a person's moral disposition, character is actually the source of all ethical—as well as unethical—conduct and, therefore, of police professionalism. "Character" is the term given to the enduring traits that affect how a person sees the world, understands it, and acts in it. These traits explain not merely why someone acts a certain way now but why someone can always be counted on to act in a certain way. In this sense, character gives a special sort of accountability and pattern to human action.

Character covers a wide range of traits other than moral ones. Besides moral virtues such as honesty, courage, and loyalty, a person's character includes traits that, in one way or another, contribute to their general well-being, to their aptitude for success in life. Character traits, or virtues and vices, determine a person's readiness to learn, their inclination to reflect upon the sorts of things that get their attention. Traits of character determine a person's likelihood for happiness.

In this study, however, we are only concerned with the part of character that pertains to the moral sense or to our understanding of right and wrong. When we consider the attributes that distinguish human beings from animals (built for the upright posture, opposed thumbs, a brain with a frontal lobe, language, culture), all these differences are fulfilled in our capacity to be sensitive to good and evil, right and wrong. Teleologically speaking, all of these defining human attributes complete themselves, or come together, in the possession of a moral sense.

6-1 ● WORKING ON IT

Our discussion will focus on the elements of character and some of the positive, conscious things people can do to promote good character in themselves. To begin with—and as obvious as this may seem—it is important to realize that having good character is something that one must work at. It doesn't happen automatically or accidentally. In the movie *The Color of Money*, when the young up-and-coming pool shark (played by Tom Cruise) asks Fast Eddie (played by Paul Newman) how he can achieve Fast Eddie's mastery as a pool hustler, Fast Eddie says, "Ya gotta be yourself, kid. But on purpose."

A. Being Yourself . . . On Purpose

While we have already discussed the notion of **integrity** in another context and utilizing another, alternative definition, it is one of the traits that is most important when we discuss how the individual can work at his or her character in a positive way. Many people consider "honesty" to be the definition of integrity.

This is only partially correct, for integrity is a particular kind of honesty. A person who possesses integrity is a person who lives their life in concert with their personal philosophy. Whatever their particular values and perspectives in life, individuals who have integrity behave in ways that do credit to their ideals. People who stand up for what they believe in, particularly when it is inconvenient to do so, have integrity. Concomitantly, when people say one thing and yet do another, we call this **hypocrisy.** Having integrity involves behaving in a way that is consistent with one's philosophy.

> *"If you've got integrity, nothing else matters. If you don't have integrity, nothing else matters."*
>
> —Former Senator Alan K. Simpson, Wyoming

© Pictorial Press Ltd/Alamy

Paul Newman as "Fast Eddie" gives advice to a young pool shark (played by Tom Crusie) in the 1986 movie *The Color of Money*.

Because this is so, integrity is not merely one of the many virtues that indicate good character. It is of critical importance because it can be—it must be—worked on. People must endeavor to behave in ways that give due credit to their principles. Those who work at this, who on a regular basis pass ethical "tests" by doing the right thing and showing integrity, indicate

BOX 6.1

BURGLARS IN UNIFORM

Police officers are the recipients of an extraordinary number of opportunities to become involved in criminal activities. Temptation is ever present on the job. They prowl in the middle of the night, when no one is around, when shop doors might have been left open, and when watchful eyes are sleeping. Furthermore, they are approached by citizens who wish to get into their good graces by padding their incomes with bribes or graft or free goods and services. They interact with drug dealers and pimps and numbers runners who are all too willing to protect their nefarious enterprises with payoff money. When police officers take advantage of these opportunities they show a lack of integrity. It sounds axiomatic, but it is absolutely critical that the modern, professional police officer understand that this type of hypocrisy is in fact a part of the history of American policing—and a part that the new professionals must eschew in any event.

by their actions that they are actively working on living a moral life. When a person "takes the easy way out" or does the most expeditious or self-serving thing, instead of that which they consider to be right, they are wanting in good character.

Another positive trait that is of particular importance with regard to working on one's character is industriousness or tenacity. In the police officer's workaday world, there are those individuals who tend to be **"soldiering"** along through their careers. That is, they tend to do as little as possible on the job in an effort to stay out of trouble, remain as safe and secure as possible, and collect their paychecks without becoming involved in solving the problems that plague the lives of their citizens. When a person lacks rigor in this way, they open themselves up to living an inconsequential life. A police officer who lacks the trait of being hard working or diligent is merely marking time and taking up space on the street. Such an officer is in fact living an odd reality. The costs of the police officer lifestyle are great. Working at odd hours, with strange days off (in the middle of the week, in lieu of the weekend), and taking vacations when the kids are still in school . . . these are but a few of the special types of prices that must be paid to be a police officer. Why pay them if one is going to soldier on and not be serious about one's craft? Why not get a job that allows for sleeping at night, working during daylight hours, and spending time with loved ones?

The two most important individual characteristics a person (or police officer) can actively work on in an effort to live a good life are the two referred to by Fast Eddie. As the quotation indicates, a good person has to be who he or she *really is*, and be that way *deliberately*.

B. Developing One's Own Philosophy

People do not live their lives automatically or by instinct. A wolf does not have to try to be a good wolf. A wolf does not take stock of its life, resolve to be a better wolf, and act accordingly. It just does what nature has equipped it to do.

But people's lives are never-ending projects for them. Unlike animals, people must try to be themselves. A great irony of the human condition is that we have to try to be who we want to be. We try to live a certain way, try to be seen and thought of by others in a certain light. The athlete strives to stay focused. The worried single mother tells herself, "I've got to stay upbeat in front of the kids." The actor repeats the mantra, "Stay in your role." The good teacher tries to resist becoming cynical and to continue to do the best for pupils. Police officers being pressured by corrupt partners must tell themselves, "Remember who you are." We all want to be thought of in a certain way. We remember what others have said about us and we act accordingly. This is all very deliberate, more or less self-conscious. We are being ourselves, but on purpose.

People see their lives in terms of an array of real or imagined possibilities over which they exercise some control. We live in the tension between what is and what might be. This tension explains our hopes and fears, plans and dreams. It explains everything we do; it explains the coherent and unified,

BOX 6.2

DELIBERATENESS AND LEGAL RESPONSIBILITY

As a matter of legal fact, this idea of **deliberateness** is so thoroughly webbed into our common understanding of human responsibility that the legal definition of an "act" is "deliberate, knowing behavior." Generally speaking, a person is held responsible by the law only for an offense he or she knowingly commits in terms of the realistic possibilities available to him or her.

Mental impairment mitigates responsibility and changes the nature of the act. An underage child falls into a different category of offender because age qualifies against responsibility. The law takes the view that responsibility does not attach to coerced behavior; taking the cash out of the till with the thief's gun pointed at your head is not something for which you will be held responsible.

Taken together, these ideas mean that the law requires and expects people to live in the deliberate way we are suggesting.

identifiable, individual quality of our lives. When we focus on the so-called moral virtues (honesty, generosity, courage, etc.), it is important to remember that the basis of these virtues includes those features of our makeup that enable us to live a purposeful life.

There is a certain dramatic quality to all of our lives in the sense that we are often conscious of playing a role, of trying to be somebody. Police officers want to look like police officers. They want, for example, to look firm, resolute, and tough. Trying to look that way means they are trying to *be* that way. There is nothing automatic about being a good cop. Being an effective cop is not something that is simply conferred upon us when we are given a badge. It is something we deliberately, consciously do, and to one degree or another, it is something we continue to work at. We are conscious of who we are and who we want to be. But there is often a gap between the two, and we try to close that gap. Police officers live with the awareness that it is not guaranteed they will succeed. They have to work at it and work hard.

Our care about what we do takes the form of filling the gap between what we think we are and what we want to be—or how we think we are seen and how we want to be seen. In revealing what is important to us, our care shows who we are trying to be. Our personhood is not fixed in advance, and so greatly does that fact matter to us that it organizes our every move. This is a mark of our character.

While a great deal of who we are is determined early in life, we nevertheless change and adapt and grow over the course of our lives. It is only the true defeatists, the cynics, the jaded who have lost themselves to the idea that they cannot change due to some kind of external forces, who believe they have no control over who they are and their own characters.

6-2 • EMOTIONS AS A FORM OF UNDERSTANDING

Here we will differentiate between **academic intelligence** and **emotional intelligence** (or social intelligence). Understanding this differentiation is important because it is critical to the effectiveness of the modern, professional officer that he or she possess both forms. Academic intelligence informs much of what officers must accomplish in terms of their administrative tasks: legal analysis, understanding search and seizure law, interrogation, investigation, report writing, testifying in court, and a multiplicity of other tasks and roles. But emotional intelligence is perhaps even more important when dealing with conflicting citizen interests, multiple definitions of justice, problematic ethical dilemmas, and vague legal issues.

A. Academic Intelligence

We are accustomed to hearing about people's **intelligence quotient (IQ)**. The IQ is a calculated percentage that relates any individual's native intelligence (not their level of education, by the way) to the average person's native intelligence. When we talk about this type of mental capacity we are discussing an academic or "book learning" type of intelligence. People take intelligence tests and their scores are compared to those of others their age. The individual's test score is divided by the average score of people their age. The percentage number that is thus developed is a percentage that indicates where the individual belongs on an imaginary continuum that stretches between the most intelligent and the least intelligent people.

An IQ of 100 indicates an absolutely average or the middle of the pack IQ. Those with higher IQs (e.g., the average police recruit) are smarter. A person with a high IQ is capable of doing well in the world of formal education or professional training. This is because it indicates that they are capable of ingesting great amounts of information and investigating complex concepts. The IQ is a measure of *intellectual potential*. As such, it is of great importance in the organizational world of the police. But it is not the only important indicator of police officer brain capacity.

Today, when we study interpersonal relationships in the police world, we are concerned with the IQ at the selection level. When hiring rookie officers we are concerned that those who are hired to interact with the public have a basic intelligence level high enough for them to be trained to perform necessary skills. And since modern-day hiring requirements are so protracted and sophisticated, this level of basic intelligence is possessed by each and every candidate who is hired to work in any public organization. Having a sufficiently high IQ is, in other words, seldom a problem for today's public servant.

Much more important is a person's emotional intelligence (EQ). This is because while an above-average IQ is commonplace in today's officer corps, a high EQ is often wanting.

B. Emotional Intelligence

In making the point that being concerned with IQ is often of limited value in the organizational world, some authors have discussed EQ and some have discussed **social intelligence (SQ)** as alternative constructs. In our discussion here, we will not take the time to differentiate between the two. This is because EQ and SQ overlap to a great extent and because they both are alternatives to the historical fixation on IQ. Without getting into the specifics here, suffice it to say that it could be argued that EQ is a critical part of SQ and vice versa.

As we can infer from the definition in Box 6.3, the emotionally intelligent person can benefit the police organization in numerous ways. High EQ people interact well with the public, with criminal suspects, with superiors within the police organizational structure, and with subordinates as well. While IQ is important in the modern police officer, it is not something about which police leadership need spend much time worrying. In today's police world it is EQ that is sometimes in short supply. By extension, because this is so, ethical behavior on the part of contemporary police officers can also be in short supply.

The police must respond to domestic scenes when the fabric of the family has disintegrated, calls for service involving irrational people, and crowd scenes where potential violence hangs heavily in the air. They must

BOX 6.3

ONE DEFINITION OF SOCIAL INTELLIGENCE

Karl Albrecht suggests that this concept (SPACE) includes:

- Situational awareness: Reading social context and understanding **proxemics**
- Presence: Exhibiting charisma and the idea of making it about the other person
- Authenticity: Avoiding manipulation and the "snap-on smile"
- Clarity: A way with words; eloquence and erudition
- Empathy: Feeling the pain, suffering, emotions of others

help distraught and fearful individuals and must handle many situations that require a steady and reassuring hand. All of society's ills and people's problems are visited upon the everyday police officer on the beat. The best officers are the ones who are able to handle the vagaries of those daily encounters with people who are at their worst. Not only must officers deal with irrational people, they must be able to handle their own emotions through these energy-consuming and difficult circumstances. Furthermore, responding to these types of stress-laden situations and encounters is something that goes on throughout the entire professional lifetime of police officers. It never lightens up. It never gets easier. One reason for police officers leaving the profession is that some of them burn out dealing with this reality.

Officers with **"street smarts"** are usually the ones who can work through those daily situations and encounters, and then go home to decompress. They have learned to grant to themselves enough time to work off the continuing stresses of responding to difficult incidents and dealing with people who are at their worst. For many years we called the really socially skilled officers, the ones who could seemingly balance their emotions, "unique," "special," or "super professionals." As it turns out, these people are emotionally smart. They are able to get through daily high

The study of "emotional intelligence" is now a major field of emphasis in the psychology of interpersonal relations, leadership and motivation study, and organizational theory.

© Dean Mitchell/Shutterstock.com

energy situations with little physical effort. They rarely get into altercations. They infrequently receive citizens' complaints. And they don't often draw their weapon or use force unnecessarily. In general, they are more personally self-aware and centered, and professionally they tend to move up the chain of command rapidly due to possessing these positive characteristics.

Such officers have always appeared to possess some kind of special quality that is difficult to pinpoint. Something in their backgrounds or personal psyches has usually been credited with allowing them to behave in such psychologically healthy ways. Something quirky or even charismatic has always been considered to be the cause of their superiority. But today we have clearer explanations of the qualities these individuals possess. They are part of the ethical frame of reference about which we are talking.

C. Emotions and Empathy

This entire discussion about care and interest points to the fact that emotions as well as reason ground the moral virtues. Our discussion about the relation between possibilities, personal identity, and care shows that emotions are themselves modes of moral response. Our emotions determine what is morally relevant to us and, in some cases, what is required of us. When police officers see a gang member "tagging" a city bus, a drunk driver careening through traffic, or a tourist who has just had his or her wallet stolen, those officers have an immediate and visceral response to what they see. This emotional response is a gauge of what interests them, what they find significant in the scene, and what they understand about it. To act rightly is to be emotionally engaged—it is to act in a way that brings to bear the lessons of the heart and not just those of a calm intelligence. An act motivated by the right reason but lacking in the right feeling is merely correct. It does not necessarily show good character. (See Box 6.4.)

When we recognize that we have done something wrong that is of moral consequence to another, we not only feel bad for them, we feel remorse. Our remorse is our recognition of the wrong we have done and of the person we have become in so doing. This reveals that when a man hits his wife, for example, he gets more than he bargained for; he gets himself as a wife-beater. When a wife lies to her husband, she gets herself as a liar. Whether we like it or not, that's part of the deal we make when we do something: We become identified with what we have done. The rest of the world recognizes this about us; and even though we may try to deny or rationalize it, we recognize it, too. What else accounts for the rationalizations and the common effort to shift blame?

To feel remorse is to judge that we did something wrong. Remorse is not so much caused by what we understand, as if there were first the insight into what we did and then the feeling of remorse that follows. Rather, remorse is a form of understanding the seriousness of what we did and what we have morally become. It is a common experience for us to note that in situations where remorse seems called for, a person's lack of remorse shows

BOX 6.4

A PARADOX ABOUT POLICE OFFICERS

It is commonly thought that police officers are cynical types, expecting the worst in people. They see all of the worst behavior humanity has to offer and begin to expect the worst from everyone. The drunkard, the gang member, the insane person, the true degenerate, the vicious predator, the ignorant victim, the self-centered thief, and a host of other negative people necessarily come into the lives of police officers.

But oddly enough, a number of studies indicate that most people become police officers because they want to help people. No matter how jaded they may end up eventually, most police officers begin their work with this in mind. They are moved to do good works.

It is a paradox that caring for victims, helping the truly vulnerable, and wanting the world to be different—working toward just that end—combines with these negative experiences to make many officers removed and aloof. In other words, it is not that police officers do not care, but precisely because they *do* care that, in the long run, makes many of them lose faith in people.

us a lack in their depth of understanding. Or, in showing that the situation had a different significance for them than it did for us, their lack of remorse shows that what was real and stood out to us about the situation was not real to them.

The point here is to note that what we understand to be the reality of a situation is a direct function of its significance for us, of what interests us about it. Our emotional response is our grasp of what matters. We react emotionally the way we do because we are seized with a certain reality—outrage at seeing the strong prey upon the weak, the good person unjustly treated, the victim bleeding in the street, the child unprotected from harm by ignorant parents, and so on. Just as remorse is a form of understanding the seriousness of what we have done, so too, pity is a form of understanding the pain of another. Emotions such as remorse and pity are natural aspects of moral judgment.

A further implication of what we say about the whole complex of care in our lives is that moral response does not assume impartiality. In most of the professions that deal with people (medicine, social work, nursing, teaching, police work), we hear a lot of talk about being objective. While it is true that medical decisions or the application of the law must be done fairly and in an impartial manner, we are arguing here that this does not imply the professional must not care about people. Impartiality in certain situations is a mode of fairness; it does not signify a lack of care.

One of the criticisms leveled at all of these "caring" professions is that the people with whom professionals interact tend to be seen as cases rather than as people. This tendency develops because, as if they were on an assembly line, patients and students and citizens move by the professionals and, in the name of impartiality, their individuality is not acknowledged. Impartiality is necessary in the sense that professionals are not supposed to show favoritism. But here we are saying that impartiality can go too far; it can develop a cynicism and a coldheartedness in the professional that impedes the ability to make moral decisions.

Seeing the morally relevant features of a situation shows moral sensibility and moral character and is a part of a morally appropriate response. Pursuing the right response does not begin with making choices but with recognizing circumstances relevant to some desired end that counts as good. Knowing how to see the relevant particulars is a mark of morality. Character is expressed in what one sees as much as in what one does. Therefore, morality begins in character.

When a police officer notices an incident that calls for attention, the ability to see the relevant particulars of the scene is as much a matter of emotional awareness as it is a rational matter. Often, officers see what they see because of and through their emotions. So, for example, a feeling of indignation makes the cop sensitive to the cruelty of a mugger, just as pity opens his eyes to the pain of the person mugged. The officer's emotional dispositions create a relevant point of view for seeing what is important in the situation. The professional officer notices feelings that might otherwise go unnoticed by a detached or uncaring person—witness the cops at the Puerto Rican festivities discussed in Box 6.5.

Emotions, then, are absolutely vital to an intelligent, ethical perspective in life. Moreover, emotions are educable. Just as a child learns the multiplication tables, dates, and historic names, we can learn what our feelings mean. When it matters to us, such as when we are trying to be good police officers, we can learn to feel differently about people's life situations and perspectives.

© Lisa F. Young/Shutterstock.com

It is an unfortunate reality that many police officers suffer from emotional jadedness.

BOX 6.5

AN EXAMPLE OF POLICE JADEDNESS

In a recent example in New York City, police officers stood by at a Puerto Rican celebration and let a gang of men molest and rape women. What did these officers see when they looked at the incident? Did they consider the molesters' actions "funny"? Did they rationalize "that's the way those people behave"? Did they avoid getting involved and doing their jobs because "women like that kind of thing"? What does the fact that dozens of officers took no action reveal about what they understood and about their character?

6-3 ● ETHICAL PERCEPTION

There is an important difference between appropriate and inappropriate anger, appropriate and inappropriate fear, and so on. When anger is inappropriate, it is excessive or not called for. There is a gap between what the angry person understands, which the anger expresses, and what he or she ought to understand. Police officers are regularly angry (outraged) by unlawful behavior—such as being confronted by a burglar who breaks into a family's home and takes precious possessions—but this anger must be appropriately channeled into the desire to take legal action. It cannot rationalize **"curbside justice"** by allowing the cop to deliver a beating as punishment for such behavior. This first kind of anger (driven by empathy for the victim) is not only understandable, but it is an important part of what motivates the professional officer to act. The second kind of anger (driven by a desire for revenge) is dangerous for the professional as it rationalizes the use of excessive force and convolutes the entire meaning of the justice system.

Before officers decide how to act, they must first understand that the situation requires action—something the cops in the New York incident described in Box 6.5 did not see. The decision to act will come from a realistic reading of the situation. Those things that stand out as being important are determined by an officer's moral sensibility. Therefore, much of the work of good character rests in knowing how to construct a situation, how to describe and classify what is going on. This takes practice. And in doing this practice from day to day, police officers have no good reason to be bullheaded about the way they see things.

Only a foolish person believes his or her way is the one and only way to judge situations. The truth is very much the opposite; the desire to be a decent person—the desire to be a competent police officer—requires that we remain critical of ourselves. We must be open to inquiry and questioning, from ourselves and from others, and this requires us to continue to reflect on the purpose of our conduct. Only in reflecting on conduct in actual situations on the beat can police officers reflect on themselves, their lives, and their professional competence. "Did I do the right thing? Could I have solved this situation differently, in a more just manner? Did I really have to use force, or could I have talked the kid into the car?" These types of questions need to be asked again and again as the officer changes, grows in competence, and learns.

We can have control over our emotions. We know how this works. Through collaboration with other officers and citizens, through listening to and identifying with the viewpoints of others, an officer's vision becomes expanded and enlarged. This moral vision improves, and with it the ability to detect relevant facts. The open-minded officer comes to learn different ways to read situations and different questions to ask to see the scene with improved clarity and understanding. How to see becomes as much a matter of inquiry as what to do. Such inquiry and dialogue establish the route to long-term understanding. As is true in all occupations, in law enforcement there is a pronounced tendency to think there is one way to handle a detail—and that in an officer's early days on the street, he or she learns this one way. We are saying this idea is foolish and that in operating this way, officers limit their ability to continue to grow and to become the best, most competent professionals they can be.

The key is to cultivate a pride in remaining open to questions. Probably no one thing is more telling of a person's character than the ability to be critical of himself or herself. All the other moral virtues and the possibility of learning or improving rest upon remaining open to the world. Every person has much to learn from life. Wisdom consists of accepting that fact.

> *"There are no great men, only great challenges that ordinary men are forced by circumstances to meet."*
>
> —Admiral William F. Halsey, U.S.N.

6-4 ◉ SUMMARY

Our character produces plans that express an overall unity of purpose, an identifiable plot line, in the story of our lives. Moral judgment is best understood as a set of judgments about possibilities because the decisions we make involve assessing our possibilities in terms of the way they fit into our overall concept of what is good. Many of the choices we make concern long-term intentions, and such future thinking reveals the kinds of people we are trying to be. This is what is meant by the claim that choices exhibit character.

People live their lives in the tension and openness created by the flow of such possibilities, and for that reason the concepts of justice and the good are bedrock principles in a moral life. These moral concepts flow directly from the relationships, experiences, and predicaments of our lives. They constitute images of the different possibilities available to people and their differing notions of the good. These moral concepts do not come from some abstract, universal ideas. Because police work is carried out at the level of procedural justice, police competence is unavoidably bound to good character.

Emotions are a critical element in moral understanding because we perceive the morally relevant facts of a situation through our emotional responses. And our emotional responses also reveal what we morally understand about both a given situation and ourselves. To a great extent, we choose our character, because our emotions are educable. That is, we can change the way we feel, the way we respond, as we become aware of what it means to us and about us.

Having done a significant amount of reflecting about character, what it is and its importance, we now turn to two chapters that will introduce several ethical theories that discuss how to make moral judgments. As opposed to our character-based discussion here, we will now discuss rule-based sets of principles for approaching ethical questions. The difference in these two approaches will become clear as we proceed through the next two discussions.

6-5 ◉ TOPICS FOR DISCUSSION

1. One of this chapter's subjects is the idea that we strive to be somebody and to be perceived in a certain way. Discuss how we want to be seen by others on the street in our roles as police officers. What is it we are trying to be like out there?

2. Discuss the difference between being objective and impartial (not being "too emotional" as professionals) and being so remote from human suffering that one doesn't care. How can dealing with people in crisis develop a jadedness and cynicism that make an officer ineffective at seeing what is important in a given situation?

3. Discuss how to handle a detail involving a large group of partying teenagers. First, discuss locker-room truisms, rules of thumb, that you have heard about how to do such a job. Second, critique these rules of thumb and consider alternative ways to do the job. Note that the reason for having this discussion is to emphasize the idea there are many ways to handle any type of detail—there is, in common vernacular, "more than one way to skin a cat."

4. Discuss emotional intelligence. What differentiates it from academic intelligence? Can you give examples of each? Examples from civilian life? Police-related examples? Why do the authors suggest that emotional or social intelligence is even more important than academic intelligence for the modern police officer?

6-6 ⊙ ETHICAL SCENARIO

Box 6.1 suggests that sometimes police officers fall victim to the multiple opportunities that the job presents for criminal behavior and become burglars in uniform. What if you were to become aware of the fact that some of your fellow officers were burglarizing on the beat? Do you believe that you have a personal ethic that would allow you to ignore subcultural norms about always being supportive of other officers and take action as a police officer against what is called "police crime"? What might you anticipate as the potential personal costs of doing so? Would you feel awkward around other officers after taking such action because of letting down the group? On the other hand, might you feel superior in some sense because of taking the higher ground? Finally, what sort(s) of police misconduct might you feel comfortable reporting? Burglary? Taking money from pimps in exchange for not arresting prostitutes? Planting evidence on suspects? Harassing citizens? (In later chapters, we will engage the substantive difference between these and numerous other forms of misconduct. At that time, we will engage the fact that it is easier to work against some forms of misconduct than others. Not all types of police deviance are equal in their impact upon the subculture and/or upon justice.)

6-7 ⊙ WRITING EXERCISE

Construct an essay differentiating between the common idea of intelligence quotient (IQ) and the contemporary emphasis upon what analysts are calling both emotional intelligence (EQ) and social intelligence (SQ). What are the differences? Can you think of specific examples of how people can have one and not the other? Furthermore, include in your analysis a police example or two of how the oft-cited idea that police work is about "common sense" relates to these two rather new ideas in the world of interpersonal relations. Given the emphasis upon constitutional law and sociological/criminological theory involved today, we know that academic intelligence is absolutely critical for the professional police officer. And yet, it is still true that without common sense (in today's parlance, emotional intelligence/social intelligence) it is impossible to develop competence in police work.

6-8 ⊙ KEY TERMS

academic intelligence: Natural trait that involves the ability to learn complex concepts and study difficult subjects.

curbside justice: Propensity of some police officers to deliver their own brand of "justice" (usually in the form of physical violence) to suspects on the street.

deliberateness: Being self-aware about one's actions and statements.

emotional intelligence (EQ): Trait that relates to the ability to interact with other people with insight, compassion, and effectiveness.

hypocrisy: Lack of integrity or a lack of congruence between one's philosophy and one's actions.

integrity: Trait involving behaving in congruence with or in concert with one's philosophy.

intelligence quotient (IQ): Numerical calculation that places individuals in relation to the intelligence of the average person.

proxemics: The study of personal space, having to do with how close people can/should be to others when interacting with them.

social intelligence (SQ): Level of sophistication in dealing with other people in social situations.

soldiering: Doing as little work as possible on the job; getting the job done by doing as little as possible.

street smarts: Common sense; police term for those officers who are good at dealing with problems on the street, regardless of their academic intelligence or formal education levels.

CHAPTER 7

Ethical Formalism

Chapter Outline

"You don't do things right some of the time. You do them right all of the time."

—Vince Lombardi, football coach

Ethical theories can be divided into several major categories along different lines of distinction. For our discussion, we will emphasize one basic differentiation. Some ethical theories formulate and encourage the individual to follow absolute rules about what is the good and about a person's duty to behave in a certain manner. There was a universal rule that was predetermined, indicating how the individual would calculate when deciding what course of action to pursue. When an ethical question appears, a "what should I do here" type of quandary, the ethical individual refers to preexisting principles. As we noted earlier, these sorts of philosophies are deontological—that is, they are philosophies of *moral obligation.*

Alternatively, other theories focus on the long-term utility or usefulness of moral decisions and suggest that only outcome is important. More precisely, they stress that the outcome of maximizing benefit to others is the decisive moral issue. When faced with an ethical question, the person adhering to these philosophies makes a calculation. In calculating what to do when making choices between behavioral options, the second type of theory involves taking into consideration the specific situation a choice presents. Such **situational theories of ethics** are not absolutist. On the contrary, they suggest it is most logical (and morally defensible) to make choices that may vary from situation to situation—driven by a concern for the consequences of such choices. **Utilitarianism** is such a theory, treated in Chapter 8. Utilitarianism is called *teleological* because a certain outcome, or end-state, is what defines the nature of the act, and not the act itself or adherence to a rule.

In this chapter, we focus on the former. We will take a look at the most important deontological theory in history: the school of ethical formalism, defined by **Immanuel Kant.** First, a brief visit of other absolutist schools of ethical thought that have been embraced by humanity for several millennia.

7-1 ● THE ABSOLUTIST SCHOOLS

It might seem odd to spend so much time—an entire chapter and even more—on a theory that appears to be of limited value. Especially when discussing the ethical parameters of police work, where we know that discretionary decision making is so omnipresent and critical to the endeavor, why is it relevant to discuss absolutist principles? Since it seems to be axiomatic that they are not of much usefulness in the real world, why bother?

The answer is that such discussions about deontological theories are about duty. And duty is a central theme in any discussion of the adherence to the law, of behavioral accountability, and of human responsibility in general. Duty comprises a large part of what parenthood, military service, public service, and of course police work are about. Before turning to Kant himself and the modern notion of absolute duty, we will take a moment to reflect upon how this side of the deontological/teleological debate has been couched throughout history.

A. Duty to God

The idea that a person's duty is absolute has its roots in ancient history. Far back in time, before the invention of the written word, we know that people understood that their duty came to them from God. Religion was the starting point, the touchstone of duty. The child learns from his or her earliest days that one can ensure oneself to be good, ensure oneself of being a real man or real woman, by obeying God's commandments. The idea was that "It is right because God said so."

Consider once again the Biblical story of Abraham's readiness to kill his son. This story about the father of the modern Western religions (Judaism, Christianity, and Islam) is a parable about how a man was willing to kill his own son—violating perhaps *the* essential rules of self and familial preservation—in order to show his absolute devotion to God. God told Abraham to slay his own son, and he was prepared to do it.

All of the world's great organized religions suggest that, rather than being made by humans, ethics are God-given. That is, rather than being discovered or concocted by intelligent human beings, definitions of the good and rules of right conduct are given to the human race by a supreme divine authority. This authority might be the God of Abraham, the gods, or the Great Spirit. Human beings find out about theses rules from the great religious works of their traditions that came down through history such as the Bible, the Koran, or the Torah. The rules that religion brings to us are absolute pronouncements from an ultimate authority and are not alterable.

In discussing how to fashion an ethic to live by, we are going to focus on principles and issues of character that are determined by people themselves. However, everything we say about Kant, utilitarianism, and our own "ethic to live by" can be seen as perfectly consistent with religious belief. Part of our ethic involves avoiding absolute pronouncements in favor of a more practical, situation-guided idea of how a person develops his or her own character and makes choices with regard to how to behave.

B. Natural Law

Similar to this idea that principles of absolute duty come from a god that has a human-type personality is the school of **natural law**. This perspective suggests that such principles come from the natural order of things. Not (necessarily) wedded to the idea of a personal god, natural law adherents—both ancient and contemporary—believe that the absolute principles of duty come to us from the natural world. The ethical standards that guide human behavior are objectively derived from the nature of human beings and the nature of the world. In the Roman Republic, we find Cicero writing that natural law consists in reverence

BOX 7.1

RELIGIOUS DUTY

Near the end of World War II, the Japanese military realized that they were destined to lose the war in the Pacific. Some of them were suicidal, but some of the more rational leaders wanted to prolong the war as best they could so that the end-of-the-war negotiations would be as favorable as possible. In order to do so, they utilized *kamikaze* attacks against the American navy. Japanese pilots would fly airplanes loaded with explosives and extra gasoline and crash them on purpose into American warships. Of course the end result of this was the death of the pilots. These were, in every sense, suicide missions.

The pilots flew their missions willingly. They went to certain death. Why? Why would men go into combat assured that they would not survive? The answer had to do with the religious views of the Japanese at that time. The pilots were members of the **Shinto** religion. This religion worshiped the emperor as a living god. When a pilot died in the service of the emperor, he was honored at the Yasukuni shrine. This was the only shrine where mere mortals were vetted in Japan. In fact, the emperor himself went to this shrine twice each year to honor Japan's dead military men.

So these pilots died for their country . . . and they died for their emperor . . . but they also died for their religion. It was their duty to do so.

for the gods, duty toward the fatherland, parents, and relatives, gratitude and readiness to forgive, and respect for all those who are superior to us in age, wisdom, or status. One can and must derive law from the laws of nature, for the law of nature is the power of nature, and for this reason it is the norm of right and wrong.

Natural law adherents may very well believe in a God—several natural law theories come from religious theorists such as **St. Thomas Aquinas**—but the duties that humans must accept are not directly written down or spoken by God. Unlike, say, the Ten Commandments, the natural law is ascertainable through rational thought.

Just as the laws of physics and of chemistry are discoverable by reason, so too are the laws of morality, society, and government. These natural laws specify the duties that humans owe to each other. The natural law constitutes the principles of **practical rationality**. Every human being, because he or she has the power to be rational, possesses a basic knowledge of the natural law—the nature of things.

St. Thomas Aquinas posited that all people know immediately, by incli-nation, what constitutes the good. He suggested that, among other things, people know that they should pursue life, procreation, knowledge, society, and reasonable conduct. This philosophy was expanded by the French philos-opher **Jean-Jacques Rousseau** during the **Age of Enlightenment**. He sug-gested that human beings are good by nature and that abnormal wickedness, evil history, and inappropriate institutions corrupt that nature. He further suggested that all people are bound to each other and to their society through a **social contract** that is implicit in all of our actions. The knowledge of it is, again, natural and possessed by all humans.

It is important for us to focus here for just a moment because the funda-mental principle of natural law is that good is to be done and evil is to be avoided. This is critical for our discussion because later on it informs our ethic to live by.

C. Ethical Formalism: Kant's Theory of Duty

Today, absolutist theories are most prominently represented by "ethical formalism." Immanuel Kant was the founder of this school of thought. An enthusiastic supporter of the French Revolution, Kant maintained that one ought to think autonomously, free of the dictates of any external authority, in-cluding the authority of religion. Kant argued that the source of the good lies not in anything outside the human subject, either in nature or given by God, but rather is only the *good will* itself. A good will is one that acts from duty in accordance with the universal moral law that the autonomous human being freely gives itself. This law obliges one to treat every person—understood as an agent of rationality—as an end in himself rather than (merely) as means to other ends the individual might hold.

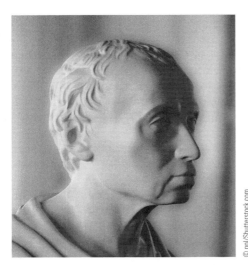

Rationality is our governing trait, the trait that, in Kant's estimation, makes us human. And rationality is the same for everyone. The parameters of reason, like the laws of mathematics, do not vary from person to person. They are not determined by context or situation. They are not a function of the desires or needs of individuals. If we are interested in living rationally, and that's a big "if," we must act in a way that is consistent with reason. This means that the reason or motive for our conduct must be the motive that could apply equally to everybody in this situation. This is Kant's principle of morality, and it involves an absolute duty to behave according to the stan-dard of reason under all circumstances.

© ppl/Shutterstock.com

Immanuel Kant, the great philosopher.

People who take reason to be their guide, independent of other considerations, are Kantians in some form or other. Whether they realize it or not, these people believe that the right, the obligatory, the morally good, is determined by only one thing: the intention that lies behind an action, the reason for which it was done. They believe the whole moral worth of an act comes from the nature of its motivation and not from what the act brings about (or its consequences). They believe that what the person tries to do has moral value, not what the person causes by the act. In focusing exclusively upon intention, ethical formalists believe there is an absolute principle (the **Categorical Imperative**) upon which ethical choices must be based. No consequence-based calculations enter into this absolutist view of duty.

Kant pointed out there are many factors involved in successfully accomplishing something. Over most of these factors, a person exercises no direct control. Through no fault of their own, people may not be skillful enough or may not know enough to succeed in accomplishing a good deed. Other people may not cooperate or may work against the would-be good deed doer. Or circumstances may get in the way. As important as these factors obviously are, they cannot count in assessing the moral worth of an act because morality relates to a person's frame of mind, to his or her "heart," and not to facts about the world. Morally speaking, doing something for the right reason is all that matters.

The Categorical Imperative. We agree with Kant in this: there are other considerations that make an action right, good, or obligatory besides the goodness or badness of its consequences (the outcome). We agree that certain features of an act itself make the act right—for example, the fact that it keeps a promise, or that it is fair or kind. We might also agree that sometimes other facts that are external to an act make it right or obligatory on us—for example, that it is commanded by God, or by patriotism, or by one's dying mother. "I did it because that's what she wanted. It was her last wish."

With specific regard to Kant's view of morality, he has provided a rule called the Categorical Imperative that tests the moral validity of any action. The rule is "categorical" because it applies universally to all situations. It is "imperative" because it has the force of a law of reason and is not in any respect optional. It is absolute. Kant gave three formulations of the Categorical Imperative, but we shall restrict ourselves to two of the three: "Act only on that maxim which you can at the same time will to be a universal law." In this statement, Kant claims that an act is right only if the motive or reason for which it is done can be imagined to apply equally to everybody. The second formulation is explained in Box 7.2.

With this imperative, Kant was saying several things at once. First, when people do something voluntarily, they must always act on a rule they can formulate or explain to themselves. This means when people act on their own initiative, they must know the reason why. Blind obedience to a rule, not accompanied by an understanding of the intention of the rule, is not satisfactory.

Second, a person is choosing and judging from a morally defensible point of view if (and only if) he or she is willing to universalize the **maxim**.

BOX 7.2

 ## Two Formulations of Kant's Categorical Imperative

1. "Act only on that maxim which you can at the same time will to be a universal law."
2. "So act as to treat humanity whether in your own person or that of any other, in every case as an end, never as a means only."

That is, people will choose to do the right thing if they are willing to imagine they are creating a rule—a rule that should be acted on by everyone in a similar situation, even if they turn out to be on the receiving end. This is a philosopher's presentation of what people often refer to as the Golden Rule: "Do unto others as you would have them do unto you."

Third, Kant tells us that doing our duty has a moral value by definition. That is, irrespective of what consequence it brings to the world, a dutiful act is ethical in and of itself. Having the will to cleave to a duty (good will) is sufficient to make a person's behavior ethical.

Unlike those philosophers who emphasize the rights people own as people, Kant emphasized the duties they owe as people. Most of the acts traditionally regarded as duties can be thought of as deriving their obligatory character from one primary obligation—the duty to treat people as ends in themselves. Reason connects every motive to those of other people, and identifies a person with the actions of all others. In consciously willing some act, a person sees that all people are members of a "kingdom of ends." This is the source of personal dignity: this connection of reason provides a sense of the ultimate worth for each person. We have a station in life to maintain; we have our own responsibilities as men and women and as rational creatures that it would be shameful to repudiate—the nobility of humanity. We have to live up to our end and destiny as human beings; to do otherwise would be to let the whole race down.

An Example: Making Promises. Let us take one of Kant's own examples of how he applies his rule. He supposes a person makes a promise but doesn't intend to keep it. The person's maxim about making promises might be expressed this way: "When it suits me, I will make promises—but also, when it suits me, I will break promises." Kant says a person cannot consistently will (desire) that this maxim be universally acted upon. A person can easily "will the lie, but not a universal law to lie." He is saying that people cannot will that they themselves be lied to when it suits someone else's interests. This makes no sense.

Kant is not arguing that a person must keep his or her promises because the results of everyone breaking promises, when convenient to themselves, would be bad. (As we will see in Chapter 8, this is how a utilitarian would run the argument.) Instead, Kant is contending that you cannot even will such a maxim or

BOX 7.3

ABSOLUTE DUTIES

We live in an era where a great deal of emphasis is placed on cultural diversity. One of the logical problems for Kantians today is that, because different cultures create different norms, values, and laws, there is serious debate about whether or not duties exist that are absolute. Here are some suggestions about what might be included in a list of such absolute duties:

- Every child deserves to be loved.
- Married people should keep their wedding vows.
- Parents have a duty to protect their children from harm.
- It is always wrong to torment animals.
- Cruelty is always wrong.
- There is no circumstance in which pedophilia is permissible.

Do you agree with some, most, or many of these "absolute" duties? Can you think of others? Or do you think there are no absolute duties?

rule to be universally acted on because in so doing you would be involved in a contradiction. He is saying that, at the same time, a person cannot (1) will that people be able to make promises and have them accepted as binding, and (2) will everyone also be free to break promises to suit themselves. Such a maxim is self-defeating. If a person acts on the maxim that to make deceitful promises is acceptable, then the "institution of promise making" is meaningless.

Kant's philosophy of ethics thus focuses on the intention of people's acts. It considers their consequences uncontrollable and, thus, irrelevant. He means to infuse into people the ideal that their duty is absolute. No amount of rationalization, whether it be self-serving or aimed at some community good, can be used to challenge the maxims included in this absolutist perspective of ethics. Right is right, and it is right all the time.

7-2 ● THE STRENGTHS OF KANT'S ABSOLUTISM

Suppose a police officer, doing his duty, arrests a marijuana smoker at a large rock concert. The arrest results in a brawl between police officers and dozens of teenagers. The principles of ethical formalism suggest that, because pot smoking is illegal—everywhere at all times—the arrest was appropriate. Utilitarian logic (which we will discuss in Chapter 8) suggests that the consequences of the arrest, a riotous situation that developed out of relative calm, were bad and thus the action taken (the arrest) was wrong. From the utilitarian perspective, even though marijuana smoking is against the law, making an arrest under these circumstances would have negative consequences that outweigh the positive duty to enforce the law absolutely.

The above example is a good one for several reasons. It illustrates a commonplace form of police discretionary decision making. It makes a good case for police officers to use their heads and hearts instead of being absolutist in their decision making. It seems, therefore, to make an argument against the principles of ethical formalism. But ethical formalism has strong supporters everywhere in the world. There is good reason to argue that "rules are rules" and, using an old police adage, "we don't make the rules, we just enforce them."

Whether people know it or not, they often argue in support of ethical formalism's absolute principles because they value the rule of law and understand that in discretion lies a problem of huge significance. Too much discretion can mean an end to the rule of law. Allowing rule enforcers—the police in the case of our discussions—to "use their heads" can too often mean they cease to apply the law as it is written. They may use the freedom that discretion creates for them to control the streets in an arbitrary manner. Even when supported by the people in a community or in a neighborhood, the exercise of power without reference to preexisting rules can bring about the sort of tyranny the rule of law was invented to overcome.

The Qadi (also spelled Khadi, Cadi, or Kadi) has absolute power where moral judgment is concerned.

© World History Archive/Alamy

Tyranny is the "exercise of power cruelly or unjustly." Tyrannical rule by a person or group of people who are not accountable to anyone was a part of history for thousands of years before the invention of the idea of law. It was the tyranny of the southern slave system that was the major cause of the Civil War. It was the tyranny of the Japanese and the Nazis that brought America into World War II. And tyranny is still a part of the contemporary world. It was the tyranny of the Serbs that brought the American military to Kosovo in the late 1990s.

The central idea of democracy is that the people get together, or their elected representatives do, and formulate the rules by which society will be governed. Then agents of this consensually created state (the police) apply those rules on the street. If the rule appliers exercise so much discretion that they are not actually following

BOX 7.4

KHADI JUSTICE

In North Africa, there are tribes that have lived for thousands of years without what we would call a formal legal system. When disputes between individuals arise, instead of trials with juries and judges, problems are brought to the Khadi. The Khadi is the lawgiver. He decides disputes using the general direction of the Koran (the sacred Islamic text) and his own moral principles. The Khadi answers to no one. His decisions don't have to be consistent, and sometimes they are not. One dispute may be decided one way on one day, and the next day a similar dispute may be decided another way.

People who study comparative legal systems call this type of absolute decision-making power **Khadi justice**. It refers to the ultimate in discretion. No rules, no principles, no laws are referenced—only the personal understanding of the decision maker about what is right serves as the grounds for dispute resolution.

the rules, then whoever ends up being arrested will believe he or she has been singled out for unfair treatment. If, in other words, discretion is abused, then the rule of law ends and the rule of cop begins. See Box 7.4.

If this abuse of discretion develops, then society ceases to be built upon consensus and the police become a law unto themselves, as the Redcoats once were. This then refers back to one of our central themes. The police are the law in the realistic sense that their decisions determine what the law means to millions of people. But they must be governed by a commitment, an absolute (Kantian) duty, to serve the law just as they serve society and the people. If they begin to act as if they really are the law in every sense, then the police destroy the essence of what America is: a country ruled by individual freedom, representative democracy, and justice for all.

Thus there are good, practical, legal, and ethical reasons for accepting what Kant says, or at least some of it. But the Kantian, absolutist position has problems associated with it. It is toward a consideration of those problems that we now turn.

7-3 ● A CRITIQUE OF KANT AND ABSOLUTISM

For all of the "rule of law"–related strengths that it possesses, Kant's position creates difficulties. We have to be careful, because when we carry out the implications of his position it becomes possible for an action or rule of conduct to be morally right even if it does not promote good over evil. That is, the logical extension of focusing on a person's intention is that the morality of an act is *not* measured by the difference, for good or ill, it makes in the life of anyone. It is right simply because of some other fact about it (e.g., it is commanded by God, or by religious faith, or by the law) or because of its own nature (e.g., it is reasonable). For ethical formalists, acting in conformity with absolute rules is morally valid regardless of whether doing so promotes a good or makes a difference in someone's life.

Let us take a police work–related example. A teenager with no criminal record is stopped for being out after curfew. The teen is cooperative, sober, and genuinely apologetic for this behavior. In fact, the officer involved finds that the child was driving home from seeing her ill grandmother after a Tuesday night high school basketball game in which the teen played. Irrespective of any analysis about the interests of justice, the law against curfew demands that the child be cited. An absolutist approach to the duty to always obey the law no matter what the circumstances would suggest to the officer that a citation must be issued. The teen's act was against the law and therefore was wrong. The officer's act of issuing a citation invokes the law and is therefore right.

Taking this Kantian view, we run into a problem. Any act, by itself, is right or wrong. The act's moral quality is completely determined only by its own moral quality. This is circular logic and suggests that the position is no real position at all. Put more clearly, we are suggesting that the moral worth of an act must depend, at least in part, on something beyond itself, on something about the real difference it makes in the lives of people. We mean that the morality of an act must be directly linked to the good or evil consequences it produces for someone. It follows that in order to know whether some behavior is right or wrong, one must first know what is good and whether the act in question promotes or is intended to promote what is good. Otherwise, how would one know what behavior was right?

In the example cited above, the officer's choice to issue a citation must be related to the impact that it might have on a teenager with an otherwise clear record. Sticking to the absolute duties of enforcing the law at all times might very well impact the teen's life in a way that is not morally defensible.

A separate problem with Kant arises from conflicts between duties. For example, one duty, according to Kant, is to tell the truth. Another is to protect people from harm. Unfortunately, it is possible for these two duties to conflict with each other. It is possible, in other words, that lying might help someone in trouble. Would Kant lie to a **Gestapo** agent who was looking to arrest Jews if he (Kant) knew where they were hiding? One may very well be able to will a specific rule that permits lies in a certain kind of situation (like this one)—"It is okay to lie to Gestapo agents, who are up to no good." But you cannot will a universal law that blankets all exceptions to the law of truth telling. Such a maxim might read, "Tell the truth, unless you think it's best not to." Such a maxim is no maxim at all.

Furthermore, even if we admit that the criterion of the Categorical Imperative rules out certain actions as immoral (for example, lying or deceitful promise making), must we agree that all our moral duties can be established this way? Is the "universality" test enough? We think it is not, especially for the police officer.

Consider loners who don't like people and wish to exercise the freedom to be left completely alone in life. We can readily imagine such people being able to will the universal maxim "People should not help others in need"— even when it is they who are in need. To follow such a maxim would be a disastrous idea for police officers. For the police to operate under the maxim that they ought not to help people would be for the central role of the police to be abrogated.

Another problem is that Kant does not tell us how to determine whether rules are moral rules or not. The "rule" that "you should always button the bottom button first" certainly has nothing to do with morals. But it is a rule of thumb that many observe. In our discussions about character (Chapters 5 and 6), we pointed out that morality begins with the recognition of a moral situation, of morally relevant facts, and that a certain kind of response is required. Kant's test of maxims does not help us at all with this problem of determining what are moral issues.

Thus, it seems for maxims to be considered moral duties, it is not enough that you be able to will your maxims to be universal. Since Kant's ethical theory is not concerned with the promotion of good in the world (good consequences, that is) but only with intentions, his idea of universalization reduces to nothing more than a requirement to act in a fashion that is logically consistent with what one wills or wishes. The mere fact that your behavior is consistent with your ideals is certainly not enough to make behavior ethical. Nazis who killed Jews because they thought it was the right thing to do were certainly not behaving in a morally defensible way.

For Kant, rationality—not the goodness brought into people's lives— is the most important feature of morality. This is to praise rationality for its own sake. A strictly Kantian police officer, then, when coming upon a man who has murdered his wife, can only say to him, "You're a traitor to reason! You've violated the rational nature of your wife!" Thus, there is more to the moral point of view than being willing to universalize one's rules. Kant and his followers—focusing on rationality and consistency only—fail to see this fact.

One additional problem for a democratic system is presented by Kant's absolute formulations. Following rules in an absolute way and cleaving to the absolute duty to obey the law can create terrible consequences for people when the law is unjust. When this happens—and history is full of examples— Kantians can be guilty of ignoring higher notions of justice and the good in favor of blind obedience to rules.

One of the paradoxes of law is that the enforcement of democratically instituted laws can sometimes be just as tyrannical as the enforcement of the wishes of a few all-powerful people (czars, kings, and dictators). That is, the majority does not always make laws that are just and equitable.

In the American South, for one hundred years after the Civil War, a system of segregation kept blacks in poverty and sent their children to poor schools while most whites lived in relative ease. In Europe, for hundreds of years, Jews were forced to live in ghettos and were denied the rights of ordinary citizenship. For generations, Irish Catholics were not allowed to vote, own land, or send their children to school. In each of these examples, a majority of the population agreed with these policies and made laws supporting this racism. Thus, democracy is no guaranteed cure for injustice and inhumanity.

BOX 7.5

THE NUREMBERG TRIALS

After World War II, some of the powerful Nazis who were responsible for sending millions to death camps and to the gas chambers were put on trial in Germany after the war. At these **Nuremberg Trials** the defense some of them presented was that they were only following the laws of their country at the time (the 1930s and early 1940s). It was, in fact, true that behavior such as fraternization between Jews and Gentiles had been made a crime in Germany at that time. Such crimes were punishable by being sent to the camps. Sex between these races was a crime. These are only two examples of what the law said in Nazi Germany.

Political scientists who study the period tell us that, in the early years of the Nazi reign, these laws were very popular with a majority of Germans. Adolph Hitler had obtained power through the democratic process in Germany in 1932. The question for us here is, what happens when, through the democratic process, laws are passed that are immoral? What happens when a majority of people holds such racist ideas and turns them into laws? This creates what political scientists call "the tyranny of the majority."

Does a law enforcer have a higher duty than to enforce the will of the people as represented in written laws? Did good Germans have a moral obligation to ignore the laws of their land and behave in ways that they considered moral and just, irrespective of what the absolute dictates of German law (in the Nazi era) said?

Thus blind, absolute, Kantian obedience to the law can be disastrous for minority rights and for the interests of justice. As we shall see in Chapter 8, there are ethical schools of thought that approach moral decision making with a situational view. Such systems as utilitarianism encourage the individual to focus on doing good in a way that takes into account the substantial impact (the consequences) of one's choices on the lives of others and on the good of the community.

At Nuremburg, Nazis were put on trial for "crimes against humanity" in an effort to hold them to answer for their death camps wherein more than 11,000,000 people were put to death. Shown here is the Auschwitz camp at Birkenau, Poland.

In summation, Kant's philosophy has several major drawbacks. First, it does not help us with conflicting duties. Second, it cannot allow for reasonable exceptions. Third, we cannot tell whether a maxim is a moral one or not. And fourth, minority rights (that reference higher moral principles) can be sacrificed in the name of blind obedience to duty.

BOX 7.6

KANT: PROS AND CONS

The Strengths of Absolute Rule Application
- It ensures equal treatment of people similarly situated.
- It develops a respect for the law and for law appliers (police).
- It limits the impact of personal prejudice.
- It makes the law understandable, consistent, and (thus) fair.

The Drawbacks of Absolute Rule Application
- It allows majorities to persecute minorities.
- It does not allow law appliers to be creative professionally by using their minds and hearts in deciding what is fair and just.
- It can inhibit justice by treating people unfairly, given their circumstances.

7-4 ⊙ SUMMARY

The thrust of this discussion goes in two opposite directions. On the one hand, we have sided with ethical formalists and agreed that the objectivity and fairness of the rule of law are necessary to make sure individual prejudice does not rule the streets. To best organize a system that in a just way determines what sorts of conduct are acceptable, a society must be ruled by laws that are administered on the streets in a fair manner by people who are accountable for how they apply those absolute rules. They are accountable, in a democracy, to the people who wrote/made the laws.

On the other hand, rules of conduct are almost invariably too rigid. They do not make allowances for the variables of life, for people's strengths and weaknesses, for those who attempt to do the right thing but fall short due to poverty, ignorance, or fate. Absolute rules do not do a very good job, in short, of determining whether the conduct of human beings is acceptable or not. They are not alive enough, sympathetic enough, flexible enough, or realistic enough to be applicable to real-life situations all of the time.

The mother who speeds while taking her child to the hospital emergency room, the first-time shoplifter, the man who punches his wife's lover, the homeless person who steals a coat to stay alive on a winter night—all of these are examples of people who would be arrested under an absolutist system. And they are, equally, examples of people who might be left alone by a flexible, thoughtful, and arguably more just system that was designed to have some insight into the human heart. There are "exceptions to the rule," something for which Kant makes no allowances.

So (1) the police must cleave to the rule of law, and (2) the absolute application of rules (laws) has severe drawbacks associated with it. What are we to make of this dichotomy? The answer is that the law, the absolute rules written down in the penal code, needs to be viewed by the professional police officer as one tool in an arsenal of tools used to maintain order, to protect lives and property, and to serve the community. When tempered by honest, intelligent, educated, ethical professionals through the screen of their discretionary decisions, the law is useful in creating a safe, livable atmosphere on the street wherein people may pursue their own visions of the good life.

In using the law as a tool in the effort to create such an atmosphere, the police promote justice, equality, and freedom. They understand the reasoning behind thinking that the law must be absolute and, equally, they understand the reasoning behind the idea that the law must be aimed at creating happiness for the greatest number of people on a day-to-day basis (see Chapter 8). This most democratic of ethical principles is our next stop along the road to developing a fully enriched understanding of police ethics.

7-5 ⦿ TOPICS FOR DISCUSSION

1. Think about the theory of natural law. What might be an example of a "law of nature" that is applicable to human society? Regarding feeding one's family? Sex? Familial responsibilities?

2. Discuss the suggested list of "absolute duties" in Box 7.3. Do you agree with this list? Would you add other duties to it? Would you exclude some of those suggestions presented?

3. Discuss police work–related examples of how different duties can conflict. How can the duty to apply the law in an absolute manner conflict with duties toward individuals, with the interests of a community, with the duties that one has to one's fellow officers, etc.?

4. Discuss immoral laws—laws that are supported by a majority of people but which (we might argue) should not be applied by ethical police officers, focusing on higher moral principles. History is filled with examples. What are some?

7-6 ⦿ ETHICAL SCENARIO

In the study of ethics, an important differentiation is made between those theories that are deontological and those that are teleological. Suppose officers are confronted on a regular basis with details in and around the campus area of a college town. Such circumstances bring police officers into regular contact with underage drinking. Given the fact that it would be impossible to arrest all underage drinkers—due to limited jail cell space and court docket time—how should officers make their arrest/no arrest decisions regarding this type of criminality? Should such decisions be made on a deontological basis or a teleological one? What is the difference and why do you believe as you do about it?

7-7 ⦿ WRITING EXERCISE

The text suggests that Kant's categorical imperative is tantamount to "the Golden Rule" of the Bible. What is this rule? Do you believe that it is, in fact, the same as Kant's rule? Construct a discussion of how and why these two concepts might be analogized, even though Kant's philosophy is given credit for being much more sophisticated than the biblical admonition.

7-8 ⦿ KEY TERMS

Age of Enlightenment: An era in history, approximately the 1700s, when men revered human rationality and applied the logic of scientific reasoning to all subjects; a philosophy of liberalism and democratic values that hastened the end of the aristocratic tradition.

Categorical Imperative: Immanuel Kant's ethical principle of the universalizability of maxims and the dignity of all persons.

Gestapo: Nazi secret police, notorious for rounding up Jews and other "enemies of the state," and taking them into a form of custody that meant almost certain death.

Immanuel Kant: Ethical philosopher most noted for founding ethical formalism, the absolutist, deontological school of thought.

Rousseau, Jean-Jacques: French philosopher; part of the Enlightenment; first suggested the idea of the social contract.

Khadi justice: Situational type of justice dispensed by the lawgiver of the Bedouin in Africa.

kamikaze: Japanese suicide pilots who attacked American warships near the end of World War II.

maxim: A motive; a personal reason that is the motive for conduct.

natural law: Set of ethical theories suggesting that the laws of human behavior and social interaction come from a higher source, perhaps God, rather than being manmade; the reason of nature.

Nuremberg trials: Post–World War II trials of Nazis aimed at holding them accountable for war crimes and a new category of crime, crimes against humanity (known as the Holocaust).

practical rationality: The method by which the heirs of the Enlightenment obtain the natural laws of the world.

Shinto: Religion that, along with Buddhism, is practiced by a large majority of Japanese.

situational theories of ethics: Methods of analyzing right human conduct that are different from time to time depending upon circumstances.

social contract: A notion coined by the English philosopher Thomas Hobbes, and then adapted by Rousseau, that the original form of life is a "state of nature" in which there is no state or social order, and that people give up their freedom to a government in order to receive protection.

St. Thomas Aquinas: Religious philosopher famous, among other things, for being a member of the school of natural law.

utilitarianism: School of ethical thought founded by Jeremy Bentham and John Stuart Mill which suggests that the right thing to do is determined by what consequences it has for the majority.

CHAPTER 8

Utilitarianism

Chapter Outline

"The utilitarian doctrine asserts that we should always act so as to produce the greatest possible ratio of good to evil for everyone concerned."

—John Stuart Mill, *Utilitarianism*

As outlined in Chapter 7, doing one's duty is a laudable and defensible way to live. Certainly it is much of the time. But such an absolutist approach sometimes ignores the consequences of doing one's duty. The intention-focused

BOX 8.1

KANT VERSUS MILL: AN EXAMPLE

Suppose a police officer stops a motorist for speeding. Confronting the driver, the officer finds that it is a mother racing to the hospital with a sick child. The officer's knowledge of emergency medicine is such that it is clear the child is in no immediate danger—the young mother is simply overreacting to her child's illness. What should the officer do?

Kant would say the driver was speeding and speeding is illegal. The circumstances, a mother driven by protective fear, are irrelevant. Furthermore, Kant would suggest that the officer could only allow the motorist to proceed without being cited if the officer could will that this be the way in which all such motorists were always treated (a universal law). The implication of such a universal law would be something like this: "One cannot speed unless one thinks there is an emergency situation involved." Because people might define "emergency" in many ways—including being late for a class, for example—strict Kantians would not wish to will such a law. Thus, Kantians would favor the issuance of a citation in the interests of justice.

From Mill's perspective, the police officer should consider the greatest good for the community. This might entail considering (1) that the hysterical mother is not a threat to drive this way all of the time, (2) that other mothers equally situated might very well behave in the same way, (3) that motherhood involves the protection of one's children as a duty that must be taken seriously, and (4) that the long-term best interests of society would be poorly served by issuing such a woman a citation for a moving violation. Thus, Mill might suggest that the officer calm the woman down, explain to her that the child is not in danger, exhort her to drive to the hospital in a more safe manner, and let her go in the interests of justice.

approach of Kant has its drawbacks. His idea that the consequences of an act do not factor into the evaluation of the morality of the act largely ignores the actual impact of behavior upon the lives of others. Such a focus makes a sort of game out of ethics, a game that is not primarily concerned with the important impact a person's behavior has in the real world.

For police officers in particular, such an absolutist, duty-oriented focus is shortsighted. Police officers are substantive, fact-oriented people. That is, when crime occurs out on the streets they must find out what happened and who was responsible. They *must* focus upon factual guilt. Theirs is the business of determining "who did it" and putting handcuffs on them. While the criminal justice system focuses upon procedural guilt, police officers do not. In fact, as we have seen earlier in our discussions, some police officers are so often frustrated by this differentiation between factual and procedural guilt that they begin to fall into Dirty Harry–like behavior.

The utilitarian school was developed by two nineteenth-century Englishmen—first **Jeremy Bentham** and later **John Stuart Mill,** its most famous proponent—as a response to these problems. These two philosophers began with a pronounced concern that Kant had misunderstood some of the real-life implications of the absolutist perspective. They suggested that for people to ignore the outcomes created by their actions was to invite disaster. All sorts of evils could eventuate from such a shortsighted approach to the study of right conduct in the world. And so they created an entirely new philosophical school of thought determined to solve some of the difficulties of Kant's approach.

8-1 • DEFINITIONS

By the term *utilitarianism* we mean the view that the sole, ultimate standard of right and wrong is the principle of utility. In everything we do, we are to seek the greatest possible balance of good over evil in the world. Taking this perspective, when judging what is the right or the wrong thing to do in life, the only criterion to be considered is the good or evil (the consequences) a choice would bring into the world. The final appeal in making ethical choices must be to analyze the comparative amount of good produced by an act or, rather, the comparative balance of good over evil it produces.

John Stuart Mill was a **hedonist** (pleasure seeker) in his view about what is good. He claimed that the moral end of action is the greatest balance of pleasure over pain. But utilitarianism is an ethic

JOHN STUART MILL

John Stuart Mill, the famous English philosopher.

© Mary Evans Picture Library/Alamy

that does not entail any particular theory of the good. While a utilitarian assumes the notion that good exists in the world, the lack of a specific definition of what constitutes the good is a drawback of utilitarianism.

Utilitarianism is democratic in a sense. Utilitarians believe that, in deciding ethical questions, a calculation is made regarding the best means to desired ends and which choice would maximize the good for the greatest number of people. If we understand utilitarianism this way, the principle tells us we are to distribute good to more people rather than to fewer when we have a choice. The principle of utility thus becomes a double principle, for it tells us (1) to maximize the balance of good over evil, and (2) to distribute this as widely as possible.

Police officers are faced with duty-related challenges a lot more often than are ordinary citizens because they make so many important decisions in the lives of others and because they moralize for others on a regular basis. Due to the general duties their office imposes upon them, police officers are

BOX 8.2

THE LIMITS OF ABSOLUTE DUTY

In St. Petersburg, Russia, in the fall of 1917, the Russians were losing the war (World War I) to the Germans. Times were terribly hard for the Russian people. Bread riots broke out. People who were literally starving to death took to the streets to protest the sacrifices the war was forcing on them and to demand food for themselves and their children.

There were so many angry people in the streets that the police could not quell the situation. The government called on the military to help with policing. The Russian Navy, in turn, called on the sailors from the local naval base. These men were ordered to take up arms and go into the streets—as police—into combat against the starving poor people.

The sailors refused. They rejected their duty to the Czar, to their country, to the Russian Navy, and to the law. They did this under the threat that they might be shot. Something moved all of these sailors to deny these duties. Something told them that to fight against their own compatriots was not right, that it was not ethical. Something suggested to them that theirs was a higher duty on that particular day.

And history notes this act was one of the reasons the Russian Revolution was born, at that moment, on that day, at that time.

consistently struggling with such ethical questions as "Do I do my duty or do I take the easy way out?" Certainly, we would accept the argument (made by Kantians) that the ethical officer, just like the ethical citizen, should always do the dutiful thing. Duty being absolute as it is, our character is determined by how often we stick to doing the right thing, no matter what the cost is to us personally.

Yet what if duty (to the law or to your fellow officers) dictates you do something that is wrong? What if the consequences of doing your own personal duty are that someone else's life is ruined or, at the very least, harmed? What then?

A. The Happiness of the Majority

For Kant, happiness was irrelevant to ethics. In his moral philosophy, he regarded happiness as irrelevant or beside the point. Happiness is a by-product of action, not a rationally defensible principle of action. Ethical duties were determined logically. They created an absolute system of behavior, and the consequences of that system for individuals or groups of individuals were irrelevant to whether the act was moral or not. If doing one's duty was difficult and/or if it did not make a person happy, that had nothing to do with the overall importance of the integrity of what is being morally preserved.

The utilitarian school began with the principle that a person should act in a way that would create the greatest happiness for the greatest number of people. When faced with a moral dilemma—a choice between two courses of action, both of which appeared to be ethical—the moral person would calculate the difference in cumulative happiness for the most people and decide which action was best. As noted above, this is an ethical perspective that involves calculations about consequences.

For example, if confronted with an arrest/no arrest decision, the police officer following utilitarian principles would consider the long-term implications of each option. If a first-time offender is to be given a warning and let go instead of being arrested, it must be done because the police officer believes that the good of the community ("the greatest number") is being pursued. The logic might be that to arrest a first-time offender would place that person in a situation in jail where he or she would learn from more hardened criminals how to misbehave in still worse ways. This might create more crime in the long run. Or the logic might be that spending too much taxpayer money on a minor offense would be bad.

There are obviously some important and attractive consequences to behaving in this utilitarian way. As we pointed out earlier in this chapter, sometimes doing one's duty can create hardship, pain, and even tragedy. Sometimes the police keep starving people from food because it doesn't belong to them. Sometimes the police ignore dishonesty by businesses and corporations, actions that hurt large numbers of citizens, because it involves torts and not crimes. Sometimes the police ignore upper-class drug use, upscale prostitution, and white-collar crime and pursue exclusively lower-class offenders because their crime is more visible, because it is easier to pursue to conviction, and because that is what they are told to do by politicians and administrators.

In these and any number of other ways, the police are doing their duties (sticking to the law as written and following their orders in an absolute way). But perhaps in doing so the police participate (indirectly) in perpetuating misery for society's most downcast members. The utilitarian would say that in all of these examples the police should make their own calculations as to what would be the best thing to do. Because a much larger majority of people would benefit from police behaving in a way that is contrary to their apparent duty, the utilitarian would encourage the police to go ahead and ignore the Kantian, absolute devotion to do what is "dutiful."

For utilitarians, what is "right" is determined in a different way. And as Americans who believe in democracy, we tend to see that the utilitarians do have a good point.

B. Individual Happiness

If the happiness of the majority, of the "community" in some sense, is the major focal point of utilitarianism, there is another, more personalized focus upon which calculations about happiness might turn. That is, what of the

BOX 8.3

THE POLICE AS UTILITARIANS

Before the focus on crime control became primary, the American police, especially in big cities, were general problem solvers and service providers. They performed all sorts of functions that did not fit well into other existing parts of city administration, such as keeping weather records and being responsible for public health. As one author notes, "Homeless drifters, by the late 1850s, were given nightly lodging in the station houses; by the 1870s, in the bigger cities, tens of thousands of homeless were put up in this fashion annually. In hard times, policemen sometimes ran soup kitchens for the hungry." [Roger Lane, *Policing the City: Boston 1822–1885* (New York: Atheneum, 1967)]

Thus, the police officer was considered a combination social worker, public service provider, and community organizer for a long time before the changeover to crime fighter. Is today's call for community-oriented policing just an attempt to bring back some of that service-oriented focus?

happiness of the individual? In deciding what action to take regarding ethical questions, what if we consider what would be "best" for the individual citizen, for nurturing relationships, or for keeping particular individuals from being hurt?

Instead of focusing on what the consequences might be for the majority of people, utilitarians might also focus on the best course of action for the people involved in an immediate situation. The officer operating in this way might ask, "How should I act to best be of service in the lives of the persons involved in the detail I'm now on?" Especially when no obvious law enforcement–related choices are involved (an arrest/no arrest decision is not being made, for example), an officer might focus on the needs, feelings, and interests of the people with whom he or she is dealing.

For example, what if a homeless person has become a regular problem on the beat? Instead of focusing on how to deal with all homeless people or on what laws might be used to incarcerate the individual (ethical formalism), the police officer might decide to take action that would focus on this particular person's needs. Could the officer help this person find a job? Could the officer help to provide this person with immediate relief in the form of food, shelter, counseling, or job training? To do so might be seen as something other than a standard police function. But given the service role of the police, taking such an individualized form of action is easily rationalized as an appropriate option.

Operating in this manner does not mean that other interests are ignored. Certainly, to solve one homeless person's immediate problem would be in the best interests of the community at large. It would also be in the best interests of justice and crime control (ethical formalism). Thus, several bases can be covered at one time when dealing with the immediate, particularized, personal problems of individual citizens.

The homeless person represents just one commonplace example of how police officers, especially in the age of community-based policing, can help individuals in a way that has many positive impacts on the community and on crime fighting. Mentoring individual teenagers to keep them out of gangs and/or away from drugs and crime is another example, as is helping elderly people. Police officers can aid the elderly by helping them with their winter heating problems, by referring them to elder-care programs that provide food, by obtaining transportation help from social welfare agencies, and so on. If time permits—that is, if there is time away from crime fighting and order maintenance details—the police can be of service to any number of citizens who are unable to care completely for themselves.

Contemporary police officers have at their disposal all sorts of skills and contacts not enjoyed by society's truly dispossessed. In using these tools to solve individual problems, the police are performing all of their functions at once. And in particular, they are acting as community-oriented problem solvers, as agents of change who use their significant powers in the name of doing good for individuals and for the general populace.

C. The Advantages of Utilitarianism

So utilitarianism gives us another set of ideas to ponder. Instead of constructing absolute sets of principles that must be acknowledged and followed at all times and under all circumstances, utilitarianism suggests ethics are situational. Either in focusing on the general good of the community or on the good of the individual citizen, this school underwrites police discretion directly. It suggests that most of the time the police ought to calculate what they think is the best course of action. When making these individualized, particularized, situationally driven decisions, the police use their own logic, pursue their own understandings of the good, and exhibit their character. Thus, an idea that has been flowing through our entire discussion is once more given support: The police are the law, and their personal ethics are critical to the generation of justice.

Suggesting that the police solve problems one at a time and exercise such a tremendous amount of discretion is not a frustrating reality to the modern professional. Instead, it makes police work an exciting and dynamic profession. It points out that every day on the job is challenging, that every

BOX 8.4

TWO KINDS OF UTILITARIANISM

In the world of philosophy, theorists make a differentiation between two types of utilitarianism related to our discussion. **"Rule utilitarianism"** and **"act utilitarianism"** involve making Mill's calculations in two different ways.

- **Rule utilitarianism** Focuses on the good of the entire community/society. It makes calculations of good versus evil that relate to long-term "rules" for all situations that are similar. When faced with an ethical question regarding what to do, rule utilitarians ask, "In the best interests of the majority, what should always be done under the circumstances I am facing?"

- **Act utilitarianism** Focuses on individual happiness. It makes calculations of good versus evil that relate to the interests of only those immediately involved in a given question. Act utilitarians ask, "What should I do to promote the greatest good and remove the greatest evil for those immediately involved in the decision with which I am faced?"

Note: The strengths and weaknesses of these views are the same— and they are at the heart of this chapter's analysis of what is positive and what is troublesome about the utilitarian view.

detail may end up going down a different path, and that the individual police officer has a tremendous amount of latitude—and therefore, power—to do good for the community and for individual citizens. In this sense, the utilitarian school presents the most exciting and yet challenging statement of the importance of the role police officers choose to play in society. It makes the most eloquent statement possible about the reason why police work is a rewarding and important calling.

8-2 • THE LIMITATIONS OF UTILITARIANISM

After evaluating the strengths of utilitarianism, we must now consider its drawbacks. If we regard good and bad consequences as the sole criterion of moral worth, and that indeed is the primary focus of those who have problems with Kant, then we run into several serious problems with utilitarianism.

A. Calculating Good and Evil

First, there is the problem of comparing different amounts of good and evil. Consider the famous **"lifeboat problem"** as an example. A lifeboat in a storm-tossed sea is dangerously overloaded and is foundering. To give at least some people a chance of surviving, the first mate decides he must throw a small number of people overboard to make the boat seaworthy, otherwise all will surely die. If he uses a strictly utilitarian reasoning, the first mate must compare the relative good of the larger group of people to the relative evil done to the smaller number.

But how can one possibly do this? Do we really want to say that two lives are "more valuable" than one just because two is a bigger number than one? Is it tolerable for us to imagine that the few should be sacrificed for the sake of the many? And what happened to the idea that a human life is of infinite worth? Attempting to calculate relative goodness and evil is thus a central problem for the utilitarian school.

B. Minority Rights

A second problem is of equal significance. A particular act may be morally right or wrong due to something other than the amount of good over evil it produces. Just because more good for more people might be produced by an act, it might still not be considered moral.

© AF archive/Alamy

This scene from the 1943 movie *Titanic* illustrates the lifeboat problem.

Harkening back to the absolutist ideas of Kant, it is easy to criticize the very practical, democratic nature of the logic of Mill. A classic example of how Mill can be criticized involves the institution of slavery.

Suppose that enslaving 10 percent of the population, working them day and night, and not paying them for their labors, could produce a better life for the other 90 percent. Then, would a utilitarian conclude slavery is morally right? Sure, 10 percent of the people are enslaved—and evil is brought into their lives. But the great majority are afforded a better life—good is brought into their lives. Are we to accept that there are no absolute principles (such as, in this case, "slavery is immoral")? Are we to believe that producing more good than evil will define any act as "right"?

As Americans, we are born and raised with an appreciation for democratic rule. One of the principles that is most dear to us is that of majority rule. In response to thousands of years of rule by individual tyrants or small groups of aristocratic elites, America was the first country ever created with democratic rule as one of its most basic, guiding principles. And because this is so, it might appear that the utilitarian focus upon creating the greatest good for the greatest number of people would be a particularly American kind of philosophical approach to determining right conduct.

But utilitarianism presents us Americans with a particularly thorny problem. What about the rights of the minority? History is full of examples of the oppression of minorities at the hands of self-serving majorities. Even American history has examples of this. From the treatment of the natives who lived on this continent before the arrival of the white Europeans to the evils foisted upon blacks by slavery to the placement of Japanese-Americans into concentration camps during World War II, America is not without a history

BOX 8.5

MINORITY RIGHTS

The most systematically organized genocide in the history of the world occurred in Nazi Germany right before and during World War II. What is difficult for many of us to believe is that Adolph Hitler, the primary organizer of this travesty, was elected to office by the German people. And even after he outlawed competing parties and took away the civil rights of various minority groups in addition to the Jews—gypsies, Catholic priests, communists, socialists, union organizers, many academics, and handicapped people included— he was fabulously popular among the majority of free Germans.

Unfortunately, the utilitarian school of ethics has no answer for the criticism that this is an example of how it can be used to rationalize the excesses of democratic rule.

of visiting outrageous repression upon some of her own people. There is not much doubt that a majority of Americans supported each of these examples of policies instituting suppression during most of the time when they were in place. And the logic of utilitarianism has no response to the criticism that it rationalizes this type of oppression.

C. Equal "Moral Scores"

A third problem relates to solving ethical dilemmas: choices between equally utilitarian courses of action. One can readily imagine that two possible courses of action, A and B, would produce the same balance of good over evil. Then the utilitarian must say that the "moral scores" of the acts are the same. There is no basis for choosing between them. It still may be, however, that they distribute the balance of good in different ways. Action A may give most of the good to a relatively small group of people, while action B may spread the good more equally over a larger segment of the population. In this case, it seems that utilitarians would tell us A is unjust and wrong and B is morally preferable.

For example, a purely utilitarian calculation would rationalize taxing the wealthy at a rate of 90 percent of their earnings and taxing the poor not at all in an effort to maximize overall good. Some people might (and do) support such a taxing policy. But certainly those who have accumulated great wealth as a result of hard work and intelligence would make the argument that to take away the fruits of their labors is immoral. Utilitarianism does not help us with this dilemma.

D. Deterrence: "Punish Anybody"

A fourth criticism—and for police officers perhaps the most troublesome—involves one of the central roles the police play in society, that of deterring criminal activity. Utilitarian logic is always used to rationalize deterrence. Crime is deterred among the majority because a few criminals are caught, imprisoned, and punished for their crimes. Furthermore, crime is deterred partly because the police are present to threaten arrest, threaten the use of force, go ahead and make arrests, and carry through with the use of force. The more police there are and the more aggressive they are, the less crime there is. That is the presumed formula. Participating in deterrence in this way is one of the roles of the police in any society.

And then there is the deterrent effect of the machinations of the criminal justice system as a whole. In theory, the more certain and harsh the punishment is, the more effective the deterrent impact of the law. The moral rationale for punishing people, and in some cases for punishing them severely, is this utilitarian point about the impact public punishment will have on the great majority. This, for example, is the way in which many people rationalize capital punishment—its application deters others from committing capital crimes. (See Box 8.6.)

BOX 8.6

PROBLEMS PRESENTED BY UTILITARIANISM

- It is difficult to "calculate" amounts of good and evil.
- Merely being good for the majority does not necessarily make an act moral—it ignores the rights of minorities and of individual citizens.
- There is no basis for choosing between equal amounts of good and evil.
- In deterring crime, it does not matter who is punished—the guilty or the innocent.

BOX 8.7

CAPITAL PUNISHMENT

Capital punishment most certainly creates what is called **specific deterrence** by criminal justice scholars. That is, when a particular individual is put to death, he or she is never again involved in criminal activity. But it is not clear whether it creates **general deterrence** by keeping the entire population from committing crimes. Scholars argue the point endlessly, and studies indicating that it does and that it does not deter are bantered about in the debate.

But even assuming that capital punishment *does* deter crime, there is no getting around the problem that its utilitarian logic presents. It does not matter whether or not those put to death are guilty of any crime whatsoever. If some people are put to death occasionally, publicly, with as much accompanying publicity as possible, then crime might be deterred . . . but it matters not one iota if those killed are guilty. The deterrent effect will be the same if completely innocent people are executed. Here, Kantians have an excellent point about the limitations of the utilitarian school.

There is a significant problem with this formula, however. The deterrence effect is created because some people are punished. A critical ethical question for us is: What does it matter if those who are punished are guilty or not? Would not the conviction and imprisonment of an innocent person, for example, put just as much fear of the law (perhaps even more) into the minds of those who watched? In accomplishing the desired result of deterring criminal behavior in the general population, those who punish criminals do not have to be particularly careful about whom they punish. As long as some people are punished often enough and severely enough, many others will be deterred from even thinking about deviating.

While the police are neither judges nor juries nor executioners, this point about deterrence is still relevant to police work. What does it matter if those whom the police arrest and those against whom they use force are actually guilty of being criminals? If the point is to "get the word out" that there will be no toleration of misbehavior on the beat, then the police might just as well arrest and use force on anyone. It will have its desired effect as long as it is done in a public fashion so it deters others.

This dynamic about utilitarianism gives us a tremendous rule of law problem, for the central idea encompassed in the rule of law is that those who are punished deserve it. They are punished if and only if they are guilty of misconduct. No matter how much the rule appliers of the world—in our discussion, the police—may dislike certain people or groups of people (have personal prejudice against them), the rule of law states that if such people are not guilty of misconduct, they must be left alone.

To punish people for any reason other than that they have behaved in a criminal manner is to create a situation where the police are a law unto themselves. It is certainly possible to argue that such punishment is immoral. Utilitarianism's focus on deterrence suggests this immorality can be overlooked in the name of doing good (deterring criminality) for the majority. This is the

BOX 8.8

KANT VERSUS MILL

Kant's ethical formalism emphasizes:

- Absolute rule application: circumstances are ignored
- Absolute devotion to duty: again, circumstances are ignored
- Focusing upon the will/intention behind an act: consequences are largely irrelevant

Mill's utilitarianism emphasizes:

- Taking situations into account when deciding what is right
- Calculating what would produce the greatest good for the greatest number of people
- Focusing on consequences: right acts are those which, in their application, promote good over evil

height of unfairness to the unjustly punished—it is unethical. It flies in the face of individual constitutional protections that are at the heart of our society's values.

8-3 ◉ SUMMARY

This much seems clear: An action may maximize the sum of good in the world and yet be unjust in the way in which it distributes this sum. An action that produces a smaller balance of good but does it more justly or fairly may be better. If this is so, then the criterion for determining right and wrong is not merely utility, or maximizing benefit, but also justice. If justice may overrule utility on occasion, then the question of what is right cannot be answered simply in terms of the principle of utility.

So the happiness of large numbers of people, no matter how much we like the sound of it, might not be the best focal point for creating an ethical perspective. As is true with the absolutist rules and duties of Kant, the utilitarian focus has its strengths and weaknesses. And, as we hope is becoming evident, neither of these two approaches—ethical formalism or utilitarianism—will satisfy all of the needs of all police officers all of the time.

Thus, we turn in Chapter 9 to the discussion of a hybrid or combination of these two perspectives created specifically with the police officer in mind. Necessitated by both the drawbacks of these two schools of thought and by the realities of the multiple, conflicting, and vague roles the police must play, we have created for the beat cop "an ethic to live by."

8-4 ◉ TOPICS FOR DISCUSSION

1. Both in Box 8.1 and at the end of this chapter, the authors discuss examples of how Kant's and Mill's schools of thought conflict with each other. Discuss examples of police details that illustrate how officers using the two perspectives might react differently and take different action in an effort to behave ethically in the performance of their duties.

2. Consider the lifeboat example given in Section 8-2, "The Limitations of Utilitarianism." Assuming you were the first mate and you had decided 5 people out of 20 had to be thrown overboard to ensure the survival of the remaining 15, how would you choose whom to sacrifice? What factors would you take into account and why? Would age, sex, intelligence, education, health, wealth, and so on play a part in deciding who is to live and who is to die?

3. Consider the implications of the ethical problem presented by the utilitarian logic behind deterrence—that it "doesn't matter who you punish," even when you are talking about capital punishment. Whether they are guilty or not, it "only matters that you punish someone." Discuss.

4. Why do the authors suggest that utilitarianism is a very democratic and therefore American point of view? Do you agree? Why or why not? Even if it is very democratic, why is that troublesome with regard to minority rights?

8-5 ⊡ ETHICAL SCENARIO

At several points in this chapter we posit examples of why applying "the letter of the law" might be eschewed by police officers in lieu of taking a utilitarian approach to solving any given problem on the street. Suppose you are confronted by a store owner who has caught a 13-year-old girl shoplifting. She has no record with the juvenile division. She appears frightened at being caught and convinces you that she "won't ever do it again." You want to deal with the situation informally and avoid taking her to juvenile hall. What do you say to the store owner? What type of logic will you use in order to convince him that this action is not only in the best interests of the child, not only in the best interests of justice, but, in the long run, in *his* best interests as well?

8-6 ⊡ WRITING EXERCISE

Perhaps the most universally accepted argument *against* utilitarian thinking has to do with deterrence. As our text suggests, a central tenet on the list of arguments posited against capital punishment is that it does not matter who is punished for a crime, only that punishment is swift, stern, and public. Write an essay about deterrence, how this argument works, and how police officers must take care in this regard; they must avoid any propensity to "punish just anybody" in order to maintain order on their beats.

8-7 ⊡ KEY TERMS

act utilitarianism: The idea that the calculation of the utility of a particular choice of action is sometimes made relative to the particular situation and, thus, particular individual(s).

capital punishment: Punishment that involves the execution of criminals; capital crimes include homicide, treason, and, in some places, rape.

general deterrence: The idea that by punishing some criminals, others in the general population will be deterred from committing crimes; particularly cogent regarding the debate over capital punishment.

hedonist: A person who seeks out pleasure as a primary focus of life, irrespective of other duties and obligations.

Jeremy Bentham: One of the fathers of utilitarianism; raised John Stuart Mill as a son.

lifeboat problem: A classic discussion in the world of ethics—utilitarian ethics in particular—is what should be done to save the majority of people in a sinking lifeboat if several people must be sacrificed for the good of the rest.

Mill, John Stuart: One of the fathers of utilitarianism; author of perhaps the most famous explanation of individual rights, *On Liberty;* along with his wife, an early pioneering author in support of women's rights and social welfare legislation.

rule utilitarianism: The idea that the calculation of the utility of any particular choice of action should be done relative to the entire community or society as a whole.

specific deterrence: The idea that by incapacitating a criminal that particular individual is deterred from committing other crimes.

CHAPTER 9

An Ethic to Live By

Chapter Outline

"There is no other story. A man, after he has brushed off the dust and chips of his life, will have left only the hard, clean questions: Was it good or was it evil? Have I done well—or ill?"

—John Steinbeck, *East of Eden*

We have presented several schools of thought about ethics and discussed several approaches to living a good life. Kant gave us an absolutist perspective. He suggested that duties are fixed and universal and that no amount of rationalization should keep the good person from pursuing the path of righteousness. Furthermore, Kant said that because too much is left to chance, too much is out of our personal control in the world, our ethics should be judged only by analyzing the intentions we have. The impact of actions in the real world cannot fairly be considered when analyzing personal morality. The practical consequences of acts cannot reasonably be regarded as a factor in morality.

The utilitarians gave us another perspective. They posited not that "rules are meant to be broken" but that life is just too complicated to suggest that

BOX 9.1

POLICE RESPONDING TO A HIGHER DUTY

On October 4, 2000, in Kolubara, Yugoslavia, thousands of people gathered together to protest. Their concern was that the results of a recently held democratic election were being ignored by their government. The sitting president was refusing to swear in the candidate who had defeated him in the election.

The police were called in to break up the protest, using force if necessary. After a tense confrontation, the police, themselves Yugoslavians, refused to follow orders and use force on their own people. Some took off their police uniforms and went home. One police officer said to an American reporter, "I'm fed up with this. I'm taking my [police] hat and throwing it away. The police [here] are more democratic than you think."

A strict Kantian analysis of this action by hundreds of police officers might conclude these officers had done wrong. They had not stuck by their absolute duty to the government and to obey orders. But our ethic to live by would suggest these police officers did the right thing. They refused to do harm to their own people and thus helped to ensure the democratic takeover of the newly elected president. Thus, we are saying this officer had a **higher duty** to take off his cap and side with the people.

the long-term impact, the implications of sticking by absolute duties, can be ignored. When we make ethical decisions, they wanted us to think about the greater good of the community and/or the good of the individuals immediately involved in a decision. They suggested that if cleaving to some absolute duty might do harm to the community or to the individual, then such a duty might very well have to be circumvented.

In this chapter, we will put together what we have called an **"ethic to live by"** for the contemporary police professional. After a brief review of why Kant and Mill are too limiting, we will construct a practical ethic for the police officer. It will be an ethic that can be applied to day-to-day situations on a regular basis. It is not a "how to do it" guide but rather a general set of principles from which the professional can view all ethical questions and dilemmas.

The ethical theory that we develop here is a hybrid of sorts, a combination built out of certain aspects of Immanuel Kant's theory of duty and John Stuart Mill's idea of utility. Our account differs from these philosophers chiefly in the importance we give to the idea of character. While theirs are principle-based ethics, ours is character-based, and in this we are closer to Aristotle. For Kant and Mill, the question that is most relevant to ethics is "What ethical principle applies to this situation?" For us, the first question is "What kind of person do I want to be?"

That is, we take very seriously that people have histories, that in whatever situation a person finds herself she can only view it from the perspective of that history and this always makes her situations unique to her. The perspective of that personal history constitutes the "interior" life, the emotional life, of a person. Kant was afraid of this when he went to such lengths to draw attention away from experience, from ego and emotion, from the self. For this reason, he restricts consideration of the good to the "good will," and does not credit the factual circumstances of people's lives as being susceptible to good and evil.

For Kant and Mill, ethical discussions begin with the problem of making specific choices; for us, to begin with decision-making rules assumes too much. For them, ethics is largely a matter of subscribing to a single rule of behavior, while for us it is a matter of how to live. But before we enter into that discussion we must consider the problems associated with each of the major schools of thought already presented.

Morality is rooted in and grows out of character. For us, the first question is, "What kind of person do I want to be?"

9-1 ● THE LIMITS OF KANT AND MILL

We have argued that sensitivity to relevant moral issues is a trait of character. We have suggested that it can be cultivated. Also, we have advanced the idea that this sensitivity is an inherent aspect of moral judgment. Knowing how to see is as much a part of ethical conduct as knowing what to do. What we recognize as the morally relevant features of a situation is a direct indicator of the kind of people we are, for the things that catch our attention determine how we size things up and what we decide to do. The decisions we make are a product of our personal background, something both Kant and Mill regard as irrelevant to the integrity of moral choice. We can thus say that knowing what to do is the natural consequence of knowing how to see. The importance of this fact reminds us that morality is rooted in and grows out of character. When aiming at moral and professional competence, character is the target.

But there remains the moral issue of knowing what to do. If moral principle without good character is powerless, then certainly good character without moral principle is blind. In other words, it is not enough to be a morally sensitive person. A good heart is never enough. We must also know how to think. Character governs what we pay attention to and what we think our obligations are, if any, in any situation. Good character shows itself in a person's habitual tendency to understand the decent, the non-self-centered thing to do, and what is good for everyone involved. That is the purpose of good character.

A. Kant: Duty Trumps the Good

Kant denied that people should consider utility (consequence) in determining their ethical perspectives. He said that because no one can control the actions of others, and because no one can know with certainty what the impact of his or her own actions will be, people should do their duty without reference to its consequences. Kant believed that if people attempt to do their duty—as determined by universalizing their intentions—then they are behaving ethically. The often-heard justification that someone "means well" is a Kantian distillation.

From the perspective of policing the streets, there are several practical reasons to question Kant's ideas. These have to do with numbers and money. If the police were to operate as if each and every law suggested to them an absolute duty to make arrests, America's jails, courtrooms, and prisons would be filled beyond their capacity. The entire criminal justice system would grind to a halt. And it would take little time for this to occur. The consequences for the system in terms of expenditures would mean that any reasonable semblance of justice would be denied to anyone and everyone.

But there is more. For the limitations of ethical formalism are more than merely pragmatic. Taking Kant's view, an act by itself is right or wrong; therefore, the moral quality of the act is determined only by the moral quality of the act. For Kant, the maxim that "a police officer ought to enforce the law" means any police officer who enforces the law is acting ethically—no matter what the consequences. Thus, citing a speeding motorist who is en route to the hospital with a bleeding gunshot wound is to act morally.

The circular logic of this claim has already been pointed out. The nature of an act, by itself, cannot make it a morally good or bad thing to do, because we find it absurd to imagine that the morality of an act is a function of the "good will" of the actor only, and has nothing to do with the promotion of good or evil in somebody's life. We find it incredible to think that moral consideration of another person is measured only by our respect for that person's rational nature, and does not involve concern for their actual welfare. How can moral concern for the human dignity of the other (Kant's position) involve only the right and wrong of how we treat them (our act), and not involve caring about what helps or hurts them? Referring to a previous example, how in the world can the suffering of a starving child, in and of itself, not be an evil in the world?

In the above example, citing all speeders in order to enforce the law at all times may not be morally defensible. Thus the moral worth of an act must depend, at least in part, on something beyond itself, on something about the real difference the act makes in the lives of people. We mean that the morality of an act must be directly linked to the good or evil consequences it produces for someone, including for the actor himself or herself.

So, in our (utilitarian) conception of good, when we say, "A man is as good as his word"—a Kantian-sounding line—we are really talking about a commitment to others and not just about the integrity of the actor. If people "stick to their word" but the promises they make are to fellow gang members and involve robbing a bank, is it the Kantian conclusion that they are behaving ethically when they rob the bank?

B. Mill: What Counts as Good?

Given these problems with Kant, in combination with others that we have discussed earlier, it would seem that Mill's utilitarianism, with its focus on consequences, would be the answer for police officers searching for an ethical perspective. Kant would fill jails and prisons to capacity. His ethic would clog courts and probation and parole offices. Mill, on the other hand, would infuse the law with both a practical concern for the costs of police action and a consideration of the implications for justice of everything that the police do.

But there are problems with Mill, too. Suppose an action produces far more good than evil. Taking the utilitarian perspective, Mill would say such an action is moral. But it takes us only a moment to think up any number of troublesome examples of this principle in action. Suppose a police officer decides to shoot a local gang leader or a vicious drug dealer. Wouldn't the evil of committing that murder be outweighed by the good it brought to the community as a whole? Suppose the police beat up every speeding

BOX 9.2

"Burn It Down"

When doing research in Kansas City, Missouri, one of the authors encountered a woman who lived in the inner city, right in the heart of gang territory. She mistook the author for a member of the police department because he was asking questions about attitudes toward the police and how they dealt with gangs.

Once the woman convinced herself that the author was a police officer interested in fighting the gang problem, she said that an abandoned house across the street was a "shooting gallery" for heroin users that was often used by the neighborhood gang. She stated, "Why don't you boys come on down at night and burn it down? I'll have a barbeque and invite the whole neighborhood over so no one would be watching. No one will ever know!"

Utilitarian logic would suggest that for the police to commit arson and burn such a building to the ground would be an ethical act, for the good that it would bring to the community would outweigh the evil of police officers committing a felony.

motorist. After a while, wouldn't everyone slow down? And wouldn't driving be much safer? It would be easy to make up a long list of such "practical" evils the police might pursue that are all, on balance, good for the greatest number of community members. (It is a fact of life that in **totalitarian states,** where the police have the power to do such things, there is very little street crime—the deterrent effect of having vicious, brutal, and unethical police officers is great.)

Mill's notions about allowing the individual to make calculations about consequences would tend to turn the police of America loose to become involved in Khadi justice. It could hasten the end of the rule of law and usher in the rule of cop. It might very well eventuate in such a disrespect for the dictates of the law, created as they are by the people for application in their own communities, that life on the street might resemble life in countries where, as noted above, the police rule with an iron fist. It might create police power without limitation, allowing them to follow their own personal views of how they should behave and what their duties are.

We have tried to show that we cannot be satisfied with the principle of maximizing good over evil as our sole basic standard of right and wrong. In particular, we have argued that we must recognize a principle of justice or fairness to guide our distribution of good, and that this principle of justice is independent of maximizing the balance of good over evil.

9-2 • AN ETHIC TO LIVE BY: MAXIMIZING THE GOOD IN A JUST WAY

We realize, therefore, that a particular act may be morally right or wrong because of certain facts about it other than the amount of good or evil it produces. And what we have just said suggests we should recognize two basic principles of obligation: the principle of maximizing good and some principle of justice. The resulting ethic would be something like this: We ought always to maximize good in a just way.

Our position is deontological or Kant-like because, for us, (1) right conduct is determined by conforming to a moral principle, and (2) conformity to the principle is an absolute requirement. But our ethic would be much closer to utilitarianism than Kant would ever allow because it requires, as fundamental to moral judgment, that we be actively concerned about the good and evil in the world.

As it stands, however, this view is still faced with the problem of measuring and balancing amounts of good and evil, and, since it recognizes two basic principles, it must also face the problem of possible conflict between them. This means that our theory must regard its two principles as principles of *prima facie* (a standing obligation, unless disproved), not of actual, duty. That is, there are always exceptions to this general obligation. Also, it must allow that the principle of justice may take precedence over that of maximizing good.

To our minds, this theory of obligation is close, but not quite right. Whether we have even a *prima facie* obligation to maximize good over evil depends, in part, on whether it makes sense to talk about good and evil in quantitative terms—that is, talking about "amounts" of good and evil, as if they were units that could be added, subtracted, and numerically compared. Assuming that it makes at least rough sense, it is not easy to deny that one of the things we ought always to do, other things being equal, is to bring about as much of a balance of good over evil as we can.

We find it hard to believe that any action or rule can be morally right, wrong, or obligatory if there is no good or evil connected with it. This does not mean there are no other factors affecting their rightness or wrongness, or that our only duty is to pile up the biggest stockpile of what is good, as utilitarians think. But it does imply that *we do have an obligation to do something about the good and evil in the world.*

In fact, we claim that people do not have any moral obligations to do anything that does not have some connection with what makes somebody's life good or bad, better or worse. Even justice is concerned with the distribution of good and evil. In other words, *all of our duties, even that of justice, presuppose the existence of good and evil and some kind of concern about their existence.* To say this is to say not only that we have no obligations except when some improvement or impairment of someone's life is involved, but also that we have a standing obligation *whenever* this is involved.

The preceding considerations provide the basis of the theory we will now develop.

A. The Principle of Beneficence

The obligation to make people's lives better (including our own) as well as to prevent harm from coming to them suggests this basic principle: One ought to do good and prevent evil. If people did not have this most basic obligation, we would not be moved to try to bring about as great a balance of good as we possibly can. The police in particular must rise to the challenges of this obligation. Because on the street, on a minute-to-minute basis, they make life-influencing decisions for others, police officers are the individuals in our society who ought to be most directly driven by this obligation.

In other words, in applying the law, in maintaining order, and in providing service to people, the police bear a positive responsibility to do good. They do this by using all of the tools at their disposal to protect the weak from the ruthless, the innocent from the vicious, the young from those adults who would use them as prey, and so on. On the other hand, they bear an equal responsibility to prevent evil. It is not just enough to do good deeds when called upon. That is half of the general charge of the police. They must also work with all the power they possess to prevent evil from occurring and abiding. Taken together, these two duties constitute beneficence. This beneficence principle is a neat and concise statement of what police work is all about. There is no better way to gather together all of the axioms and mottos and platitudes written about police work than this: We should do good and prevent harm.

The reason we call this the principle of beneficence and not the principle of benevolence is to remind ourselves that it asks us actually to *do* good and not evil, not merely to approve of it or to want to do so. **Benevolence** means "good will, charitableness, kindliness." To be benevolent is to think well of people and to attempt to act well toward them. It is, in a Kantian sense, intentional— it is all about the general attitude toward others of having good will.

But beneficence means more. **Beneficence** involves doing good deeds, acting charitably, and behaving in a kindly manner. In other words, beneficence is active and not intentional (concerned merely with a person's intentions). It is not enough, in our discussion of ethics, for police officers to think good thoughts and wish people well. As we said in our criticism of Kant earlier, mere intentions do not "make it" on the street. They are not enough. If it is anything at all, police work is action oriented. The police must engage in doing good and preventing evil. They cannot stand on the sidelines in life and merely have good will. Police officers are umpires or referees, not merely spectators in people's lives.

BOX 9.3

PRINCIPLE 1 = BENEFICENCE
The obligation to do good and to prevent harm.

B. Implications

Our principle of beneficence implies four things (see Box 9.4). First, a police officer ought not to inflict harm on others or do evil. There is an axiom from the physician's code of ethics, the **Hippocratic Oath,** that says doctors should "first, do no harm." This is a good principle for all professionals to follow. The obvious implications for police officers should not be difficult for us to deduce. In the performance of their duties, police officers must take care at all times to act such that they do not bring more evil (or harm) into a world that is fraught with evil in the first place. When citizens call the police for assistance, they first and foremost ought to be safe in assuming that difficult situations and complicated problems will not be made worse when the police arrive. Police officers should exercise their arrest powers with great care. They should be **circumspect** about their application of force. And they should be focused upon their own professionalism to such an extent that under no circumstances does their arrival bring "trouble."

Second, a police officer ought to take seriously the obligation to prevent evil and harm. For police officers, this means they must be proactive with regard to uncovering evil and alleviating pain and suffering. In an age of COP, wherein the police are asked to be actively engaged in preventing crime, this admonition stands out as the central idea. Preventing evil and harm before they occur involves a number of strategies. But perhaps most important is the commitment to actively pursue the causes of crime before they have time to fester and grow. The proactive nature of COP requires that the police behave as criminologists or sociologists or, even, social welfare workers. Together with community leaders, they should strategize about the creation of evil and then work to prevent it.

Third, a police officer ought to remove evil. The police cannot, must not be anonymous citizens in uniform. They cannot stand on the sidelines and ignore the evil deeds of anyone, especially society's most powerful. To do so would be to abrogate completely the central rationale for having the police in the first place. Society gives a great deal of power to police officers, even allowing them to use lethal force on occasion. The police officers of America ought to be driven by a concern about this power and should always use the

BOX 9.4

IMPLICATIONS OF THE PRINCIPLE OF BENEFICENCE

1. One ought not to inflict evil or harm.
2. One ought to prevent evil or harm.
3. One ought to remove evil.
4. One ought to do or promote good.

© lenetstan/Shutterstock.com

The medical doctor's Hippocratic Oath begins by saying, "First, do no harm."

power they possess to prevent evil. When officers use force or make arrests, they ought to do so in the name of removing evil and harm from the lives of honest citizens.

Muir would suggest a particular way to conceptualize this. Recall that his professional officer has an integrated understanding of the morality of coercion. If and when coercive power is the only option available to them (exhortation and reciprocity having failed), the police must not hesitate to act in a forceful way to remove evil. They may not behave as avoiders, watching from the sidelines. Theirs is a positive, definitive responsibility in this regard.

Fourth, a police officer ought to promote good. While this seems to be an obvious point, it requires a moment's reflection. No longer driven merely by calls for service but actively operating as agents of change in their communities, the police of today must take seriously their responsibility to do good works. This can involve any number of endeavors, from acting as mentors for troubled youth to taking care of the problems of the homeless to helping elderly citizens with any number of age-related difficulties.

The police of today, under COP, should do more than look at the crime that happens in the world, but engage quality of life issues in their communities. COP involves both sides of the formula underwritten in our principle: The police must be positively engaged with and actively working for their communities both in preventing evil directly and in doing good works. Driven by Muir's tragic perspective of life, the police must engage the problem of evil and surmount it, never backing away from their responsibility in the name of being safe and/or careful of their own situation. In other words, they must have courage and tenacity on the street.

9-3 ● THE PRINCIPLE OF DISTRIBUTIVE JUSTICE

Beneficence is important, but not all of our obligations (and decisions) can be derived from the principle of beneficence. This principle does not tell us what is "due" to each person, only that we ought to do good and prevent evil. So the question remains, "What is due each?" or "What are the rules for the comparative treatment of people?" In other words, how do we distribute justice?

BOX 9.5

PRINCIPLE 2 = DISTRIBUTIVE JUSTICE

We ought to make the same relative contribution to the goodness of the lives of others.

A number of criteria have been proposed over the years in an ongoing discussion of how to distribute resources, status, and justice in a moral society. A central tenet of **Western liberalism** suggests that justice involves dealing with people according to their merits. That is, those who are more worthy receive more. Translated into the world of economics, for example, this principle underwrites the institution of **capitalism.** People obtain more money (economic wealth) if they work harder, develop better products, provide better services, and so on. Capitalism says that in the business world these people are more worthy than those who are lazy, unproductive, unimaginative, and so forth.

Modern democratic theory is based, in contrast, upon the idea that everyone should receive precisely the same amount of political power. This we do by allowing everyone to cast one vote, and only one vote, in elections. This is called the egalitarian principle of distributive justice ("Equality" in Box 9.6).

It simply means that the most fair and just way of distributing political power is to spread it equally among everyone. This may seem to be the only rational way to conduct elections, but it is not. If elections were run with deference to the merit principle, for example, then people's votes might be weighted so that some count for more and some for less; smart, educated, or rich people might have their votes count for more than others "because they deserve it." In politics, we have clearly decided in America that the egalitarian principle should prevail.

BOX 9.6

THEORIES OF DISTRIBUTIVE JUSTICE

(Or, how goods, services, status, and justice should be distributed)

Merit	=	People should receive according to their relative merit.
Equality	=	People should receive exactly equal amounts.
Socialism	=	People should receive according to their need.
Virtue	=	People should receive according to their goodness.

Karl Marx ushered in a revolution in thinking when he suggested the base level logic that supports socialism and communism.

A third way of distributing justice is related to **Karl Marx**'s principles. Marx was the father of **communism** and **socialism** whose *The Communist Manifesto* (1932, co-written with Friedrich Engels) suggested that everyone ought to receive society's benefits according to their needs. While many Americans hold some distinctive prejudices about communism, this way of allocating resources, status, and justice is neither evil nor irrational. In fact, all of us are members of small groups that distribute resources and power in this way. These groups are called families. Members receive medical treatment, education, and money not equally but according to their needs. Someone in a family who has special needs—who requires glasses, for example—gets them even if no one else needs them. This way of allocating resources is not related to merit nor is it equal in its impact.

For our purposes, we will focus on Plato's idea of moral virtue. In *The Republic*, Book I, Plato suggested that we use virtue as a criterion in judging "what each is due." The more virtuous a person is, the more resources he or she receives. This, too, is a morally defensible method of allocation. It says that those who behave themselves are rewarded in ways that those who do not behave are not. It says that those who work harder get more. It says that those who are smarter receive deference for their intelligence, and so on.

As one can readily see, Plato's idea includes the principle of merit. But merit, as historically applied by other philosophers, can include social standing or class. A person can receive more because of his or her position in society and not just because his or her actions are more virtuous. Thus, the virtue principle goes further than merit. It suggests that people who behave in a virtuous manner, by being hardworking, intelligent, and educated (with which the merit principle agrees) are joined by those who show compassion, kindness, and empathy. All of these are considered important virtues, and anyone who is virtuous must receive "credit" for being so in terms of the distribution of justice.

Now, we can only use virtue as the principle upon which to decide the distribution of justice if each individual has an equal chance to develop virtues as much as he or she is capable. Life deals with each of us differently. What about the beaten and abandoned child? What about the veteran with serious injuries? Before virtue can be adopted as our standard for resource distribution, we must all have had the same chance to achieve it.

Therefore, we suggest that we ought to modify Plato's position to say that our second criterion of morality shall be: "We ought to do what we can to give each person the same conditions for achieving virtue." And thus, justice means making the same relative contribution to the goodness of people's lives—namely, that they be supported in "making the most of themselves."

How does this relate to police work? Certainly, the police cannot be expected, even in the COP era, to right all of the wrongs that have been done to people. The police cannot reconstitute the major institutions of society so they are equitable and fair. We do not and cannot suggest this. But what we can suggest is that police officers focus on the theoretical discussion here and apply its principles to the things on the street they can control. This means the enlightened, competent, ethical officer needs to think about several things at once.

First, it is important to understand that treating people fairly does not mean treating them identically. Because of their circumstances, strengths, weaknesses, abilities, and so on, people might be treated in different ways by the police but still be treated "fairly." In other words, treatment that takes life's variables into account might mean different treatment for different people, but it also means if citizens were equally situated in life (had the same opportunities, education, abilities, and so on) then they might be treated in exactly the same way.

This might sound confusing, so an example is in order. In the interests of justice, a police officer might cite one motorist for double-parking and allow another to go uncited because he or she was in a great hurry taking a child to a hospital emergency room. Both motorists might be equally guilty of causing a traffic problem, and the egalitarian principle of justice might require that precisely the same action be taken in both cases. But in the hospital-related example, the motorist is allowed to move the car later, without penalty, due to the circumstances involved. In such an example, both motorists were treated fairly (given their different circumstances) and equitably (they both would have received leniency if they both had a medical emergency), but they were not treated identically.

Second, our concept of justice does not mean the actions of the police will make people's lives equally good. A decision not to arrest one person may make only a marginal difference in his or her life. The same decision granted to another may make a tremendous difference. Consider, for example, that avoiding a speeding fine of $150 might have little impact on a rich person's life but could make a great impact on that of a poor person. The police cannot control this reality. It is but one example of life's unfairness that is out of the hands of uniformed police officers.

Thus, the police must use their discretionary decision-making powers to further the interests of justice in a way that attempts to treat everyone fairly. But we can neither assume that such treatment will always be exactly the same nor that it will impact people's lives in a similar way.

We have argued here that justice is not driven by, but neither is it independent of, the principle of maximizing benefit (the principle of utilitarianism). Justice is driven by the principle that we ought always to promote the good

BOX 9.7

DISTRIBUTING JUSTICE FAIRLY

We have noted that penalties, such as fines for speeding, impact people in unequal ways. This reality is being changed in some European countries through the imposition of what are called "day fines." When people are fined for minor infractions, they are fined the equivalent of one or two (or more) days' worth of wages. Thus, a day fine meted out for the crime of drunk driving of "five days" might cost a doctor $5,000, a teacher $1,000, and someone living at the poverty level $250. Arguably, this practice hits everyone fined in an equally forceful way. This is an example of how some countries are wrestling with the idea of how to distribute justice fairly.

because we understand justice as the principle that we ought to make the same relative contribution to the goodness of people's lives. Justice is the principle that implements the good, and without justice, the principle of promoting the good cannot live. The existence of justice is inescapably necessary for the realistic possibility of promoting and maintaining goodness in people's lives.

9-4 ◉ SUMMARY

The basic idea of our argument is that (1) our single, most dominant moral obligation is to care about and promote goodness where we can, and (2) this obligation requires the further principle of justice, now identified as equal treatment. The first principle asks us to be actively concerned about the goodness and evil of people's lives, while the second asks us to be fair in the way we deal with people.

The principle that we ought to promote the good constitutes an absolute and universal requirement, and there is no other principle as fundamental to the idea of an ethical life as this one. It is absolute because there can be no exceptions and universal because it applies to everybody. From this one principle springs every moral duty we have. The principle of justice is responsive to the principle of promoting the good and is understood as the implementation of it. Therefore, without our first principle, justice has no meaning; but without justice, promotion of the good and prevention of evil is impossible.

Must we recognize any other principles of right and wrong? It seems to us that we need not. As far as we can see, all of the things we may wish to recognize as moral duties (kindness, honesty, courage, etc.) and all our judgments about what to do in specific situations originate in these two principles, either directly or indirectly. From the first principle follow various specific rules of *prima facie* (at first view) obligation, for example those of not injuring anyone and of not interfering with another's liberty. From the second principle follow others, like equality of consideration and equality before the law. Some—like telling the truth, not being cruel, or not tormenting animals—may follow separately from both principles. Others, like keeping promises and taking care of one's children, may be justified on the basis of the two principles jointly.

We began our discussion about moral judgment by arguing that the concepts of "the good" and "justice" can be understood as the chief organizing principles of human life and that they emerge directly and necessarily from the most fundamental kinds of human experience. Our "ethic to live by" is a fusion of these two principles. We determine what to do in this or that situation by consulting the usual moral rules we are familiar with (be loyal, don't gossip, be kind, etc.). But our discussion has shown that the way to tell what moral rules to live by in specific situations is to see which rules best fulfill the joint requirement of promoting the good and justice.

We are constantly being "questioned" by life, by the world, with regard to whether or not we are living a good, ethical life. But being asked to live this way has the force of an imperative, for we really have no choice but to heed the request. That is, we have no choice if we want to be found worthy, if we want to live a decent life, if we want to do competent work. The profession of policing guarantees nobody is questioned in this way more than the police officer. Police officers' responses depend on nothing as much as how they see themselves, and this is entirely a matter of character.

9-5 ◉ TOPICS FOR DISCUSSION

1. In an effort to better understand the principle of beneficence, consider this idea of promoting good and preventing evil. Discuss examples from everyday life of how people might behave so as to follow this rule. Then discuss police-related examples of how one might apply beneficence on the job.

2. Refer to Box 9.6. Discuss examples from everyday life in which each of these different methods of distributing justice might be considered morally defensible.

3. Police officers attempting to promote justice cannot undo all of the unfairness and inequality in the world. But what can they do? In the COP era, what types of actions can police officers take on the job that might have a positive impact on the lives of citizens who are the most needy in our society? In other words, how do police officers behave in today's world as "agents of change"?

4. Recall Muir's definition of the tragic perspective in life. How does that idea inform our discussion here? In other words, how would Muir's professional officer behave in order to do honor to our ethic to live by?

9-6 ◉ ETHICAL SCENARIO

You arrive at a detail involving a domestic disturbance. A couple are argu-ing loudly enough to have necessitated the call from neighbors. Two small children and a young teenager are in attendance. As part of sorting things out, you run everyone for records and warrants. The father is clean and the teenager is clean, but the mother comes up with an outstanding warrant. It involves a traffic violation that has turned into a $180 warrant. The father is arrogant and verbally abusive. The mother is sober and cooperative. The teenager is sober, but obviously intimidated by the father. The warrant is large enough that you are prone to serve it. After all, it's not merely a $30 parking ticket warrant.

But you stop to think: What would the impact be of "doing your duty" and arresting this woman and taking her to jail? Two small children would be left alone with an irate and potentially (your police officer's sixth sense tells you) abusive father. You have no right to take the children to the shelter, as the father is there, sober, and warrantless. They are his kids. You cannot take them away from him.

The first part of our ethic to live by suggests that doing no harm is your priority. Taking the mother away in handcuffs—while perfectly legal and proper—would do all sorts of bad things for this little family. It might impact upon the little kids in a particularly negative way. It might set the teenager against the father. What do you do? Do you cleave to our axiom and "not inflict evil or harm"? If you let the woman slide (with a lecture about taking care of the warrant) you would be ignoring one of your primary functions, to enforce the law, but you would be cleaving to our ethic.

9-7 ◉ WRITING EXERCISE

Review Box 9.7 and write an essay about "day fines." What are they? What is the alternative way of levying fines for criminal conduct? What is the ethical frame of reference behind the idea of day fines? Do you consider this idea inter-esting and provocative as an alternative to how we do things here in America? Would you change our fine structure toward such a system? Why or why not?

9-8 ◉ KEY TERMS

beneficence: Actively doing good.

benevolence: The disposition to be good or to be charitable.

capitalism: Competitive economics focused upon the idea of an open marketplace; part of the ideas that were central to the development of Western liberalism that did away with the aristocratic tradition.

circumspect: Attending all consequences or circumstances; exercising discretion and paying heed to personal behavior.

communism: The economic system envisioned by Karl Marx in his numerous works, especially *The Communist Manifesto*; involves a democratic control over all aspects of life through a dictatorship of the people.

ethic to live by: We ought always to make the same relative contribution to the good of people's lives; our formulation of the perspective appropriate for a police officer to take onto the streets.

higher duty: The idea that sometimes the requirements of a situation mean taking heed of principles that are more synoptic or esoteric, rather than those that are immediate and obvious.

Hippocratic Oath: Promise that medical doctors make when they commit themselves to their profession.

Karl Marx: The father of communism and, to some extent, socialism; also considered by sociologists today to be the father of conflict theory.

socialism: Economic system that puts control over major elements of the industrial economy into the hands of the government and provides a universal social welfare safety net for all citizens.

totalitarian states: Governments that control all aspects of society influencing the lives of all citizens; examples include communism and fascism.

Western liberalism: A movement beginning in the 1600s (the English Civil War) that changed the economic, social, and political systems in the Western world, moving them away from the aristocratic tradition in the direction of the construction of a meritocracy; includes the ideas of capitalism, democracy, equality before the law, religious freedom, and the ideal of a classless society.

CHAPTER 10

Judgment Calls

Chapter Outline

"A good referee should try to be invisible whenever possible. He shouldn't control or even be a part of the game, if it isn't absolutely necessary. He should just let 'em play football."

—John Madden, football coach

Perhaps the most cogent truism about police work is that it is all about common sense. Police officers make judgment calls all the time. In doing so, they apply their common sense or street sense to the complexities that human interactions create. One paradox of today's drive toward professionalism is that for all the academic learning that the modern officer obtains, out on the street there are still many, many situations wherein academic learning is irrelevant. These present themselves often. And when they do, the common sense factor is paramount. Overall, the judgment necessitated on the job is informed by academic learning, police training, and real life experiences that all enlighten the internal ethic of the individual officer.

The famous organized-crime figure Al Capone was once quoted as saying, "When I serve alcohol downtown they call it bootlegging. When they serve it on Lakeshore Drive, they call it hospitality." (Lakeshore Drive was where many of the most affluent and important people in Chicago lived at the time of the quote.) Was he correct? Are there inconsistencies in the application of the law in America? Are some laws applied to some people and not to others? Aside from how they are applied, which is of course a practical consideration, were some laws *intended* to impact some people and not others? Are there laws that are so vague it is hard to understand them, much less apply them in a fair manner? Are there occasions where different laws even conflict with each other? Are there occasions where the nature of American society makes some laws *appear* to be unfair to certain groups of people? The answer to all of these questions, of course, is yes. And because this is true, the job of being a police officer is extremely difficult from a practical perspective.

In this chapter, we will relate police officer judgment calls to our ethic to live by. Our discussion here will have to take both procedural and substantive approaches as we will engage each of the conflicts, problems, and troublesome dynamics noted above.

© debra hughes/Shutterstock.com

Police work involves the exercise of judgment on a regular basis, evaluating competing citizen interests and weighing different alternatives, one against the other.

10-1 • PROBLEMS OF PROCESS

There are troublesome questions that arise due to the frustrating and complex nature of how rules are applied. All people who apply rules or laws to the behavior of others have to read between the lines to ascertain the intent of those rules. They must discern what sorts of behavior the rules are truly meant to control. Sometimes this is because the rules themselves can be vague and difficult to fathom. Furthermore, they can actually disagree with each other. They create situations wherein police officers are required to make judgment calls.

A. When Beneficence Conflicts with Justice

In Chapters 7 and 8, we engaged the reality that ethical formalism and utilitarianism often come to alternative conclusions with regard to the optimum action for the ethical person to take. Our ethic to live by was explicated in Chapter 9 in an attempt to make sense of the conflict that Kant's and Mill's ethical perspectives create for the police. When the police make arrest/no arrest decisions, these decisions must be based on solid, irrefutable criteria. There must be specific evidence to show that the elements of a crime are present. A person is only arrested if there is probable cause to believe he or she has committed that crime. There must also be specific evidence to show this. In a country that respects the rule of law, these are absolute requirements. The right of *habeas corpus,* written into our constitution, puts these requirements about legal specificity into one of our most basic legal principles: A person has to be charged with a particular crime or be set free.

This seems to mean that police officers who perform the role of law enforcement officers are Kantians. They must be absolutists because they are dealing with people's freedom. When they decide to take away that freedom or to leave it be, police officers must apply absolute legal principles, procedural rules, and substantive laws. As we noted in the introduction, the rule of law demands that no amount of personal bias on the part of a police officer can substitute for the breaking of specific laws. If laws are not broken, then the person goes free.

Similarly, it seems when police officers are operating in the order maintenance mode, they often use as a rule, a utilitarian frame of reference. When not dealing with law enforcement–oriented decisions, police officers spend their time calculating what is in the best interests of the state and of all the people. When dealing with drunks, the homeless, parties, loud music, groups of juveniles, family troubles, and a host of other order-maintenance types of details, the police consistently calculate what to do with an eye toward what they understand to be fair and equitable in the local community. In this way, the police balance conflicting interests and act in a very democratic fashion, attempting to make decisions that benefit the greatest number of people.

Then there is the service role of the police. In this context, police officers also tend to make utilitarian-type decisions. But they are of a different sort. Neither reflecting on the long-term interests of justice in the state (law enforcement/Kantian decisions) nor on fairness and equity in the local neighborhood (order maintenance/rule utilitarian decisions), the service orientation demands an alternative ethic. It requires that police officers consider the best interests of just those people immediately involved in a given detail. This is act utilitarianism.

Because of the confusion between these types of ethical perspectives we have created our ethic to live by. But even in applying that ethical perspective, the police are sometimes confronted with judgment calls. One kind of judgment call occurs when beneficence conflicts with justice.

When justice (again, defined as fairness) conflicts with beneficence, the latter becomes paramount. This might put the police officer in a bind sometimes. But dealing with such binds (by making discretionary decisions) is a central reality of police work. Morality cannot provide the officer with fixed principles of actual duty but only with principles of *prima facie* duty. The officer's sense of morality cannot be content with the letter of the law, but must foster the disposition that will sustain him or her when he or she must decide what to do. There are often extenuating circumstances, and all that the officer's morality can insist on is that he show a fixed disposition to find out what the right thing is and to do it if possible. In this sense, the officer must "be this" rather than "do this." But it must also be remembered that "being" involves at least *trying* to "do." Being without doing, like faith without works, is dead. Doing the right thing under such circumstances is something the officer with good character takes and embraces willingly.

The bind created by the conflict between justice and beneficence involves understanding something that we addressed in our discussion of justice earlier. We must not confuse the principle of equal treatment with the disposition to treat people identically or in just the same way. Say two motorists are double-parked in front of a hospital. One raced there with a bleeding victim

BOX 10.1

BENEFICENCE CONFLICTING WITH JUSTICE

What happens when, in doing good and removing harm, the police are confronted with the reality that they cannot promote justice or fairness? For example, justice may dictate the arrest of a 12-year-old burglar, in fairness to all burglars and in fairness to all burglary victims. The question may become whether or not this duty to justice can be overridden by the utilitarian idea that the age and lack of criminal record of the child dictates another course of action? Is the duty to behave in a beneficent manner controlling? We think that it is. Beneficence is paramount, and this is a principle that must be included within an understanding of our ethic to live by.

in tow, the other doubled-parked simply out of convenience. We are saying in this section that doing good for those people may very well involve treating them differently—that is, making the same proportional contribution to the good in their lives. This is what we think is meant by Kant's insistence on the equal intrinsic dignity or value of all individuals. As long as competent, ethical officers understand that they would treat other citizens in a like manner under similar circumstances, then our ethic does provide for equal treatment in the sense of "making the same proportional contribution" to what's good for them, or asking the same proportional sacrifice.

In other words, ethical officers must be comfortable with the idea that all people who double-park at hospitals because of genuine emergencies should be let off with a warning. Equally, ethical officers must know that all people who double-park out of laziness should be cited. As long as such decisions are made irrespective of race, color, creed, class, and so on (characteristics that are morally irrelevant to the issue at hand), the competent, professional, ethical officer can be comfortable with such inequitable treatment. While in a pure sense such actions (citing one and not citing the other) may not be "just," they are beneficent. And beneficence is the controlling principle.

B. Vagueness and Overbreadth

Aside from when laws conflict, sometimes they are vague and therefore difficult to understand. **Vagueness** too tests the ethics of the police officer's decision making. A basic principle of what scholars label the **morality of law** is that for a criminal statute to carry moral authority it must be specific. It must be understandable by the average person. If someone were to read it, and they were motivated to be a good citizen, then they would be able to avoid behaving in such a way as to become the focus of the law. For example, when a person reads under a burglary statute that it is a felony "to enter into a structure, boat, or locked automobile with the intent to commit grand theft, petty theft, or any other felony" it is relatively understandable and straightforward. Nuance might be involved in determining what "intent" means, for example. But generally speaking, a person of normal intelligence and education can read that penal code section and understand it. It is specific enough and focused enough to avoid the suggestion that it is too vague to be understood.

But what about "disturbing the peace"? What does that mean? Whose peace? How "disturbed"? How about "disorderly conduct"? What constitutes being "disorderly"? Or "malicious mischief"? For legal purposes, what constitutes behavior that is "mischievous"? These and other similarly indefinite penal code sections are sometimes referred to as "catch-alls." That is, they make crimes out of the sort of behavior that is so indistinct that many, many citizens might be caught up in the web of police arrest.

An equally difficult problem is presented when laws are overly broad in their construction. By being written in a way that encompasses too large a number of citizens, laws can be thus criticized. The idea of **overbreadth** is that officers might be provided with too much power when the law is defined in broadly enough verbiage that it allows them to arrest virtually any citizen. Again, overly broad penal code sections are considered to be catch-alls. They provide the police with too much power.

Such confusion of course tends to work in favor of the police. Officers generally like it when they have catch-all sections in their local codes. Police officers like to have an edge or leverage (what's called a "lever" in police vernacular) when dealing with a citizen. It always makes a detail easier when citizens have done something arrestable. In the case of misdemeanors or in-fractions, the police don't *need* to

Anti-gang ordinances are often questioned with regard to whether or not they give too much power to the police.

arrest. But they like it when the ability to do so hangs in the air. It makes obtaining citizen cooperation much easier.

But there are several problems here. The suggestion that criminal code sections can be "vague and overly broad" is often utilized by defense attorneys to make the point that such laws are unfair to citizens in two ways. On the one hand, vague laws are unfair to citizens directly due to the inability of the citizen to understand what sort of behavior has been made illegal. On the other hand, they are unfair because the police are allowed to cast a wider net than the law ought to allow them. Despite these criticisms, and despite the fact that courts sometimes declare such catch-all sections unconstitutional (as noted in Box 10.2), virtually all state and local criminal codes include some of them.

BOX 10.2

THE CHICAGO ANTI-GANG STATUTE

In the late 1990s, the city council of Chicago passed an ordinance in an effort to help the police fight the growing strength of local gangs. The law made it a crime for three or more people to stand in the street "with no apparent purpose." On the grounds that it was "vague and overly broad" and gave unlimited discretion to police officers, the United States Supreme Court declared this ordinance unconstitutional in 1999 in the case of *City of Chicago v. Morales*. This was a classic example of a decision wherein a catch-all section was considered to be unfair to the public.

Now, what are the police to make of this? As noted above, the existence of such empowering ordinances tends to be a boon to the police. But the contemporary officer must understand that such sections are of marginal legality and, equally, *why* they are of marginal legality. Just because the police are empowered in one way or other is no excuse to utilize that power whenever possible. Our ethic suggests that the police be self-limiting in this regard. Muir told us that the police should avoid using coercive power whenever possible. We have noted several times that the use of force must necessarily be accompanied by a degree of circumspection. The exercise of any sort of police power, the use of force, or the application of catch-all sections must be circumscribed by an understanding that such acts must only be resorted to in the interest of removing evil and doing good.

C. The Harm Principle: What's a Legal Problem?

All societies must strike a delicate balance when they decide how much power the agents of the state should possess. A **classical liberal,** such as **John Locke** (who gave us the ideas of natural rights and limited government), would say that individuals should almost always be left alone to live their own lives without interference from the state or government. This liberal principle is, of course, a very American idea. (See Peter Laslett, ed., *Locke's Two Treatises of Government* [New York: Cambridge University Press, 1960].) A **classical conservative,** such as Edmund Burke (who led the opposition to Locke's ideas in England 300 years ago), would say people cannot be trusted with their own decisions. Burke called for strong government, tight laws, and increased police powers. He believed that, being ignorant and stupid, people needed to be controlled using any means possible. (See Charles Parkin, *The Moral Basis of Burke's Political Thought* [Cambridge, England: Cambridge University Press, 1956].)

In America, we have our own "classical" statement of the trade-off between the power of the state and the freedom of the individual, and it comes (again) from John Stuart Mill. In his famous essay "On Liberty," Mill suggested a formula for how much power belonged in whose hands. Mill said the individual should only be amenable to society for that conduct which directly harms another. This is called Mill's **"harm principle,"** and it is important for all police officers to remember.

The harm principle is important because it provides a good yardstick for making judgment calls. That is, often police officers must decide whether to invoke the law, to arrest, and/or to become involved in solving problems that might otherwise be solved if people were simply left alone. When this occurs, it serves the police well to remember Mill and to ask themselves whether or not someone is directly harmed by the actions of another. In other words, if there is no direct harm to others from deviant behavior, why worry about it?

For example, if loud music is coming from a rowdy party but there have been no complaints to the police about it, who cares? Or if a pair of backpackers decides to make love in the forest and no one sees them but a police

BOX 10.3

MILL AND THE POWER OF THE STATE

John Stuart Mill suggested three main reasons why decisions relating to people's personal lives (where no direct harm to others could result from the outcome) should be left in the hands of individuals and not given over to the power of the state or government.

- Usually, people know better than bureaucrats, politicians, or police officers how best to decide questions about their own lives because of their intimate knowledge of their own interests, goals, desires, and so on.

- On those occasions wherein government agents know better what is good for the citizen than people do themselves, it is still usually best to leave decisions to individuals. Even though people may make mistakes, part of our intellectual development and maturation in life is learning through trial and error.

- Given the universal propensity of governmental power over the individual to expand, we should always remain reluctant to create more governmental structures—they will almost invariably endure and, in the long run, lessen individual freedom.

officer, who cares? Or if teenagers are out after curfew on their way home from a school function that ran a little late and are minding their own business, who cares? Or if married couples are turned on by the idea of swapping partners for sexual liaisons in the privacy of their own homes and bedrooms, who cares? In these and a thousand other instances, people might break the law or behave deviantly but not create the sort of problem that one might think ought to be "the business" of the state or of the police.

Americans have a long tradition of believing in Mill's philosophy about personal harm and about keeping the government out of our lives. The competent police professional, understanding Mill and the American ideals of limited government and individual rights, must avoid the tendency to feel frustrated when this ideal is put into action. That is, one of the overt manifestations of Americans' agreement with Mill and their belief in the principle of limiting governmental power is their propensity to be suspicious of the police and of police power. The intelligent police officer understands this and makes allowances for people's very natural "American-like" behavior in (often) distrusting the police.

10-2 ● SUBSTANTIVE PROBLEMS

But there is more. Police officers are presented with judgment calls because of the specific substance of what laws are meant to accomplish. This has nothing to do with how indefinite the laws might be or with how difficult they are to apply. Some judgment calls originate from the fact that the laws were meant at the outset to deal with human interactions that might more properly be left alone. Alternately, some laws perpetuate inequities in society for which the police have absolutely no answers.

A. Victimless Crimes

While we may all applaud the harm principle and believe the state and the police should keep out of people's lives whenever possible, one dynamic in contemporary American society stands in the way of applying this ideal. As one might imagine, when people analyze the concept of **"victimless crimes,"** crimes for which there are no specific, individual complainants, Mill's philosophy is always in the forefront of discussion. This is because victimless crimes involve no direct harm to others. And a remarkable number of Americans agree in leaving victimless crime alone. Studies indicate, for example, that large numbers of people believe citizens should be left alone if they are gambling, reading "smut," viewing pornography, or enjoying consensual adult sexual behavior in their own homes.

One of the classic victimless crimes is drug use. Given the monumental effort being undertaken in America and throughout the world in the name of the "drug war," the application of the harm principle to drug use is a major stumbling block for the police. Estimates of the numbers of Americans who have used illegal drugs range above the 70 million mark. Furthermore, any number of studies indicates that about 12 percent of the population—regardless of socioeconomic level, race, or class—use illicit drugs. Thus, a

BOX 10.4

THE CHARACTERISTICS OF VICTIMLESS CRIMES

- Consenting participants on both sides of the criminal act (such as prostitute and "John," gambling partners, illicit sexual partners)
- An ongoing demand for the goods/services that are provided
- Significant amounts of official corruption due to high profits and the absence of witnesses/complaining parties when officials (usually the police) interact with criminals

huge number of Americans, not merely those who use crack and heroine in the inner cities, create the demand for illegal drugs on an ongoing basis.

This creates several problems for the police. First, such black market profits tend to create corruption because officials, police officers included, can be bought off by drug dealers who possess incredible amounts of money. For the purposes of our discussion

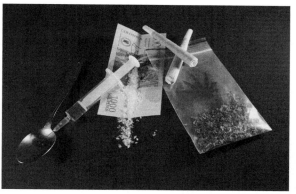

© Roland Spiegler/Shutterstock.com

Victimless crimes are characterized by the huge profits their purveyors enjoy, the black markets that the demand for their goods and/ or services create, and the official corruption that is often associated with them.

of police ethics, the drug war creates a black market that almost invariably seduces some police officers into lives of crime. Victimless crimes always produce this dynamic. Second, the empowerment of gangs in America, linked as it is to the tremendous profits made available because they have taken over the drug trade in many places, puts the police under great stress and into harm's way on streets where gangs carry increasingly powerful armaments. Just as occurred during **Prohibition,** today's police are under increased stress in numerous ways due to the machinations of the drug war.

Third, and more relevant to our discussion here, because drug use does not directly harm anyone other than the user, the involvement of the police in the drug war creates a philosophical problem relative to Mill's concerns about personal freedom. Many Americans resent the injection of the state's power into the lives of citizens unless the lives and property of others are in jeopardy. Gambling, prostitution, and alcohol-related crimes are all examples of the sorts of criminal behaviors wherein the police operate along a sliding scale. Obvious, flagrant, public violations, especially when someone complains about them, are often prosecuted. But consensual, adult, private violations can be, and in most jurisdictions usually are, ignored.

For practical reasons, we have to put the policing of drug use aside and keep it off this list. The individual police officer, no matter how sensitive he or she might be to the paradoxes of the drug war, can hardly be expected to stand in the way of such a large-scale endeavor. It is true that a steadily increasing number of citizens, analysts, politicians, and even police officers have become opposed to this war. But a majority of Americans, a majority of police officers, and certainly a huge majority of police administrators are still in favor of its prosecution. Given that the police are supposed to be accountable to public opinion, the law, and their departments' orders, we must keep drug use separate from this discussion of the harm principle and other victimless crimes.

Thus, our discussion of the harm principle must carry a "drug war asterisk" next to it. But generally, aside from the realities of fighting the drug war, Mill's harm principles translates into police work in this way: Police officers ought to leave people alone, not take official action, as often as possible—when no one else is directly harmed. With the exception of felonious crime and, of course, violent crime, police officers, like "good referees," should try to be invisible. Barring violence, felony crime, or direct harm to others, police officers ought to be a part of life's scenery.

B. American Inequities

We have noted from the outset that an important function of societal values and laws is to determine who gets what, when, and how. The police are situated at the flash points of those situations wherein citizens interact, struggle, and fight for what they consider to be their fair share or what they are due. The police will always catch some level of flack due to being the referees in the struggles between citizens. This is in the very nature of things. But they also are put into unfortunate situations when those struggles have to do with social inequities or ongoing social problems. The police are the recipients of the brunt of civilian contempt when in fact there is nothing whatsoever that the police have to do about the problems that people face.

To wit, the American police work in the industrialized or "developed" society that presents its citizens with the largest inequities in the world. The gap between the rich and the poor in America is huge—much greater than in any other developed country—and it grows every year. Executives make over 200 times what entry level workers make in American corporations, something that is unheard of everywhere else around the world. Furthermore, the dynamics associated with racial disparities in America are important. For as much as it *appears* that non-white people have made progress in the past several decades, it is nevertheless true that such institutions as schools are as segregated today as they were in 1954 when the Supreme Court declared (in theory) an end to such segregation. Crime is greater than in any other industrialized country. Our schools lag far, far behind those in other advanced countries. The underclass in this country suffers from deteriorating rather than improving wages, working conditions, vacation opportunities, retirement possibilities, and living conditions generally.

Now this might sound like an anti-American diatribe. Nothing could be further from the truth. The authors believe heartily in the promise of the American dream and in the possibilities that this country has traditionally presented to a majority of its people. But these facts about today's American social and economic fabric are incontrovertible. They present to the police a set of working conditions under which people struggle in ways that they do not have to in other industrialized countries. And as the people struggle with each other and with the system, as they steal from each other and visit violence born out of frustration upon their fellows, the police are drawn in. The police are situated between the struggling classes of people wrestling with these economic conditions. The stress brought upon the police is great and, arguably, they need to understand these realities more than police in any other advanced country. Because this is so, the individual officer's ethical frame of reference is critical; it informs his or her world view in a way that may (or may not) help in wrestling with the problems visited upon members of the American underclass.

At the beginning of this chapter, we quoted Al Capone, the notorious hoodlum. He suggested that laws are often applied in an inequitable way. Unlike our discussion here, his point was not a reflection upon how unequal treatment might very well be just, of course. He was suggesting that the law was applied unfairly in favor of political and economic elites.

10-3 ● SOLVING ETHICAL DILEMMAS

We often hear that people show their character when they are faced with ethical questions. In life we are sometimes faced with a choice between doing the right thing and doing the easy thing or the safe thing or the comfortable thing or the hedonistic ("feel good") thing. People show what they are really made of when they decide how they will behave under such circumstances. Life presents everyone with such questions on a regular basis. Do I pad my tax returns with false deductions or tell the truth? Do I stick to my marriage vows or pursue the good-looking co-worker? Do I lie to my kids about my drug use when I was a kid or do I "come clean"? In this way, life presents everyone with large and small ethical choices to make that involve balancing the right thing to do against the easy thing to do.

But things get more complicated than this. Life also presents us with ethical dilemmas: choices between conflicting duties. An ethical question may be hard to answer. But when one does the right thing in facing an ethical question, even though it might be difficult, one is left with a good feeling about oneself. When a person tells the truth, cleaves to his or her spouse, acts loyally, behaves like a good parent, and so on, that person gets the satisfaction of knowing that his or her good character is being exhibited.

But what happens when you have to decide between two courses of action, each of which has a good, solid, ethical duty attached to it? What happens when a genuine **ethical dilemma** presents itself? Police officers, more than most people, are faced with such decision making because they so often have to decide between the conflicting claims of diverse people. Often on the street, both sides in a dispute are right, both sides are arguing from perfectly reasonable perspectives, and both sides are making moral claims that are defensible. What does the police officer do when confronted with such dilemmas?

Criminal ethicist Joycelyn Pollock attempts to help the individual decision maker (in our discussion the police officer) with such evaluations.

BOX 10.5

POLLOCK'S ANALYTICAL STEPS TO CLARIFYING ETHICAL DILEMMAS

While there is not "one way" to decide between conflicting ethical duties when making behavior choices, criminal ethicist Joycelyn Pollock suggests several steps be taken by individuals who seek to clarify an ethical dilemma. Her steps are:

- Review all the facts—not future predictions, not suppositions, not probabilities, but what is known.
- Identify all the potential values of each party that might be relevant—life, law, family, and self-preservation.
- Identify all possible moral issues for each party involved.
- Decide what is the most immediate moral or ethical issue facing each individual.
- Resolve the ethical dilemma. Make an ethical judgment based on an appropriate ethical system (e.g., our ethic to live by) and supported by moral rules (such as "one must always follow the law").

Joycelyn Pollock, *Ethics in Crime and Justice*, 3rd ed.
(Belmont, CA: Wadsworth, 1998)

After reading such a list one might be frustrated that it does not give a specific explanation about how to solve such dilemmas. But the complicated nature of life on the street dictates that thoughtful analysts and experienced practitioners will only be able to provide us with such general sets of guidelines as these. Because there are millions of sets of facts, sets of circumstances, and sets of participants in the world, the competent police officer can only be given approaches and cannot be shown all solutions for dealing with real-life dilemmas.

So Pollock tells us, in essence, to be as careful and thoughtful and thorough as we can, given the pressures of time on the beat. Make sure the facts are clear. Make sure assumptions, prejudices, and predictions are left out of decision making. Be clear what the relevant interests are, what ethical duties present themselves to all parties, and what constitute the most immediate ethical issues.

Consider this example. Suppose you are on a detail where a husband has been accused of abusing his wife. The accusation comes from her mother, the grandmother of the children who stand around you as you survey the situation in the family's living room. The wife looks shocked and exhausted—as if she might very well have been attacked by her husband. On the other hand, she has no wounds showing, no blood flowing, no visible trauma. She says that he did not assault her. She is obviously afraid of the man but is adamant that he should be left alone.

The grandmother is equally adamant about having seen an assault, about the need for the police to take the man to jail, and about her duty to protect her daughter and grandchildren. What do you do? There is, of course, no single answer to this question. The physical state of the people involved would need to be assessed. Are they drunk? Drinking? Using drugs? The history of the family would have to be taken into account. Have you been there before? Has the husband been arrested for abuse before? Has the wife herself complained before? What is the relationship of the grandmother to the family? Is she in the home on a regular basis? Has she complained before? Do you, the officer on the scene, believe that she means well and truly wants to protect her daughter and grandchildren? Or is she trying to break up a marriage for her own reasons?

These and a dozen other variables need to be taken into consideration. When you do this, considering Pollock's chart can be helpful. Rather than swimming in all of these details and rather than making an intuitive decision that might be ineffectual, the competent professional will attempt to analyze the problem logically. The ethical duties of the mother, father, and grandmother, not to mention those of the police, must be considered.

The duty to protect people from abuse (removing evil) must be considered and weighed against the duty to keep the family unit together (promoting good). Using our ethic to live by, the police officer may not see an apparent solution, one that answers the "what to do" question in a precise manner. While we believe our ethic is an important compromise between other schools of thought, we cannot argue that it solves all such dilemmas in a concrete way.

For who, in the middle of a hot detail and under the pressure of time and multiple stressors, has the time to write all of this down and do such calculating? The answer, of course, is that no one does. But we (and Pollock) are not suggesting that officers do so. We (and she) are suggesting that in training sessions, in informal discussions, in reviewing how past details have been handled, and so

Police officers are often confronted with dilemmas wherein each of several alternative actions presents a logical and ethical choice . . . and the options conflict with each other.

BOX 10.6

THE POLICE OFFICER'S CRAFT

Almost half a century ago, one of the social scientists who first studied the police, Bruce Smith, wrote about the art of the police officer, the officer's critical role in administering justice, and the ethics of the endeavor:

"The policeman's art . . . consists in applying and enforcing a multitude of laws and ordinances in such degree or proportion and in such manner that the greatest degree of protection will be secured. The degree of enforcement and the method of application will vary with each neighborhood and community. There are no set rules, not even general principles, to the policy to be applied. Each policeman must, in a sense, determine the standard to be set in the area for which he is responsible. Immediate superiors may be able to impress upon him some of the lessons of experience, but for the most part such experience must be his own . . . thus he is a policy-forming police administrator in miniature, who operates beyond the scope of the unusual devices for control. . . ."

Bruce Smith, *Police Systems in the United States* (New York: Harper and Brothers, 1960)

on, competent police officers can and should go over these types of options when they have the time. If they do, their competence, as a function of their effectiveness in dealing with ethical dilemmas, will grow.

This is just one common example of a type of ethical dilemma presented to the officer on the beat. Viewed relative to appropriate ethical perspectives and related to moral rules that make up the officer's understanding of the good life and of the important elements of community, such dilemmas need not present police officers with frustration. Understanding that theirs is a limited role, that they cannot solve all the world's problems, police officers who approach such problems and make judgments based on these principles will more often than not be acting as competent professionals.

10-4 ◉ SUMMARY

More than 50 years ago, sociologist Jerome Skolnick suggested that police work was something between a blue-collar type of trade and a white-collar profession. He suggested that the combination of academic knowledge, street sense, particularized skills, and intuitive logic cops needed to possess made their occupation something like that of the fine craftsman.

Skolnick was the first to talk about how the potential of violence colored the police perception of the street. He first discussed how police officers tend to be very much against the exclusionary rule and, thus, the due process system as it operates. Even before Dirty Harry existed as a screen character, Skolnick anticipated his arrival. Weaving together their roles as legal paraprofessionals, social workers, street level psychologists, discretionary decision makers, and policy developers, he even noted well in advance of others the terrible drawbacks of fighting drugs on the streets the way it is done in contemporary America. Skolnick was ahead of his time and broke the ground for much of what we know and say today about the sociology of the police.

Today, we are suggesting this definition be amplified, pushed one step further. For when the increasingly complex set of knowledge and skills (the craft) is modified and applied through a screen that puts the entire job into an ethical frame of reference, police work becomes a genuine profession. Making the types of judgment calls we have discussed here is the essence of the professional's role in this modern era. And it is driven, as we have said numerous times, by individual police officer character.

10-5 ◉ TOPICS FOR DISCUSSION

1. Discuss the idea that the two parts of our ethic to live by, beneficence and justice, can conflict. First consider examples from civilian life where they conflict. Then discuss police examples. In each case discuss why beneficence must be the controlling principle.

2. Discuss victimless crimes. What are examples and what are the elements they all have in common? With an eye toward Part III's discussion of particular types of police misconduct, consider why victimless crimes almost invariably produce police corruption.

3. Discuss the difference between an ethical question and an ethical dilemma. First, consider examples from life in general. Then discuss examples from police work.

4. What are the elements of the police officer's "craft"? How would you describe the types of practical skills involved in being a good, competent officer?

10-6 ◉ ETHICAL SCENARIO

You stop a car for missing its current license plate tags. After some preliminary inquiries, the driver allows you to search the trunk. He does this because he says that it is not his car, he borrowed it from his roommate (who is not present). You are, in fact, able to confirm the story that the car does not belong to the driver. In the trunk are drugs. The young man—who is clear of records and warrants—is a student at the local medical school. You are convinced that he knew nothing about the drugs. What do you do?

You are not only able to arrest him (on a charge that may very well end his chance at a medical career), but you can also impound the car and keep it under forfeiture laws (something that your department has emphasized is an important policy goal). A good felony bust and a good legal seizure are within your grasp. What do you do, and why?

10-7   WRITING EXERCISE

So much time and effort has been spent since 1969 in the pursuit of the War on Drugs that it is a very, very touchy subject in the police world. The overwhelming majority of police officers and administrators are committed "drug warriors." They accept America's drug laws and participate in the war willingly. On the other hand, not only are there a substantial number of citizens who are in favor of legalizing drugs, but a steadily increasing number of police officers, a "substantial minority," are as well. In the midst of this controversy, the American police officer must soldier on.

Write an essay about victimless crimes, focusing in particular upon drug laws. Discuss the classic elements of victimless crimes, which of course include huge profits, an ongoing demand, and official corruption. Discuss how this corruption is created by the fact that (1) so much money is involved, and (2) often there are no specifically victimized citizens present at times of potential arrests. (In fact, drug dealers and police officers are usually the only people present, and the dealers want the police to take some payoff money and just go away.) Include a discussion of these realities in your essay and include the debate about how legalizing drugs might lessen police corruption of authority. Finally, take your own stand on the issues involved. Where are you with regard to, say, the legalization of drugs—marijuana in particular?

10-8   KEY TERMS

classical conservatism: School of thought that was created as a reaction to liberalism; suggested that people were greedy, self-centered, and driven by evil impulses and thus they need to be controlled by powerful governmental agencies and institutions.

classical liberalism: School of thought created during the Age of Enlightenment; suggested that society's political, economic, social, and legal institutions be organized along the lines of a meritocracy, as opposed to the aristocratic tradition that preceded it.

ethical dilemma: Situation wherein a choice must be made between competing courses of action, each of which is ethically defensible.

habeas corpus: Latin for "bring forth the body" (of evidence); Anglo-American legal principle that citizens must be charged with a specific crime or else be let free.

harm principle: Developed by John Stuart Mill, this idea suggests that an individual citizen is only amenable to society for that conduct which directly harms the interests or persons of others.

John Locke: One of the fathers of Western or English liberalism; wrote extensively on the ideas of meritocracy, individual rights, equal opportunity, and political organization.

morality of law: Principle relating to the specific requirements that are endemic to any morally defensible legal system, such as the requirement to have publicized laws, to have consistency between how laws are written and how they are administered.

overbreadth: Legal concept having to do with laws that are not narrowly focused enough and, thus, avail the police of too much power.

Prohibition: The attempt in the United States between 1920 and 1933 to prohibit the distillation, distribution, and possession of alcohol; led to the creation of organized crime, due to the financial boon which illegal alcohol (drug) sale provided.

vagueness: Legal concept having to do with laws that are not specific enough to be fair when administered on the street.

victimless crimes: Crimes wherein no particular, individual citizen is victimized, such as drug use and sales, prostitution, gambling, and the possession of pornography.

PART III

On the Street

It is time for us to consider more practical questions. First, we must engage in an analysis of those forms into which police misconduct falls. There is not just one type of misconduct. Rather, there are many. Some of them are particularly troublesome and some are trivial in their import. After reflecting upon them, we will move on to examine the causal roots of misconduct—and perceived misconduct. Again, the causes are sometimes inadvertent and unimportant and at other times crucial to the delivery of justice on the street. Finally, we will discuss some practical applications of our ethic to live by.

CHAPTER 11

Types of Police Misconduct

Chapter Outline

"All power tends to corrupt, and absolute power corrupts absolutely."

—Lord Acton, 1834–1902

It is always uncomfortable for police officers and police leaders to confront the topic of police misconduct. These people know how hard it is to be a cop on the beat. They understand the stresses and violence involved. They are confident that the overwhelming majority of police officers do the very best job they can against the odds. Thus, those in police work tend to want to shy away from this negative subject.

But no amount of avoidance will change the reality that police officers, like people in any other line of work, are sometimes guilty of misbehaving. The power the police possess is great. They are licensed by society to take away people's freedom, to use force, and even to use deadly force. It is perhaps more important for the police officers of America to "behave themselves" than it is for any other political, social, economic, or legal actors. In this chapter we will discuss the various types of police misconduct into which police officers sometimes fall. We will take time to understand the differences between these types and to outline the characteristics that define police deviance in a way that makes our discussions of police ethics more clear and focused.

It is more than a little ironic that we now finally come to the subject that so often is the *only* topic of discussion when police ethics are discussed. As we pointed out in the very first few pages of our journey here, the standard police academy consideration of police ethics was (and still is in many places) nothing more than a set of warnings about the several sorts of misconduct into which police officers sometimes fall. Here in a chapter about the typology of five sorts of police misconduct, we will discuss something akin to what was always discussed in those "here's how not to mess up" discussions.

Of particular importance in this chapter is the idea that there are numerous types of misconduct and an equal number of types of causes. Because this is so, police review systems, police supervision models, and police disciplinary mechanisms need to be multi-faceted.

11-1 ● STANDARDS OF CONDUCT

To begin, we need to explore briefly what is meant by **"police deviance."** When people deviate, they break norms of conduct that are prescribed for them. Norms can be defined as cultural values, moral tenets, social customs, or codified laws. Of course, people (and police officers) can break any number of norms and behave in deviant ways without becoming the subject of anything other than disapproval. If people pick their noses in public or talk too loudly in theaters or say bad things about a dead person, they may make us think ill of them. By doing these things they may invite people to think they are ignorant, stupid, rude, or insensitive. Such disapproval is powerful stuff and it controls how we dress, talk, and act most of the time. But such deviance is only informally sanctioned.

However, sometimes people transgress distinctive, written rules of conduct. When they do this, they are subjected to the operations of the institutionalized systems that are society's official behavior-control mechanisms. When people break the law, they may be arrested, jailed, tried, convicted, and punished. Similarly, when a cop breaks the rules of conduct set up for the police, he or she may be accused, investigated, found guilty, and punished. In the case of citizens, the criminal justice system does the work of holding them accountable. In the case of the police, police review systems, internal affairs units, or civilian review boards do the job.

Police review systems can be considered mini-criminal-justice systems. They investigate allegations of misconduct and make findings about the guilt of accused officers. These systems come in all shapes and sizes. They have a thankless job to do in attempting to hold the police accountable for their actions. Police review systems operate after the fact. That is, they deal with accusations of misconduct after they have happened. Our task in this book is to talk about internalizing standards of ethical conduct so police officers do not break the rules in the first place. We are, therefore, making the point that internalized ethics are more important than prescribed rules. The institutions of the family, schools, churches, clubs, and so on internalize standards of behavior for all individuals. The police subculture, training mechanisms, and discussions such as occur in this book do so for the police.

This begs us to ask, what standards are the standards of conduct to which the police must be held accountable? As was true earlier in our discussion of the roles of the police, the standards to which we hold the police are multiple, conflicting, and vague. Thus, as was true of police roles, there will always be some confusion about where we should find the yardstick to evaluate police behavior.

A. Cops as Legal Actors

First, and some would say foremost, the police must answer to the law. Everything a police officer does must be legal. When applying codes and statutes, police officers must know the codified law, charge appropriately, investigate effectively, and write reports that are legally tight and include the appropriate elements.

BOX 11.1

MULTIPLE STANDARDS OF CONDUCT

- Police officers are legal actors.
- Police officers are political actors.
- Police officers are administrative actors.

On the other hand, when dealing with citizens and suspects the police must also know procedural or case law. They must treat citizens with deference to the constitutionally prescribed rights all Americans possess. They must know under what circumstances they can stop and field-interrogate people, how and when to admonish suspects of their rights, when they can and cannot make warrantless searches, and so on. Here, too, the police must be legally precise.

B. Cops as Political Actors

However, the law represents only one set of standards for the police. A second set of standards comes from the constituents in the neighborhoods they serve. The police must be political actors in responding to the desires of their communities. They are **"streetcorner politicians,"** as author William K. Muir labeled them. In today's era of COP the police are asked to form bonds with the community, to encourage neighborhood groups to inform them of their desires, and to behave in a responsive manner, taking such feedback into account when they police the streets. So the police must be held accountable to standards of conduct prescribed by the people.

This may sound easy. But trouble can arise when these two sets of standards conflict. When the people ask the police to do things that are not legal, as they do more often than one might think, there is a distinctive conflict between these two sets of standards (see Box 11.2). People will regularly ask the police to do "whatever it takes" to get rid of drugs on the streets, to break up local gangs, to curb domestic abuse, to protect children from guns, and so forth. Not being police officers, and not caring (really) about what the law says, citizens expect the police to take effective action against these evils and to do it without making excuses.

Because it is not clear how to resolve such conflicts, the police and any system that attempts to hold them accountable for their actions are put in a bind. Should the police harass people whom they know to be drug dealers or gang members, whether or not they are observing the Constitution? Should the police target known drug dealers for special treatment even though there is no legal evidence against them? Should an individual police officer threaten to "personally kick the c___ out of you" to deter a wife beater from doing it again? All of these tactics are arguably effective in doing things a majority of the people in the community may very well want done. But they are not legal.

C. Cops as Administrative Actors

The police are legal, political, and administrative actors, all rolled into one. In the administrative arena, the police must live by the rules of conduct set down by police professionals in police department **general order manuals.** This third set of standards makes up the "nuts and bolts" of police work. These standards are the focus of much of the training the police experience. They are police-specific in that neither the law nor the people have much to say about them.

BOX 11.2

ASKING THE POLICE TO DO THE IMPOSSIBLE

Police officers interact with citizens who often want what is legally impossible: for the police to get gangs, drugs, and guns off of the streets of America in any way possible. It is not at all uncommon for people to suggest that the police "round up" gang members randomly. Equally, people are often perplexed by the fact that the police will not search known drug houses or stop drug dealers' cars without cause. The intricacies of the law are lost on those whose only focus is the peace and quiet of their neighborhoods and the safety of their children.

Driven by unrealistic images from television and movies, American citizens on the street often believe in and support Dirty Harry–like behavior. Nobody outside of the criminal justice system cares much for constitutional limitations or for the intricacies of legal processes. They want action and they want results. They want their children protected. No amount of excuse making about how difficult this might be will suffice. As they see it happening in the entertainment media, citizens wish that the police would "clean up the streets" . . . and they have not the slightest hesitation in supporting the most draconian of police tactics in doing so.

© Zbynek Jirousek/Shutterstock.com

In some departments, the general order manuals are made up of volumes and volumes including hundreds of rules, regulations, and procedures.

Neither the courts nor the people care much about how to fill out appropriate forms, how to handcuff a suspect, how to search a prisoner, how to transport an arrestee, and so forth. All of the general orders or specific "how to be a cop" regulations that cover such behavior are written by police managers. General order manuals include dozens, sometimes hundreds, of rules relating to job performance. These include regulations about tardiness, taking sick leave, grooming, proper uniform display, and so on. The police must abide by these rules and will be punished if they ignore them.

Thus, police officers must answer to three separate sets of standards.

They must observe the law, respond to the community, and follow professional regulations. Of course, being human beings and operating under great stress at all hours of the day and night, they will sometimes violate the norms of conduct that are included in these standards and be guilty of misconduct.

11-2 ● TYPOLOGY OF MISCONDUCT

Police misconduct falls into five distinctive category types. To illustrate the differences in these types, we begin by discussing two sets of parameters that define them. Two questions must be asked of police misconduct for us to fit such misbehavior into its proper place in its typology.

First, was the misconduct done in the name of personal gain? Whether it takes the form of money, goods, services, or other types of trade-offs, when police officers misbehave sometimes they are looking to enhance their own material well-being. Concomitantly, sometimes they are not.

Second, did the misconduct involve the use of the police officer's position of authority? Did the cop(s) "sell the badge" in exchange for something? Whether it involves protecting criminals from arrest or arresting certain criminals to enhance the business of others, police officers sometimes use their state-granted authority as a bargaining tool to get something accomplished that is improper. On the other hand, sometimes their state-granted authority has nothing to do with police misconduct.

Once these two questions are answered, police misconduct can be classified. Four types fall into a table, and one exists outside of that table. This may seem to be just an academic exercise, but it is not. The consequences, methods of investigation, punishments, and political fallout associated with each of these five types of misbehavior are different—sometimes very different—from each other. Furthermore, our ethic to live by can have very different things to say about the relative immorality of the various types.

Table 11.1 shows how four of the types of police misconduct are determined by applying the two questions above. Let us discuss these types individually.

TABLE 11.1

TYPES OF POLICE MISCONDUCT		
	Was Personal Gain Involved?	
	Yes	No
Yes	Corruption of authority	Noble cause corruption
Did The Officers abuse their Legal Authority?		
No	Police crime	Ineptitude

A. Corruption of Authority

Police officers are guilty of what we label **"corruption of authority"** when they use their legal authority (badges) to obtain personal rewards. This takes several forms. Payoffs are sometimes obtained by police officers to protect certain criminal enterprises, such as gambling, prostitution, and drug sales. Money is handed over to the police, and arrests are not made. **Shakedowns** are sometimes undertaken wherein police officers proactively demand money from people, normally small business operators, in exchange for "letting them off easy" with regard to city ordinances and so forth. **Graft** is sometimes accepted on an individual basis, from a motorist in exchange for not giving a ticket, for example.

B. Police Crime

Sometimes police officers will become involved in criminal activities while on duty that do not involve the use of their offices. Cops will sometimes use the opportunities that being on duty, particularly at night, afford to them to burglarize businesses or residences. Sometimes when a theft has already occurred, police officers will take merchandise or money and report it as part of the original theft. When this type of misconduct happens, cops are misbehaving to obtain personal gain. But they are not trading off their positions of authority to do so. This is **police crime** or professional crime. This type of misconduct is considered different from either of the above two types.

Those who study police corruption of authority (and police crime, too) have developed a labeling scheme to illustrate different levels of misconduct. They refer to **"grass eating"** and **"meat eating."** We will discuss this differentiation and how it helps us understand the generation of these types of misconduct.

Grass Eating. Grass eating involves two types of police behavior (or misbehavior). First, it entails a nonsystematic, individualized type of personal gain–related misconduct that sometimes develops from individual police–citizen interactions. This type of misconduct is not proactive in the sense that the police who become involved in it do not seek out citizens as victims and do not attempt to glean large amounts of graft. Thus, grass eating includes accepting cash in exchange for not writing a moving violation, obtaining police discounts, eating free food, drinking free coffee, and so on. While these activities are all unacceptable because they do harm to the image of the police and the law, they nevertheless are considered by students of police misconduct to be minor in their importance.

Second, grass eating involves the acceptance by some police officers of the large-scale, organized (meat-eating) misconduct of others. That is, grass eating also involves looking the other way and not reporting/taking action with regard to the personal gain–related misconduct of others. Thus, some police officers who never take payoffs of any kind can still be considered to be grass eaters if they become aware of meat eating and take no action to stop it. This type of behavior involves another transgression against our ethic. It ignores the duty to remove evil.

Meat Eating. **Meat eating** involves proactive, systematic, organized payoffs. Examples include narcotics officers who accept money on a regular basis in exchange for not arresting certain drug dealers, vice officers who accept money from pimps in exchange for not arresting their prostitutes, and beat cops who regularly shake down businesses and demand protection money from them. When officers actively seek opportunities to obtain personal gain and organize systems for accepting and covering up such behavior, they are meat eating. (Again, when anyone else in the police world sees this happening and looks the other way, they are grass eating.)

The Slippery Slope. Numerous authors in several different fields of deviance study have discussed the idea of the **"slippery slope"** (see Box 11.3). This idea suggests that when people begin to deviate, they do so in small, incremental ways. But once a person strays from norms and rules of conduct, he or she begins to slide down a slope that leads to greater, more pronounced forms of deviance. Thus, kids begin with shoplifting and then graduate to burglary and perhaps even armed robbery. Business people begin with phantom tax deductions and eventually bury large amounts of income in elaborate tax evasion schemes. And so it goes.

With regard to police officer misconduct, the slippery slope idea suggests that grass eating supports meat eating in two ways. First, some officers who first accept small gifts such as free coffee or free meals eventually will begin to normalize accepting more significant gifts such as money from drug dealers or pimps in exchange for allowing these people to violate the law. Especially in departments with a history of organized corruption schemes— and these departments still exist—where misconduct is rampant, the slippery slope idea suggests grass eating is the precursor to organized, systematic corruption. Thus, grass eating develops into meat eating.

A second way grass eating relates to meat eating is that, as discussed above, grass eating also can involve looking the other way when meat eating occurs. When officers are discovered to be involved in organized, systematized payoffs, grass-eating officers ignore it. For large-scale, organized payoffs to continue indefinitely, there usually must be a tacit acceptance of this behavior by officers who are not directly involved. Thus, even if grass eating does not create meat eating, it perpetuates it; grass eating by the many is necessary for meat eating by the few.

Thus, the slippery slope idea suggests small-scale graft is unacceptable because it cannot be differentiated from large-scale graft. While there certainly is a quantitative difference between a free cup of coffee and taking large amounts of money from drug dealers, the slippery slope idea posits that there is no qualitative difference.

BOX 11.3

CAN A "LITTLE BIT OF GRAFT" BE A GOOD THING?

In an era when community-based policing requires police officers to create permanent bonds with their communities, a number of strategies are being used to accomplish this task. One such tactic, suggested by authors such as Robert Kania, is for individual police officers to move closer to the people on their beats by accepting graft of the minor sort, such as free cups of coffee, free meals, or police discounts. The idea is that people and police officers will bond and feel closer to each other through this sort of personalized interaction.

Those who believe in the slippery slope idea of police misconduct are strongly opposed to this argument. They see the acceptance of such minor gratuities as grass eating, which will almost invariably lead to meat eating. Thus, some believe Kania's idea is a genuinely dangerous one for today's police officers. For them, there is no such thing as "minor" amounts of unethical behavior. They, being believers in ethical formalism, reject the utilitarian idea that some graft can be good.

There is another school of thought that cuts through the middle of this argument. Aristotle would say that such community-building, minor gratuities are acceptable if the officer(s) involved possess the good character not to consider such gifts as bribes. In other words, as long as officers treat those who give them free coffee appropriately, fairly, and without preference when they become involved with the police in legal situations, accepting such gifts is ethical and appropriate.

(Note: For a discussion of this debate about "acceptable levels of graft," see Joycelyn Pollock's *Ethics in Crime and Justice*, cited elsewhere herein.)

C. Noble Cause Corruption

To review, noble cause corruption involves police officers misusing their positions of authority but not for personal gain. Noble cause corruption presents a paradox for the student of police ethics because it involves behavior that appears to be unethical to those who view it from the outside but that is often considered ethical by participants. This type of paradox is not present in our previous two types of misconduct. While some police officers will succumb to the temptation to become involved in the corruption of authority or in police crime, it is clear those types of behavior are unethical.

But because of its very nature, noble cause corruption is accompanied by its own internal rationalization. Police officers who are involved in noble cause corruption are reluctant to acknowledge that it is unethical behavior because they believe it is necessary to get the job of policing done. They are involved, as the label states, in a noble cause, that of putting criminals behind bars or deterring criminal activity. Unlike those involved in police crime, for example, cops involved in noble cause corruption believe they are doing the right thing. This makes stopping such misconduct very difficult.

An additional problem with noble cause corruption is that the police can receive positive feedback from people in their communities when they engage in it. That is, citizens often want the police to get the job done at any cost. Police officers are told by people they see every day to "get the gangs out of our neighborhood," "get the guns off the streets," "keep drugs and drug dealers away from our kids," "lower the crime rate"—and "we don't care how you do it." Thus, unlike any other form of misconduct, noble cause corruption is often accompanied by a significant amount of community support.

D. Ineptitude

There are all sorts of transgressions against departmental regulations that are considered to be police misconduct but that involve neither personal gain nor the use of police authority on the part of erring cops. Such common violations as sleeping on duty, showing up habitually late, writing poor reports, failing to respond to calls, and ignoring orders make up this category. While these are sometimes serious violations, they are neither criminal nor corrupt in their nature. They are thus considered to be merely the products of **ineptitude.**

When police officers are guilty of ineptitude, they misbehave themselves, but they do so without obtaining personal gain and without abusing their position of authority. Ineptitude does not involve making decisions, conscious or unconscious, to engage in behavior that is unethical or appears to be unethical. Police officers who fail to do their duty because they are unintelligent, uneducated, not well trained, lazy, or unskilled have not chosen to misbehave in a way that would normally move an observer to label them as immoral.

But we must not go too far with the argument that ineptitude does not involve ethical decision making. We cannot make excuses for inept officers. The responsibility for inept behavior still resides in the individual ineffective officer. Being a competent police officer involves having the intelligence, education, motivation, and skill to get the job done and thus avoid ineptitude.

If an officer lacks any or all of these traits, he or she can (and should) be retrained, reeducated, or dismissed. An inept officer ought to be personally motivated to improve and also ought to be stimulated and encouraged by experienced leaders to change. Most techniques used for dealing with ineptitude involve proactive, "no-fault" strategies that bring change without impacting negatively upon an officer's career.

When the police fail to do their jobs because of ineptness, their conduct often carries with it no *intent* to misbehave. Thus, a discussion of the causes and potential solutions for ineptitude does not engage us in considerations of culpability or blame that might be attached to conscious decisions to misbehave. Ineptitude often occurs almost inadvertently, usually without malice. Attempts to limit ineptitude, then, do not involve the sort of moralizing that all of our previous discussions have undertaken.

E. Personal Misconduct

In this category belong sorts of personal (and sometimes even criminal) misconduct that reflect on an officer's image as a police officer but that have nothing to do with actual police officer performance on duty. Here we are talking about alcoholism, cohabitation, off-duty drunk driving, and so on. This category does not fit on our chart of types of misconduct because it does not directly relate to a person acting as a police officer.

President Clinton's approval ratings remained high even when he was impeached because people considered his misconduct to be "personal" and not a reflection of the job he was doing as president.

However, we should not make the mistake of thinking that police officer behavior off duty is unimportant. It has great significance in two ways. First, it may be of general relevance to the image of a police department. When a police officer cheats on his or her taxes, for example, it can have a tremendous negative effect on community confidence in the police. Thus, an officer found guilty of "conduct unbecoming an officer" can be disciplined even if the conduct has no

BOX 11.4

THE SKEPTIC AND THE GENERAL ORDERS

"Every time something goes wrong, they make a rule about it. All the directions in the force flow from someone's mistake. You can't go eight hours on the job without breaking the disciplinary code . . . no one cares until something goes wrong. The job goes wild on trivialities."

—New York City police officer (quoted by Kappeler, et al., op. cit.)

relation to anything he or she ever did on duty. This is because the perceptions of the public toward the police are critical to maintaining legitimacy in any police organization.

Second, the way in which a police officer behaves off duty is directly controlled by the kind of person that police officer is. That is, it relates to his or her character. Because of this, off-duty behavior is just as critical as on-duty behavior as an indicator of police ethics. One does not become a different person when one goes to work. Certainly we are all familiar with the idea that people change roles when they enter their job situations. But they do not change the basic nature of who they are, how they think, and how they moralize. This element of character is constant. Thus, this category is critical to our discussion.

BOX 11.5

PRESIDENTIAL MISCONDUCT

Recent political scandals involving various U.S. presidents help to illustrate the different types of misconduct we are discussing. It is interesting to remember these events and to reflect on how we tend to consider some of them "heinous" and some of them "forgivable" depending on our personal political views.

Corruption of Authority
In his last week as president, George H. W. Bush issued a pardon to everyone involved in the Iran/Contra scandal. In doing so, he excused several people from prosecution, one of whom was about to argue in court that he was ordered to commit crimes by both Presidents Reagan and Bush. Thus, Bush's blanket pardon saved his own skin. This is corruption of authority because Bush used his power as president for his own personal gain.

Noble Cause Corruption
When President Ronald Reagan allowed Oliver North to organize the delivery of arms to the Contras in Nicaragua, using drug dealers to accomplish this criminal task, Reagan was guilty of noble cause corruption. What Reagan did was illegal, but he did not personally profit from it. On the contrary, Reagan was convinced that these crimes were perpetrated "in the best interests" of America.

Criminal Behavior
When the Watergate scandal broke, it implicated President Richard Nixon in dozens of crimes and almost all of our types of misconduct. One thing the president did was steal leftover campaign funds to

(continued)

PRESIDENTIAL MISCONDUCT (*CONTINUED*)

buy expensive gifts for his wife. This is criminal behavior that did not relate to his official capacity as president. His office simply presented to him the opportunity to commit this crime.

Ineptitude

When President Jimmy Carter ran for reelection in 1980, voters held him accountable for what millions considered ineptitude—his inability to solve the Iranian hostage crisis and to return home more than 100 Americans being held hostage by the Iranians. This was a classic example, as determined by voters, of ineptitude that had to be rectified via the ballot box.

Personal Misconduct

When he was impeached and tried in the Senate, President Bill Clinton was accused of personal misconduct. The reason he was acquitted, and the reason his popularity soared during this time frame, was a majority of Americans believed his conduct to be improper but not a reflection of the job he was doing as president. His extramarital affair was considered by a large number of people to be personal misconduct.

There is no way to apply utilitarian ethics to misconduct that involves personal gain in an effort to rationalize it. Thus, when we view corruption of authority or police crime, we are prone to take a somewhat Kantian, absolutist viewpoint. No amount of special circumstances or rationalization can make these types of conduct appear to be ethical. As Kant might say, using a position of trust to obtain personal gain is wrong, not just some of the time but all of the time and in all circumstances.

Applying our ethic to live by, we conclude that corruption of authority and police crime involve violations of the primary duty of the police, the first rule by which they must abide in cleaving to the principle of beneficence—namely, to do no harm. When the police avoid this duty and act for personal gain, the community suffers and respect for the law is impaired.

But there is a problem with taking this absolute position. First, it ignores how and why such misconduct is sometimes generated among police officers—it tends to allow us to avoid studying its causes. Second, it ignores how these types of behaviors are rationalized after the fact. While it might seem to many that no amount of excuse making could make anyone accept this type of behavior as legitimate, this simply isn't so. Some police officers do, in fact, believe corruption of authority and/or police crime are understandable behaviors.

And because they are sometimes rationalized, corruption of authority and, to a lesser extent, police crime have always been problems associated with the police. While these two types of misconduct have lessened to a great extent in recent years, they are still with us. They constitute significant problems for police administrators, for honest police officers, and for the public in general.

Personal misconduct presents another problem. In considering personal misconduct, we must enter into an analysis of what part of a police officer's private life, if any, is the business of the police department, the community, and the state. This presents a thorny issue because we live in a society that values personal freedom highly. As American citizens, police officers have rights to privacy like anyone else. Yet because they occupy roles as representatives of the state, police officers have some limits placed on their freedom of activity, even when off duty. Precisely what those limits are and should be is at issue in this chapter.

All Americans possess certain constitutionally protected rights to privacy. When, if ever, are these individual rights denied to police officers? Under what circumstances does a police officer's off-duty, personal behavior become the business of the police department or the public? More specifically, when does a police officer's off-duty personal misconduct become something that is relevant to the job on duty?

There is no simple answer to the questions posed in Box 11.6. Off-duty, personal misbehavior can cease to be one's own business and can become the concern of police accountability systems and even the public in several ways. The analytical problem is that personal misconduct exists on a sort of sliding scale. Sometimes it becomes publicized and important; other times it remains private and unimportant. There are several levels of concern for us in our consideration of personal misconduct.

Off-Duty Crime. The first and most obvious example of personal misconduct of concern to us is police off-duty crime. When a police officer is arrested off duty for shoplifting, for example, this invariably makes headlines and becomes the business of police accountability systems. Because the police are licensed to arrest others for criminal behavior, such off-duty conduct is obviously not a personal matter, as it could arguably be with other professionals. If, for example, a doctor were to be guilty of income tax evasion, it would not necessarily follow that this misconduct impacts his or her ability to minister to people's sickness and injury. But because of the role the police perform, their off-duty crime cannot be ignored and cannot be treated as irrelevant, personal business.

When it becomes public knowledge due to the arrest of a police officer, police off-duty crime immediately becomes the concern of everyone who cares about police officer ethics. But sometimes such crime does not get publicized. This can happen because the local media help to keep things quiet. Or police officers can be involved in off-duty crime and not be caught. Or they might be caught and not arrested or prosecuted. While it might not be fair

BOX 11.6

What Is "Personal" and What Is "Professional" Behavior?

In 1998 and 1999, President Bill Clinton was embroiled in a scandal that eventually led to his impeachment. While he was acquitted of the charges leveled against him, the misconduct was taken seriously by his political enemies and by the mainstream media. The sensational story involved the president having a sexual affair with a young intern in the White House.

Throughout the nearly two years the scandal played out, opinion polls taken over and over again indicated a large majority of Americans did not care about it. Several pollsters interviewed people about this dynamic, and what these citizens said is important for our discussion here. It turns out that while most people thought the president's actions were disgusting or unacceptable, they saw such sexual behavior as an issue of "personal conduct" that did not disqualify Clinton from being president. While people did not like his actions, they said it was not the business of the country but a personal matter between the president and his family.

What do you think? What would you think if the transgressor were not president of the United States but a police officer? Would such marital infidelity disqualify a person from being a cop, or is it an issue of personal, private business?

to individual officers, a sliding scale exists wherein that which gets publicized must be treated seriously and that which does not can often be avoided. This is a practical reality of "how things work in the world" that may or may not be the way we would want them to work.

For the purposes of our discussion of police ethics, we must be concerned with all police off-duty crime. But for the reasons just suggested, we have to weigh the issue of the relative level of gravity of police off-duty crime. Are police officers who receive off-duty speeding tickets to be disciplined on the job? What about parking tickets? How much are we to be concerned with the ethical dilemma of officers arresting others for what they themselves have done if the crimes committed are petty and minor? Are we not expecting police officers to be saints if we consider every minor offense to be some sort of indication of their character—or lack of it?

One might be prone to answer this question by saying that infractions, crimes punishable only by fines and not imprisonment, should be excluded from our concern here. But what if a police officer develops a pronounced pattern of driving violations that indicate a lack of respect for the law?

Off-duty drunk driving is an example of personal misconduct that is job-related.

What if an officer obtains 20 moving violations or 100 parking tickets? Should we be concerned about such offenses, even though they are minor in a legal sense?

The answer is that there is no answer. There is no one way to analyze what sort of personal misconduct should be of concern to students of police ethics. The problem presents us with a sort of sliding scale. Police officer off-duty crime is of concern to us all the time if it is felonious and/or violent in nature, some of the time if it is of the misdemeanor type, and seldom if it is infraction related. Then too, any pattern of criminal behavior can be troublesome, no matter how minor the infractions involved.

Duty-Related Misconduct. A second way in which personal misconduct becomes the business of the department or the public is when, no matter how private it might be, the behavior can logically be said to impact directly upon the ability of the police officers to perform their duties. For example, when an officer is found to have an alcoholism problem, such a problem is arguably not the sort that can be left at home when the officer shows up for work. Alcoholism carries with it certain dynamics that cannot be divorced from the workaday life of a police officer. Alcoholics can suffer from withdrawal symptoms when denied their drug; they can have functional problems relating to decision making and motor skills; and they can be prone to pursue drinking ("just one drink" is often rationalized) when working.

Thus, we have suggested alcoholism is a personal problem that has such far-reaching ramifications it cannot be ignored by anyone who seeks to evaluate the character of an alcoholic officer. A similar argument can be made with respect to officers who are involved in domestic abuse, marital infidelity, drug problems, and violence of any kind in their off-duty lives. While any and all of these types of problems can become legal issues, that is to say criminal in their nature, often they don't. Often the drug user is not caught, the domestic abuser is not arrested, the bar fighter is not prosecuted, and so on.

When these dynamics present themselves in the lives of average citizens, civilians are often left alone by the criminal justice system. We argue here that when such problems come to light in the lives of police officers, whether or not they become criminal in their nature is irrelevant. Such behavior cannot remain private because of how directly it relates to the abilities of the officers to perform their duties on the job. Thus, we are suggesting that officers who have such problems receive the type of counseling and rehabilitation that is necessary to diminish if not solve these difficulties. We are also saying that no amount of rationalizing can divorce these types of personal problems from an evaluation of the officer's on-the-job competence and ethical perspective.

11-3 ◉ SUMMARY

Our very first discussion here was about how we aimed to construct a book that approached police ethics from the ground up. We noted that traditional police training in ethics was not only lacking in terms of the lack of time spent but also in the sense that it was negative in its approach. Our idea was to talk about being a good person and good police officer first. It has taken us until now to engage the sort of negative side of things that we planned to avoid. It might seem that we have gone back on our word and changed our approach, but this is not the case.

In this chapter, we have approached a subject that is of critical importance, even though it might be negative. We have outlined a typology of police misconduct. We have noted that police misconduct comes in various, critically different forms. Furthermore, police deviance has multiple and diverse causes. In subsequent discussions regarding what to do about them, these differences in types of malpractice will be of paramount importance.

11-4 ◉ TOPICS FOR DISCUSSION

1. As is true of the various roles of the police, there are multiple, conflicting, and vague sets of standards to which they must answer. Discuss how legality and democracy in particular can conflict. What are examples of how the requirement that everything the police do be legal conflict with the contemporary, COP-driven idea that the police must be responsive to their communities?

2. When people discuss police misconduct, they have historically confused several types. In particular, people lump together corruption of authority and police (or professional) crime. What is the difference? What are examples of each?

3. Discuss the nexus between noble cause corruption and grass eating. Why is it that noble cause corruption is so difficult to deter and investigate today? What do the authors mean when they say that while meat eating is gone in most places, grass eating is alive and well?

4. Discuss the fact that personal misconduct might or might not be "the police department's business." What is it that might make an otherwise private behavior pattern into something that is relevant to the chief of police and the department?

11-5 ⊙ ETHICAL SCENARIO

Our discussion makes the point that police officers are both political and legal actors. One problem subsumed under this reality is that people will sometimes ask the police to do things that are illegal and, thus, request that they prioritize being politically responsive over being legally accountable. What would you do when the good, honest, hard-working members of a neighborhood ask you to "do whatever's necessary" to get the local gang off the streets? How might you be moved to act in "semi-legal" or "quasi-legal" ways? Would you actually be moved to act in illegal ways? If so, how would you rationalize being a criminal? If not, how would you deal with the good people who are asking you to do illegal things in the name of achieving the morally defensible end of cleaning up their streets?

11-6 ⊙ WRITING EXERCISE

Construct an essay that discusses the five types of police misconduct. Explicate how the typology differentiates between them. Then discuss why it is that for all of the discussion about internal affairs systems and civilian review boards, the overwhelming majority of allegations of police misconduct are generated internally and handled internally and informally. (Hint: This is about focusing upon the general orders and ineptitude.)

11-7 ⊙ KEY TERMS

corruption of authority: Police misconduct involving personal gain on the part of errant police officers and the misuse of an officer's official power.

general order manuals: Books filled with internal regulations that are constructed by all police and sheriff's departments.

graft: Acquisition of money, goods, or services through dishonesty and involving taking advantage of one's official position.

grass eating: Form of police misconduct that involves the acceptance of non-systematic graft or the covering up of more serious corruption.

ineptitude: Type of police misconduct that has to do with incompetence, sloth, and/or a lack of training.

meat eating: Serious form of police corruption involving ongoing payoffs or graft.

personal misconduct: Police deviance that is off duty and, thus, may or may not become the subject of internal, departmental investigation and sanctioning.

police crime: Form of police misconduct involving personal gain, but not related to the official authority of the police.

police deviance: Police behavior that goes against either legal or professional standards of conduct or against input obtained from the community under COP.

shakedowns: Element of corruption of authority involving the police proactively obtaining money from citizens in exchange for avoiding the performance of their official charge.

slippery slope: The idea that misconduct can begin with small types of misbehavior and then, incrementally, expand and change into major corruption.

streetcorner politicians: Muir's label for police officers; refers to their exercise of power over citizens.

CHAPTER 12

The Causes of Police Misconduct

Chapter Outline

> *"It is better to let one hundred guilty men go free than it is to convict an innocent man."*
>
> —American legal axiom

Just as there are several different sorts of police misconduct so too are there several sorts of causes. Because this is so, our discussions must take cognizance of different solutions, both proactive and reactive. Police accountability is about hiring individuals who have the sort of character capable of withstanding and ignoring the opportunities to misbehave experienced by all police officers at one time or another. It is about academy and in-service training that instills an internalized ethic that drives police officers to do good works. It is about police leadership that is effective at motivating police officers to behave themselves proactively, motivating them to learn from their mistakes reactively, and not sanctioning egregious police behavior.

Some police misconduct is the product of greed combined with opportunity or chance that causes people in general to deviate from society norms and laws. Some is produced of multiple frustrations experienced by individual officers that sometimes comes together and eventuates in the creation of Dirty Harry. Some is created by subcultural pressures and abnormal covenants that drive and rationalize police deviance. And some is the fruit of dynamics that are a part of the fabric of American society as a whole.

Of course, police administrators can do something about some of this. But they are nevertheless limited in their impact upon it. In the first instance, the character of individual officers is controlling in most regards and that was formed long before anyone was sworn in as a police officer. Then too, the police subculture is one of the most isolated professional groups in the world. It is known throughout the field of sociology for its solidarity. Having an impact upon causes that come from within this subculture is limited. Finally, those forms of misconduct that are produced by impetuses that are society-wide are completely out of the influence of police leaders.

We are left with the individual police officer and his or her character as the driving, mitigating force that creates (or does not create) behavior patterns that can mitigate against deviance.

12-1 ● GENERIC DEVIANCE

Students of criminology present a multitude of causes for deviant behavior. They tell us that crime is caused by rational choice, of course; this involves people choosing to be deviant after calculating the chances of being caught, the potential rewards, and so on. We will come back to this theory in a moment, for it is one of the few criminological theories that sometimes apply to police deviance. But **rational choice theory** is only one of many notions of crime causation.

Crime is also caused by behavior patterns learned as one grows up. People's nurturing environment will sometimes cause them to witness or to learn

BOX 12.1

THE POLITICS OF CRIME CAUSATION

In today's world of media-driven political campaign reporting, the "nine-second sound bite" is about all the time that candidates have to discuss issues. Thus, political debate becomes more and more simplistic over time. In the field of crime and what to do about it, politicos tend to suggest that crime has one and only one cause: bad people choosing to behave badly. Therefore, more prisons and a get-tough-on-crime attitude are the solutions required. This is almost universal.

The irony for our discussion of police deviance is that while most of the other multiple causes of crime are ignored by such simplistic speechifying, in favor of the personal choice idea, it is exactly personal choice that is almost universally the culprit with respect to police deviance.

criminal behavior patterns. Crime is caused by ineffective and disorganized social institutions, culturally transmitted deviance, or **deviant subcultures.** Some people are improperly socialized, develop **antisocial personalities,** or become genuinely **sociopathic.** Some crime is caused by the social structure that surrounds the individual. Factors such as poverty, racism, and overt class prejudice can tend to lead to crime caused by economic or other forms of discrimination. Crime is caused by biological factors such as biochemical imbalances in the brain, hormonal abnormalities, or environmental contaminants. Crime is caused by genetic propensity, neurological abnormalities, bipolar disorders, or early alcohol intake. Some theorists suggest that crime is caused by the strain (**strain theory**) that occurs when people reject either their society's culturally constructed goals or institutionally prescribed methods of obtaining those goals.

Others suggest that the struggle between the economic classes creates substantial strain that leads to crime. The poor want to be more affluent and comfortable. The struggle to obtain that comfort causes some crime. And when the economic distance or gap between the very poor and the extremely rich (society's **stratification**) is great, the amount of crime that occurs can be significant. In today's America, this gap is greater than in any other developed nation on earth. Therefore, the American police experience a type of crime that other police (again, in developed or industrialized nations) do not. This explanation for crime is called **conflict theory.**

Crime causation theories abound, and it seems that each decade brings us another one. For the purposes of our discussion, it is important to think

© emin kuljyev/Shutterstock.com

Unfortunately, the level of stratification in American society is greater than it is in any other industrialized nation.

about what types of causes might work to create police deviance. Police officers almost never suffer from any of the biochemical-related causes mentioned or from those nature-oriented causes relating to genetic make-up and so on. This is because modern selection processes are quite effective at removing candidates with those limitations. Because of their socioeconomic status, educational backgrounds, and political roots, police officers avoid most of the nurture-related causes of deviance. They are middle-class individuals of above average intelligence who are selected due to their education, stable roots, clean backgrounds, and physical fitness. They therefore suffer from neither the nature-related nor the nurture-related causal factors that can cause deviance in civilians.

However, the sort of crime that sometimes develops when greed meets opportunity or chance, referred to above as rational choice theory, *can* be a problem in police circles.

A. Greed, Opportunity, and Chance

Crime is the product of the greed of individuals combined with opportunities presented by life's circumstances. While we could take time here to discuss a number of theories about the causes of crime, we will stick to a consideration of **greed and opportunity** because they are central to the problems of police corruption of authority and police crime.

People possess a natural tendency to want to enhance their personal financial situations and that of their families. This propensity is in all of us, and it is not necessarily a bad thing. It is the dynamic that drives capitalism. The capitalistic system expects everyone to behave in a (somewhat) greedy fashion. In such an economy, all citizens attempt to further their own financial situations by competing in the open marketplace. To do this, they attempt to work harder, produce more goods, provide better services, create more significant innovations, or invent better products than their competitors. When they are successful and "win," people make more money and have (arguably) better lives than those whom they "defeat" in this competition.

Thus, when channeled in this positive way, greed works to make life better for individuals, for their families, and for the general public. In the larger scheme of things, this type of capitalistic greed produces a better life for almost everyone. It provides the motivation that drives the American economic engine that has been the envy of the world for generations.

In police officers, too, greed can be a good, positive force. To further their own positions in life, police officers may be moved to seek assignments that are difficult and dangerous, obtain positions that involve increased responsibilities, get promoted, and generally do good works and a competent job to obtain increased status and/or income. Not only is there nothing wrong with this, but it also presents to us the best example of how the capitalistic, competitive spirit can be applied to police work. Our ethic to live by might suggest that doing good, with personal greed as the rationale, is still doing good.

But when people's individual greed moves them to break the rules, to circumvent the law, and to take unfair advantage of others, it becomes a form of deviance. In the police officer, this type of deviance is particularly troublesome because it involves the abuse of the position of authority into which the criminal justice system has placed the cop on the beat. The duty of police officers is, quite clearly, to perform their many tasks and multiple roles in the interests of justice and with an eye to providing services and protection to all of society's members. When this duty is convoluted and ignored in favor of personal gain, the interests of justice are at risk.

So greed can be bad or good, depending on the character of the individual. In people who are prone to want more no matter what it takes, and who are thus prone to cheat, lie, and take shortcuts, greed is bad. It moves them to ignore their duties as police officers, citizens, fathers, mothers, and so on in favor of furthering their own situations, financial, political, or other.

When people who possess this type of character flaw are confronted with the opportunity to obtain personal gain at the expense of others, they may be prone to commit all sorts of criminal acts. Such people may cheat on their taxes, calculating that the IRS will probably not investigate their phantom deductions. They may pad a theft insurance claim, calculating that there is no way for anyone to know what specifically was stolen. Or they may take the opportunity at work to skim some money from the till, knowing that no one else is watching.

Police officers are often presented with such opportunities. The police occupy a position of trust. More often than most people, police officers are in a position to abuse that trust if they possess the type of character that moves them to do so. With regard to the corruption of authority, the police often interact with criminals—especially those involved in victimless crimes such as drug trafficking, gambling, and prostitution—who will offer to reimburse the police if they look the other way. There is so much profit involved in such types of crimes that the pressure to sell the badge by not making arrests in exchange for money is great.

But the police also have opportunities presented to them that do not involve selling their positions of authority for personal gain. At night, operating largely alone, police officers will learn which businesses are vulnerable to theft, which doors are left open, which establishments have a lot of cash on hand, and so on. When thefts occur, police officers are often presented with the opportunity to skim some money or goods before anyone else arrives at a crime scene. This, as opposed to the corruption of authority, is police crime.

The opportunities presented to the police are so great as to almost guarantee that some police officers will take advantage of them. Those who possess a certain limited understanding of their roles, of the importance of police ethics, and of the nature of professionalism will exhibit their personal character flaws in this way. They will become involved in corruption of authority and/or in police crime.

Thus, greed—which is present in all people and all police officers—will meet with opportunity—which is presented to police officers in a way that it is not often presented to civilians—to produce the tendency toward these types of misconduct. Given how much of police work is done alone and unobserved, personal character (as we have argued all along) is the one and only hedge the police officer can possess that mitigates falling into such misconduct.

B. Rationalizations

Rationalizations for police misconduct can be very similar to the **rationalization techniques** criminals use to neutralize their deviant acts. Individual officers, or small groups of them, neutralize feelings of guilt over deviant behavior using five distinctive techniques. Studying deviance in 1957, authors Gary Sykes and David Matza suggested there are several ways people can rationalize their misbehavior and avoid the normally negative self-image that goes with it. Since that time, several authors (including Kappeler et al. in Table 12.1) have applied this idea to misbehaving police officers. We will briefly review these techniques here.

First, police officers can deny they are responsible for their own actions. They can view their acts as predetermined by people, events, and situations they cannot influence. Thus, well-meaning citizens, liberal judges, the thoughtless press, "spoiled brat" intellectuals, the due process system, and a host of other people and institutions are responsible for somehow requiring the police to misbehave. An example might be the officer who takes police discounts because "the store owner would be offended if I didn't."

Using a second technique for neutralizing deviance, police officers can deny their misbehavior caused any injury. Much like citizens who rationalize cheating on their income taxes or defrauding wealthy insurance companies, police officers can tell themselves no one was really hurt by their deviance. An example might be officers who take merchandise from a burglary site rationalizing "no one gets hurt" by it.

The third technique of neutralization involves the denial of the victim. Because of the character of the victim of police misconduct, it is possible to

TABLE 12.1

◉ POLICE TECHNIQUES OF NEUTRALIZING DEVIANCE		
NEUTRALIZATION TECHNIQUE	**VERBALIZATION**	**POLICE CONTEXT**
Denial of responsibility	"They made me do it."	Citizens offer graft and the police officer takes it to be the norm.
Denial of injury	"No innocents got hurt."	Police take money from drug dealers and not honest citizens.
Denial of victim	"They deserved it."	Police thefts occur because business owners are not careful.
Condemning the condemners	"They don't know anything."	Police rejection of legal and department control and sanction of deviant behavior.
Appeal to higher loyalty	"Protect your own."	Police perjury to protect another officer.

Source: Victor E. Kappeler, Richard D. Sluder, and Geoffrey P. Alpert, *Forces of Deviance,* 2nd ed. (Longrove, IL: Waveland Press, 1998), op. cit., p. 114.

deny there was any misconduct. If the people "ripped off" are drug dealers, violent gang members, or criminals of some other type, they do not have the right to status as victims.

Fourth, errant police officers may condemn the condemners. Here, police officers may accuse those who accuse them of misconduct. Lawyers from civil liberties groups, the investigators in internal affairs, or judges who scrupulously attack corrupt police officers are all at fault. This technique shifts responsibility away from the misbehaving officers toward others.

Finally, the deviant police officer may appeal to higher loyalties. By protecting other deviant officers, by going along with corruption schemes, or by interfering with investigations into police misconduct, police officers may feel they are supporting their fellow officers and the subculture in general. In doing so, they invoke a loyalty and a duty that circumvent their duty to the law and to the community.

In these ways, erring police officers rationalize their misbehavior and avoid dealing with what we have called the duty to be beneficent. They do harm to others (in the form of meat eating or committing police crime) or they fail to remove harm (in the form of grass eating). Because it has been studied by many criminologist and psychologists, we might acknowledge that such rationalizing is understandable in some sense. But just as we are prone to deny criminals their rationalizations, we can and must acknowledge police crime and corruption of authority exhibit character flaws that cannot be tolerated in the competent, professional officer.

12-2 ● SUBCULTURAL CAUSES

Those who study what is referred to as the police subculture often speak as if there is only one type of subculture associated with police work. However, this is a simplistic idea. There are as many different types of police subcultures as there are different types of police departments. And the differences in the dynamics that operate within these subcultures are particularly pronounced when related to police misconduct.

In some jurisdictions, the police subculture is a loosely knit group of men and women who merely happen to be co-workers in the same occupation. Officers share a perspective about life on the beat, about their roles and duties, and about police professionalism and competence. Police misconduct is seen as a problem for every officer because it impacts the respect citizens hold for the police. Furthermore, when police misconduct of the personal gain type is investigated, cooperation is obtained from the overwhelming majority of police officers.

In other jurisdictions—happily a steadily decreasing number of police organizations—personal gain–oriented misconduct is normalized and at least tacitly accepted throughout the subculture. Fighting such misconduct becomes extremely difficult because attempts to hold errant officers accountable are opposed, even by those who do not participate in the misconduct. Cleaving to what many authors call the "blue code of silence," even would-be honest officers who know about corruption of authority and/or police crime often do not cooperate in its investigation. Such reluctance by grass eaters to help with the pursuit of systematic misconduct can effectively guarantee meat eaters will cover up their misconduct and pursue it on a continuous basis.

Again, this sort of personal gain–oriented misconduct harkens back to an earlier age and it is gone today from most organizations in most jurisdictions. Even where it exists, corruption of authority and police crime are rarely supported by the modern subculture. But having said this, misconduct of several types still exists today. In no particular order, we will briefly discuss several subcultural dynamics that tend to create misconduct or an atmosphere within which it can flourish. First, there is the overkill dynamic described in Box 12.2. Driven by what is at least an implicit understanding of Muir's paradoxes, police officers tend to rationalize the use of excessive force on some occasions.

Second, even though we have already discussed noble cause corruption at length, it is apposite here. The Dirty Harry problem is supported by far too many members of the police subculture. The noble cause of getting the job done being the central rationalization in support of Harry, it is troublesome

BOX 12.2

OVERKILL

Recall Muir's paradox of face, which suggests that "the nastier one's reputation, the less nasty one has to be." Whether or not they have read Muir, the police officers of America understand this concept intuitively. And because they do, there is substantial subcultural support for what is called the idea of "overkill" with regard to the use of force.

Overkill suggests that even though the police are very seldom challenged physically on the street (assaulted), when they *are* they must "win and win big." Police officers understand that it is important to send out the message that citizens should not "mess with" or "try" the local police. So the locker room axiom is "If someone hits one of us, they go to jail. If they hurt one of us, they go to the hospital." Thus, overkill is nothing other than a confirmation of Muir's principle.

that in today's ever more professional world of policing this type of misconduct still exists. It not only exists, but it is the centrally most troublesome type of misconduct today.

Third, all the frustrations of the job come together to create a subculture that is well known for its solidarity; police officers construct a Fort Apache around themselves. As noted earlier, the Fort Apache syndrome works in a cyclical fashion to take individuals who are already a tightly knit group and galvanize them into a fortified "us against them" dynamic. Clearly, such a dynamic not only can be a causal factor in creating police misconduct in the first place, it can also work to rationalize and keep misconduct from being discovered after the fact.

Fourth, there is a troublesome dynamic that harkens back to the days when the police were first distanced from the citizenry. When the reform era came along, the police—formerly closely woven into their communities as integral members—were divorced from their day-to-day, physically intimate relationship with the populace. The walking beat and the long-term relationship with people in one neighborhood were replaced with rotating beats and the squad car. As this occurred, the police necessarily and purposefully became distant. The change was purposeful because it was done in an effort to remove the temptation and/or ability to generate long-term systems of corrupt payoffs.

As the police became more distant, a new informal norm began to emerge. The more removed police began to believe in the type of Fort Apache, "us against them" isolation from the populace and to behave in concert with another axiom unheard of before that time. Today, **"never explain, never apologize"** is the subcultural wisdom. It suggests that it is neither necessary nor wise to explain anything to the citizenry. Furthermore, it posits that to apologize, even for genuine misdeeds, is to show weakness. Instead of taking advantage of the potentiality of creating a closer bond with the public that explanation can afford, the police will almost universally avoid such deferential behavior. This tends to underwrite the potential for the sort of misconduct that is produced by a distant cynicism about the public. It also supports the blue code of silence in a way that can work to sustain rationalizations for misconduct and inhibit the attempts of review systems, both informal and institutionalized, to hold the police accountable for their actions.

12-3 ● AMERICAN SOCIETAL DYNAMICS

Several dynamics are endemic to contemporary American society that help to create an atmosphere within which misconduct can flourish or, at the very least, that can rationalize its concealment. The first has to do with the level of crime and violence that exists in the streets of America. The United States is the most violent and dangerous society in all of the industrialized world. Crime statistics here outstrip those of any other developed nation, and by quite a large margin. Violence and guns in particular are in evidence in numbers that would (and sometimes do) shock the rest of the world. And because this is true, the American police are the most violent police in the developed world. This is axiomatic. Because they must exercise enough force to over come the use of illegal force, and because the use of illegal force is greater here than elsewhere, the American police end up using what would elsewhere be considered excessive force on a regular basis.

A second dynamic has to do with the degree of stratification present in the United States. We noted in Chapter 10 that the distance between the very rich and the very poor in America is greater than in any other industrialized country. We noted this for the purposes of our analysis of how the police function is complicated by judgment calls that must be made when the interests of these wildly disparate classes conflict. Here we are suggesting that some police misconduct will be created due to the necessity of the police to referee the conflict between American classes. This is so because the

© kilukilu/Shutterstock.com

Crime statistics in the United States, especially for violent and gun-related crimes, outstrip those of any other developed nation.

BOX 12.3

THE DEMOCRATIC NATURE OF POLICE WORK

For American citizens to afford themselves of the benefits of governmental action it can sometimes take a certain amount of status, expertise, influence, or money. No matter how much time is spent on discussing the "free" nature of governmental services, this is always true. Not everyone can put the government or its agents into motion.

Except for the police. A citizen need not have any money (they can call 911 on a public phone) or even leave their name (they can report crime anonymously) and the police will go flying into the night. Armed agents of the state will spring into action under any and all such circumstances. Thus, in an odd way, the police represent the most democratic of all American institutions.

police must interact with members of the underclass in an adversarial relationship on a regular basis. And this adversity will be greater than that present in any other advanced nation.

Finally, some police misconduct will be created due to what some contemporary political scientists refer to as the "semi-democratic" nature of American society. There is no doubt that in today's America, the idea that "the people" control public policy has been replaced by the more realistic idea that corporate dollars—by the billions—control policy most of the time. Specifically with reference to public laws that regulate industry, corporations control American public policy directly. However, this does not mean the people have nothing to say about what goes on in government. In the case of the police, corporations do not often attempt to control them directly. In the long run, the people of America "get the policing they want." As we have noted, a large number of those people support Dirty Harry behavior. When they viewed the Rodney King beating, millions of Americans said, "So what?" Since that is true, some of the excesses of the American police can be directly linked to the desires of the American public to have forceful policing done in our streets.

12-4 ● CAUSAL SPECIFICITY

Aside from the generic causes that we have considered here so far, the reasons for the generation of some police deviance are specific to the type of misconduct involved. For a moment then, we will discuss a couple of types of deviance and reflect upon their particular causes.

A. Dirty Harry Again

It has been almost twenty years since Carl Klockars discussed "the Dirty Harry problem" and engaged everyone in American police work with the idea that noble cause corruption was rampant and that it presented a tremendous problem for the rule of law. In a troublesome way, noble cause corruption presents

BOX 12.4

THE "EFFECTIVENESS" OF NOBLE CAUSE CORRUPTION

Several years ago, in a police jurisdiction on the West Coast, the officers who policed a high-crime area found they had a major problem with daylight burglaries on their beat. Through informants, they learned a significant amount of this burglary was being committed by a convicted burglar who had served hard time in the state penitentiary. This particular criminal was a very good burglar, in the sense that he was smart and could not be caught in the act. Thus, even though they knew he was a professional burglar and the victimizer of dozens of people on their beat, the police could not catch him.

The officers became even more frustrated when, on one occasion, the suspect was caught in the act and arrested, only to be turned loose because of a legal technicality. The arresting officers had conducted an illegal search of this suspect's car, and the evidence obtained was excluded (thrown out) in court.

Ignoring the suspect's constitutional rights, the officers began to stop him, on foot or when driving, every time they saw him. They conducted illegal searches of his car and ran records and warrants checks on a daily, sometimes hourly, basis. They generally harassed the man, taking up hours of his time and writing citations for the most questionable of infractions. He was finally given six months in the county jail for driving with a suspended license. When his six months were over and he was let out, he left the area, never to be heard from again.

These officers, following their noble cause or answering to a higher duty than they considered the Constitution to present, had succeeded in removing a threat to the people of their community. Burglaries went down substantially, and the people on the beat were happy. Thus, noble cause corruption, in the form of harassment, had worked to do a job the criminal justice system could not accomplish legally.

us with this dilemma: It appears that in behaving like Dirty Harry, police officers cleave to the duty of beneficence. That is, in breaking the procedural rules of the criminal justice game, police officers are doing good. They are removing evil people from the streets. They are deterring criminals. And because of this view, noble cause corruption is by far the hardest form of police misconduct to deter.

It takes a firm commitment to the rule of law and a solid personal resolve to live by the dictates of the due process system for a police officer to avoid such behavior and do the job in a legally and ethically defensible way. In other words, avoiding the Dirty Harry syndrome takes character. Furthermore, it involves cleaving to the second principle of our ethic to live by: It takes acknowledging that justice must be served and that it must be equally served to those we consider to be deviants.

What is wrong with using harassment, physical intimidation, excessive force, or "testilying" (to name only a few examples of noble cause corruption) if they get the job done? If it works to deter crime and to put away criminals—and if the deterrent impact of the criminal justice system doesn't work—then why not clean up the streets the way Dirty Harry did? The answer is that breaking procedural rules and thus becoming a lawbreaker involves the police officer in doing harm (the promotion of evil). Noble cause corruption substitutes police intuition (which may or may not

BOX 12.5

THE FRAMING OF RUBIN "HURRICANE" CARTER

Rubin "Hurricane" Carter, a black world boxing champion in the 1960s, had a troubled youth that included being arrested on several occasions. Despite a clean and honorable record of military service, he was hounded throughout his life by a New Jersey prosecutor who "knew" he was a bad person.

On one particular night when unknown suspects committed a murder in Carter's town, this prosecutor proceeded to manipulate witnesses and evidence in a way that put Carter behind bars for a crime that he did not commit. It took 20 years of Carter's life for him to be finally acquitted and given his freedom.

This was an example of the extent to which Dirty Harry–type thinking can create injustice. The local prosecutor, certain in his mind that Carter was a bad person and that he deserved to be behind bars, ruined this man's life in the name of doing good for the community.

©Everett Collection Inc / Alamy

Rubin "Hurricane" Carter, shown here in 1964, spent much of his adult life in prison having been framed by Dirty Harry-like prosecutors and police officers for a crime he did not commit.

be correct) for legal, fair, equitable rules of procedure. When this happens, the police may be effective in deterring crime, but they may also become involved in creating crime. In this way, the police both do harm and fail to distribute justice.

When the police misbehave in this way, it takes away the entire rational base upon which the criminal justice system rests. In a free society we should be particularly concerned that no innocent people be punished. We take great pains to attempt to ensure this. Only the guilty are supposed to be punished, and they are supposed to be punished only when they deviate. When the agents of the system misbehave and are not punished—in fact, in the case of noble cause corruption, they insist their deviance is ethical—then the rationale for the system punishing anyone is lost.

B. Ineptitude

Ineptitude is often the product of inadvertent incompetence. When this is the case, police leaders can and should treat ineptitude in a positive, counseling-and-training mode. Thus, when officers write poor reports, they can be required to receive training in this area. When officers sleep on duty, motivation to cease this behavior can come from effective leadership. Many if not most inept officers, motivated by knowledgeable police leaders, can change their inept behavior in a way that it ceases to be a problem in the future.

On the other hand, inept behavior is sometimes the product of problems that simply cannot be overcome. The lack of skills, knowledge, and perspective involved in some ineptitude is terminal in a sense. When officers are guilty of racism due to their personal beliefs about racial superiority, for example, they may have to be terminated. When officers are simply not intelligent enough to understand the nuances of the law, they may not be retrainable. And most importantly, when officers cannot or will not change themselves, when they do not respond to positive discipline in the forms suggested above, the system may eventually have to "give up" and dismiss the erring cops. Such problems involve character defects that sometimes simply cannot be corrected. Thus, not all ineptitude is solvable and not all positive, motivational approaches to dealing with incompetence in a non-threatening way will work. Police officer ineptitude is the product of several factors that can occur individually or in combination.

BOX 12.6

THE POSITIVE POWER OF TRAINING AND RETRAINING

"The secret of the chief's success in moral matters was in his use of the policemen's appetite for understanding. He extended the duration of the academy course for recruits . . . he created a series of courses for sergeants, lieutenants, jailers, communications dispatchers, the vice squad, personnel interviewers, advanced officers, and field training officers. In batches of twenty men, [the] Training [Division] incessantly conducted introductory and two-week refresher courses. Discussions, problem sets, simulation, and lectures: The techniques were always changing, but the education never ceased.

"The process was important and was established—argument, exchange of experience, openness, the whetting of the appetite for ideas, the recognition of problems, and the time for detached reflection. Training was the administration's successful attempt to respond to the moral matters in men's hearts. Training dealt as much with the moral as with the intellectual perplexities of being a policeman. Without a feeling that the world mattered, policemen often surrendered to the worst effects of the paradoxes of power. The Training Division, however, provided the motives, the tools, the stimulation, and the sanctuary busy men needed to get perspective on their lives, to redefine purposes, to challenge old assumptions, and to become morally creative. The effect was profound."

—William K. Muir, Jr., *Police: Streetcorner Politicians*

Some ineptitude is the result of poor selection processes. Some people who are hired to be police officers simply are not capable of doing the job. They lack the requisite skills, personal commitment to hard work, and integrity to be good officers. In short, they lack the character necessary to get the job done. If this is the case, then we can hardly expect positive change and we can hardly require such individuals to become the competent professionals that we desire and that the job requires. The only thing individuals who are inept can do under such circumstances—and this is hard to expect of anyone—is to accept their limitations and remove themselves from police work.

Some ineptitude is the product of poor training. Under such circumstances, police officers who possess the requisite skills to accomplish their multiple tasks in the field have simply not been given the education necessary to do so. While it is again difficult to expect this level of self-analysis from any person, such officers must be able to see their shortcomings and have the character to seek training and help to improve. As discussed in depth in our discussions about character, taking a self-critical view of one's personal abilities as a professional may be extremely difficult. But such introspection is an important part of personal character. The intelligent person realizes and deals honestly with his or her shortcomings. It is critical that those entrusted with the powers and responsibilities of being police officers possess this ability to be self-critical and to acknowledge that no one "knows it all." Seeking additional training to erase personal deficiencies can only occur if a person is willing to understand that the job of becoming a competent officer involves an ongoing commitment to grow as a good person.

Some ineptitude is the product of laziness. Police officers, like those involved in any occupation, sometimes become bored and unmotivated. Police work is a profession that is particularly prone to produce **burn-out**. It is always difficult to avoid the natural tendency to take it easy. Guided by leaders who are committed to teach and to motivate such officers, individuals who fail to get the job done due to slothfulness must recommit themselves to doing their best for their communities. This may, again, seem like asking for the impossible. But becoming complacent, then recommitting, and then becoming complacent again is a cycle into which many people fall in most professions at one time or another. The good news is that it is part of human nature, in the good person, to reinvigorate oneself on an ongoing basis. Again, it is a matter of having good character that a person sees this propensity and takes action accordingly.

C. The Special Case of Excessive Force

The troublesome nature of the problem of excessive force is that it is has multiple causes. First, Dirty Harry might use force in an illegal way to obtain information. As is always the case with Harry, this is done to get the job done, of course. And thus, in some strange way, its perpetrators believe that it is done with "good intentions."

Second, some excessive force is the product of ineptitude. This can take the form of the ever-present and always troublesome American problem of racism. There are societies in the world that are multicultural and multiracial that do a good job of maintaining a stable, working, civil, and even positive relationship between different races and ethnic groups. But unfortunately, America is not one of them. Or, to be fair, America is not one of the most successful nations in this regard. We have contemporary racial problems that are driven by the remnants of slavery and, in a later incarnation, the civil rights movement. This sort of misconduct, of course, is not to be tolerated. Given that people are "hard wired" in the first few years of life, it is hard to imagine that officers found guilty of racism on the job can be rehabilitated or changed.

Another type of excessive force driven by ineptitude has to do with poor training. Today's officer is trained in several forms of physical restraint and self-defense. This type is, to some extent, easily surmounted. Additional training can be obtained and officers who have used too much force by failing to

BOX 12.7

There Is No Such Thing as "Excessive" Force

In 1982, the famous criminologist Carl Klockars wrote perhaps the most important article ever written about the police use of force. He suggested that there really was no definition of how much force is "necessary" (and proper/legal) and, therefore, there is no definition of "excessive." And because that is true, he reasoned that police training and discussion about force is a waste of time. In discussing the application of force, we merely talk about how officers should be circumspect about it. Until some sort of definition is created, it is all nonsense.

use appropriate techniques can have their on-the-street behavior changed in a positive direction.

Finally, an additional cause of inappropriate force utilization can be related to corruption of authority and/or police crime. In using force, sometimes officers are, in essence, protecting business. Force can be used to protect those involved in nefarious enterprises with whom the police are in association. Such behavior can intimidate would-be competitors of the partners of the corrupt police. When this occurs, of course, we are talking about corruption of authority. But the police sometimes are in business for themselves, using opportunities presented to them by their positions, but not abusing their legal authority. When force is used under these circumstances, it is police crime–related.

Taken together, the multiple causes of excessive force present a complex and troublesome problem for police leaders and for all students of police ethics.

12-5 ◉ SUMMARY

We began here with a brief consideration of the fact that some police misconduct is caused by the same sorts of greed and opportunity that causes some citizen deviance. Personal choice theory suggests that sometimes people simply opt to misbehave having considered the potential rewards and punishments involved. Then we treated a multiplicity of causes, some of which related to the police subculture and some to America's dominant culture. Finally, we considered the particularly thorny issue of police excessive force. Here, our discussion implied that multiple causes can confuse anyone interested in holding the police accountable.

Now we turn to discuss what to do about police misconduct. Whether it be through administrative venues involving who is hired and how they are trained, or through informal behavior control dynamics, or through intelligent police leadership, or through the machinations of police review systems, police misconduct can be dealt with after the fact in numerous, effective ways.

12-6 ◉ TOPICS FOR DISCUSSION

1. Consider the numerous types of opportunities to misbehave that are regularly presented to police officers. Give specific examples of how each type of misconduct can eventuate from such opportunities.

2. How is it that the police subculture, even in today's modern world of professionalism and COP, can support and even generate police misconduct? What types are most prone to be supported by the subculture?

3. How is it that ineptitude constitutes the overwhelming majority of instances of police misconduct? Since most misconduct is about transgressing general orders, do you think that it is appropriate that this type be handled informally, by sergeants?

4. Discuss Klockars's idea that there is no such thing as a definition of "excessive force." Do you agree? What are the consequences of this fact?

12-7 ◉ ETHICAL SCENARIO

A business's burglar alarm sounds in the middle of the night, and a police officer responds to a hardware store. She finds that the large front window of the store has been shattered and the cash register has been pried open. When the shop owner arrives, he informs the officer that all of the money is still in the till. Then the owner says to the officer, "You know, I'll have to make an insurance report. And there will be a deductible. Why don't you take the cash? It's no loss to me." The officer is alone with the shop owner, it is the middle of the night, no witnesses are present, and the shop owner *wants* her to take the money, as a gesture of what the owner considers to be good faith and support for the local police.

What does the officer do? Of course we can agree that she should not take the bribe money. No one who is reading this book and, therefore, is interested in police ethics will dwell upon that question. But bribing a police officer is a serious felony. Does the officer arrest the man for attempted bribery? Does the officer give the man a stern lecture and a warning about the potential consequences of bribing a public officer? Does the officer give a positive, supportive speech about how those days are long gone? All of these are ethically defensible acts. Which do you favor?

12-8 ◉ WRITING EXERCISE

Perhaps the most troublesome reality about the use of excessive force is that there are multiple causes of it. Of the five kinds of police misconduct, at least three of them can lead to this type of deviance. Because this is true, there is no one "cure" or approach to doing away with it. Write an essay engaging all of the multiple causes of excessive force that you can think of. Then spend some time in your essay reflecting upon how all of this creates quite a frustrating reality for police officers, police leaders, police review systems, and students of police behavior.

12-9 ◉ KEY TERMS

antisocial personalities: Like sociopathic personalities; personality structures of people who are dangerous and aggressive, and who neither learn from their mistakes nor are deterred by punishment.

burn-out: Propensity for people in high-stress occupations to end up losing their exuberance and mental edge.

conflict theory: Built upon the analysis of Karl Marx, this sociological school of analysis suggests that social norms and institutions are controlled by economic elites that pass their desires down to the masses.

deviant subcultures: Cultures within cultures that possess their own norms and values, that deviate from the norms and values of the dominant society.

greed and opportunity: Formula that explains both crime causation and police deviance causation.

never explain, never apologize: Police axiom from the post-political era suggesting that explaining or apologizing is an indication of weakness and, therefore, is to be avoided at all costs.

rational choice theory: Crime causation theory suggesting that crime is caused by people weighing potential rewards against potential sanctions and deciding to misbehave in a rational manner.

rationalization techniques: Modes of thinking used by deviants to explain to themselves how they are not bad people even though they misbehave.

sociopathic: Form of behavior of people who are dangerous, aggressive, and antisocial and who neither learn from their mistakes nor are deterred by punishment.

strain theory: Sociological theory of Robert Merton suggesting that there exists a strain or tension between those socially prescribed goals and institutionally defined methods of obtaining the goals in any society and the goals and methods accepted by some citizens.

stratification: The level of economic differentiation in any given society, or the gaps between the economic experiences of the rich, the poor, the middle class, and so forth.

CHAPTER 13

Practical Applications

"In this life, you don't have to prove nothin' to nobody but yourself."

—From the movie *Rudy*

So, what can be done proactively about the development of ethical officers? What are some strategies that might be pursued in an effort to instill ethical conduct in the first instance, and create accountability when officers have erred? Who might influence the young officer to create and to apply a personal, professional ethic? What types of informal behavior control mechanisms might be effective in generating ethical behavior on the street? And finally, what sorts of police review mechanisms might be most effective at creating accountability when police officers have been accused of misconduct?

In this chapter we will engage first in a discussion about the most important strategies in this regard, those that are informal and have to do with leadership. Influenced profoundly by their sergeants, less so by middle managers, and indirectly by the chief, individual police officers tend to be very responsive to efforts to motivate them to create and live by a personal ethic. Sergeants in particular serve as mentors, coaches, and teachers for young police officers. In this capacity, they can influence police work for decades to come in a positive or negative direction.

Second in significance are informal administrative systems. From the police academy to the FTO to internal police review boards, police ethics can be influenced in important ways by semiformal processes. Finally, in this chapter we will discuss and compare several types of police review systems. Internal affairs processes, civilian review boards, and hybrid systems that attempt to take advantage of the strengths of each of the other two types will be explicated and compared. These review mechanisms often generate controversy due to the volatile and politicized nature of their machinations, especially where the use of force by the police is concerned.

13-1 • LEADERSHIP

First and foremost, where we are discussing informal accountability or formalized police review systems, we must consider the importance of police leadership. From police officer due process rights to the power of the subculture, there are severe limitations placed upon formalized review systems. Because of these and other, pragmatic limits of reform, the most important impact that can possibly be brought to bear on police ethics is exercised by police leaders.

A. The Sergeant

As is true with teachers and coaches, the most important leader in the life of the individual police officer is the immediate supervisor, the sergeant. When conducting his research into the police officer's experience, Muir asked his officers about the influence exerted by various actors in the departmental hierarchy. Muir found that "the chief, the deputy chief in charge of the Patrol

Division, and the watch commander were, in comparison, remote and minute men, seen from afar and infrequently. The patrol officer saw none of them as being so crucial to his own development, for good or ill, as his sergeant." (William K. Muir, Jr., *Police: Streetcorner Politicians* [Chicago: University of Chicago Press, 1978], p. 235)

How and why do sergeants maintain their critical importance in the lives of individual officers? In some places, sergeants have input into the process of assigning officers not only to particular beats but to particular shifts and teams. When doing so, they exercise a level of power within the organization that is paramount in the lives of individual officers. The sergeant is close enough to the individual officer to provide a pat on the back for positive behavior. In a profession known to be largely populated by people who often expect the worst, and who experience negative evaluations from the public on a regular basis, the sergeant can bestow respectability on an officer. In some departments sergeants can impact upon vacation assignments and days off. Even extra overtime hours can be tendered by the sergeant, and that means extra pay.

When the sergeant assists in solving particularly risky or delicate encounters, he or she actually impacts upon the safety of officers. The sergeant can take "heat" from above when negativity rolls "downhill." In departments where there are implicit quotas ("targets") for arrests and/or citations, the sergeant can steer new officers in the direction of **"duck hunting ponds."** Taken together, the sergeant can bestow "skills, knowledge, safety, self-respect, freedom from blame, friendship, better jobs, extra money, and even a sense of moral context." (Ibid., p. 240)

The sergeant should allow for innovation and tolerate mistakes on the part of subordinates. Here is where the sergeant can protect the younger, learning, growing, maturing officer from harm. The administration is just too far removed from the street officer to have much of an impact on day-to-day operations. Add this together with the fact that most mistakes are never brought to light, and the sergeant has a great deal of latitude within which to

BOX 13.1

THE SERGEANT'S STRATEGIES

- Provide specific, important rewards for good works
- Allow for innovation and mistakes
- Teach circumspection about the use of force
- Encourage the avoidance of subcultural negativity
- Motivate, coach, teach, and persuade
- Encourage the development of the personal ethic

aid the officer in the creation of a personal ethic through experimenting with what does and does not work.

Our friend Muir often tells his students that when writing one should endeavor "to teach and persuade." That is, in written work, one seeks to teach the reader about the subject matter involved and to persuade them in one direction or another. What better little phrase could there be for a contemporary sergeant to utilize to help with his or her focus when dealing with subordinates and their key role as ethical advisor? "Teach and persuade."

Sergeants provide the glue that keeps things together. Their efforts at coaching, mentoring, and teaching beat officers bring meaning to the otherwise sterile dictates of the law and of police policy. The first and perhaps most important teaching job required of sergeants is that they nurture in their subordinates an understanding of and a feeling for the ethical elements of police work. It is absolutely essential that they prepare young officers in particular

BOX 13.2

ALLOWING FOR MISTAKES

A young police rookie shows up at the scene of a domestic disturbance. When the rookie suggests to an irate husband that he must quiet down or he'll have to be "taken outta here," the husband responds with indignation and states, "If you think you're man enough." The young officer immediately takes offence to this challenge to his manhood and grabs the man by the shirt. The man responds by grabbing the officer by his shirt.

The rookie's sergeant arrives at that exact moment. He calms down the husband who, in fact, is not really any threat to the police. He separates the two, and he handles the detail without incident or arrest. Later, the sergeant sits the young officer down and talks him through the event, suggesting a number of alternative strategies for its resolution. The sergeant believes that the rookie has performed poorly—has made several important mistakes—but he understands the macho mentality of the young man. He remembers how young and inexperienced the rookie is. And he handles the entire situation informally, in a "just between you and me" manner. In this way, the sergeant acknowledges the rookie's mistakes, encourages learning, and, at the same time, develops a level of trust upon which he can depend in the future. The sergeant has "allowed for mistakes" without being too officious or judgmental. And he has probably taught the young officer several important lessons.

for the frustrations that will visit them on the street. Only if officers understand in an intellectual sense some of the troublesome, paradoxical stresses that are operable on the street, will they be able to avert some of the pitfalls of unethical conduct.

A second critical substantive piece of teaching for the sergeant relates to the use of power and force. As Klockars told us, there is no definitive understanding of what appropriate force is. So the sergeant is the key person in developing the sort of circumspection that police officers must have about the use of force. In particular, the sergeant needs to work consciously upon the subcultural norm of overkill. The immediate supervisor must understand the paradox of face, and thus why police officers tend to cleave to the idea that they have to "win and win big" when confronted by citizen violence. The sergeant must attempt to dispel the idea that excessive force has any place in police work.

Third, and in conjunction with the above point about force, the sergeant needs to do everything possible to dissuade police officers from sticking by those subcultural norms that are most deleterious to the best interests of justice. Aside from overkill, the sergeant must endeavor to lessen the distance between the police and the public. Nothing good ever comes from the "us against them" focus. A good sergeant will teach police officers that to explain or to apologize is neither a sign of weakness nor counterproductive to the interests of the police. The contemporary police officer must understand that COP requires a closely knit, ongoing relationship between police and public.

B. The Middle Manager

Caught between the proverbial rock and a hard place, the **middle manager** faces a tough challenge. He or she serves as the glue that holds together upper level policy makers and the line officers on the street. In our current COP era, they aid teams to develop day-to-day strategies that aim at implementing policy developed above. Then, as the second part of their job, middle managers evaluate implementation strategies and, also, they evaluate and assess police officers.

COP attempts to create a much more open and direct relationship between middle manager and individual street cop. In the past, the lieutenant, and certainly the captain, was such a removed persona from the individual officer on the street that they sometimes did not even know the names of all of their charges. Today, this distance is still a part of the reality of the relationship, and understandably so. If we want the sergeant to play the role of mentor and coach and teacher and so forth—which we do—then an authority figure of one sort or another must exist within the departmental milieu, and the middle manager is that person.

However, it is equally true that this officer–lieutenant/captain relationship has changed today. If we truly want there to be collegial problem solving under COP, with middle managers and sergeants as **facilitators** and resources for today's empowered agents of change on the street, then the middle manager just cannot remain as aloof as was previously the case. The middle manager must be capable of both being supportive and understanding (motivational), and being swift and ruthless (coercive), whenever either is required. Middle manager creativity is required to perform the balancing act required to do both at once, of course. So the middle manager must be at once aloof and available, and support sergeants as they influence the creation of internalized codes of ethics.

C. The Chief

Because he or she can be far removed from the individual police officer, the chief executive of a police organization can have little effect upon specific officers. But chiefs have a critically important impact when sending out messages to the entire organization. The chief of police must operate within

© Jose Gil/Shutterstock.com

The chief of police must teach democracy and legality at the same time.

an ongoing paradox, that of **teaching democracy and legality** at the same time. Police officers must be hired, trained, and disciplined on a regular basis with an eye toward ensuring that they have an appreciation for the law. Everything they do must be done legally, and this must be a serious principle that drives the organization. But also, the police must have an appreciation for democracy—for the rule of the people. Especially in an era of COP, they must understand that they serve the citizens of their community and need to be as responsive to public concerns as they can possibly be.

The people will sometimes call for the most outrageous of police actions. To ignore calls for illegal action from the citizenry, and thus ignore the principle of democratic rule, is to cleave to the law. No amount of rationalization can create a situation wherein the chief can take the easy way out and behave unethically in order to please the citizenry.

The chief can do two important things to send out important messages about ethics. First, when a person makes it to the sergeant's level there is an open window with respect to the machinations of internal affairs (IA). At that moment it is possible for the newly minted sergeant to spend a week or so in IA. Even if that experience merely involves being shown around and then interviewing a complainant or two, the idea is to make sure—in the long run—that each and every sergeant in the entire department understands the substance of the IA process and how important the chief believes it to be. Second, in order to send out an important, "no-nonsense" message about how the department is run and what is prioritized, the chief should put the best and the brightest investigators into IA. In police work it is traditional to put the most intelligent and fast-rising people of the organization into homicide and/or robbery as they pass through the ranks. This is why investigators from those bureaus or divisions are often referred to as "the varsity" by uniformed officers. The same can be done with regard to IA. If the chief takes care to place such people into IA on a regular basis, over time the subculture will learn that the chief is serious about what goes on in IA.

13-2 ● NON-JUDICIALIZED ACCOUNTABILITY

It is important to consider non-judicialized accountability mechanisms for two distinctive reasons. First, this is where and how most police misconduct is handled. It is done informally. Second, it is within this process that police leaders have their most obvious and ongoing chance to make a difference in the world of police accountability by using their imaginations and creativity.

A. The Academy

A critically important point relating to the academy was made initially in our preface. Traditional police academy training (or what passes for it) with regard to ethics is lacking in time. Cadets experience only a couple of hours worth of speechifying by someone from internal affairs in an entire 15-week academy experience. Also, the time spent is focused upon negativity, discussing how not to mess up. As we noted at the outset, this book is one attempt to create the sort of tool that can be utilized to discuss ethics from a positive perspective at the academy. Accountability and professionalism can increase if and only if academy training begins to take ethics seriously.

B. The Field Training Officer (FTO)

Of course, after the academy comes the in-the-field training accomplished with a **field training officer (FTO)** at the rookie officer's side. This process ought to be

Ethics training in traditional police academies has tended to be either minimal or nonexistent.

© Jerry Portelli/Shutterstock.com

BOX 13.3

THE CREATIVE LEADER

Some years ago at a medium-sized sheriff's department a rather wild "cop party" occurred involving numerous young deputies in questionable conduct. The behavior was neither violent nor was it made public. But it was undoubtedly the sort of misconduct that could embarrass the department if it were to reoccur.

Upon hearing rumors about the outlandish behavior involved, a thoughtful watch commander decided to react to it in an informal manner. He quietly called in several of the young officers involved and, one by one, gave them a dressing-down.

The commander (who would eventually rise to become sheriff) told each of the young men that while he understood being young and energetic, he nevertheless also knew that they could do permanent damage to their careers if they persisted in this type of behavior. Simply acting as an older, fatherly figure, the captain made a distinctive impression upon the young officers . . . and they never again were involved in such shenanigans.

This type of creative leadership is juxtaposed with how many leaders might approach such rumors, with officiousness and the machinations of internal affairs. Had that type of officiousness been visited upon the young officers, they might very well have reacted with diffidence and self-righteous indignation, buoyed up by the fact that the misconduct did not in fact ever embarrass the department or become public.

the focal point of a great deal of consideration paid to ethics in general and to the proactive creation of the individual officer's internalized ethic in particular. But several problems plague FTO programs. One is that experienced officers are given little financial incentive to participate. Furthermore, given the amount of time and paperwork involved, the average number of years of experience possessed by FTOs today has dropped down to less than two years' worth of seniority. This is hardly the ideal level of experience to create a substantively effective program.

The modern leader needs to take the FTO process seriously, as it has been proven to be an effective tool in the overall professionalization process. Motivating experienced officers to participate is critical. Upper-level leaders can be creative (utilizing choice assignments, vacation times, and so forth) to attempt such motivation. The best and the brightest veteran officers should be involved in the process.

C. Police Departmental Review Boards

Some jurisdictions have their own in-house **police officer review boards.** Most of these boards are utilized for shooting-related incidents only. They involve using the expertise of experienced professionals to analyze incidents, make recommendations for training, and sometimes for sanctioning errant officers. They operate independently of IA in most places, and their make-up is different from that of IA. Instead of having what is clearly an adversarial approach to the consideration of accusations of impropriety, shooting review boards often take a more collegial approach to their topic. Led by experienced professionals, and often populated by training division teachers and firearms instructors, the shooting review board is often a fact-finding, problem-solving group that is more interested in analysis and change than it is in retribution and blame.

13-3 ● POLICE REVIEW SYSTEMS

It is a very complicated endeavor when one wishes to compare police review systems. Nothing about it is straight-forward. There are multiple issues involved: the judicial fairness of the process, the thoroughness of investigations, the objectivity of decision making, the political "salability" of the system, and so forth. There are multiple personal interests involved. There are the rights and liberties of the complaining citizen, of the accused officer, and of witness citizens and officers. And finally, making a fair and objective analysis is troubled by perceptions—sometimes based in truth and sometimes in prejudice and mythology—of individuals and collectivities that are within and without the process. In analyzing the several types of systems that exist, the following set of criteria have been created.

A. Criteria of Evaluation

How would one compare and contrast police review systems? What questions should be asked when attempting to analyze whether the idea of civilian review, almost a century old now, is or is not more effective than internal systems? The answer comes in a multiple approach involving four distinctive sets of questions.

Integrity.   To begin with, any review system has to be evaluated as if it were a miniature criminal justice system. It has a process for receiving complaints that must be evaluated with respect to its openness. It cannot be too complicated, too inaccessible, or too intimidating. It cannot "chill" the right of American citizens to petition their government for redress of grievances.

It must conduct investigations that are objective, fair, and thorough. This cannot be accomplished with any preconceived ideas about the guilt or innocence of accused officers. It cannot favor either complainant or officer. It must leave no stone unturned in its efforts to obtain the truth of what happened. Taken together, an effective police review system must have

integrity. Whether conducted by police officers in an IA section or by civilians on a civilian review board, the decisions must be judicially correct and take cognizance of procedural law. Taken together, these are the integrity issues of the system.

Legitimacy. An issue of critical importance to anyone who wishes to compare police review systems is how people outside of the system *perceive* it to be working. That is, no matter what the substantive reality is of the system's integrity, it is absolutely crucial that people *believe* the system to have integrity. If people in the community that is being policed and in the general police officer corps believe the system to have integrity, that is an important plus. If they believe the system lacks integrity, then the system has problems. We call this criterion **legitimacy,** but it is, in fact, *perceived* legitimacy that is involved here.

Learning. Completely separate from our first two criteria is the question of police officer **learning.** Do errant officers mend their ways when they have been guilty of minor forms of misconduct? When officers are found culpable for minor transgressions and are therefore not terminated, do they change their behavior? Given the fact that almost all confirmed misconduct falls into this category, it is another critically important function of the overall accountability system.

BOX 13.4

THE (SLOW) DEATH OF THE "BLUE CODE OF SILENCE"

For generations, American police officers—both individually and as a collectivity, as the subculture taken together—were known to "cover" each other when any member of the group was accused of misconduct. Even after the invention of the idea of police accountability during the early years of the era of reform, for an extremely long period of time the police in America were known to live by the "blue code of silence." This informal code suggested that no member of the police officer corps should ever cooperate with investigations into the misconduct of others.

This code, so universally acknowledged, accepted, and observed for generations, has slowly fallen by the wayside in most places. Today, investigators into police corruption of authority in particular find a substantial amount of support from the officer corps. When doing research into police review, one of the authors found any number of examples of police officers who had been fired from their positions on the strength of investigations into misconduct (the use of excessive force in particular) *that had been initiated by other officers* and not by citizens.

BOX 13.5

CRITERIA OF EVALUATION FOR POLICE REVIEW SYSTEMS

- Integrity   = Openness, objectivity, and fairness of systemic processes
- Legitimacy = Externally held perceptions of systemic integrity
- Learning   = Propensity for errant police officers to change their behavior in a positive direction
- Cost   = Fiscal impact of review upon local budgets

Cost. Finally, we must consider how much review costs. As we shall see in a moment—when directly comparing the systems—despite all of its potential, civilian review in particular is extraordinarily expensive to operate. It is far more expensive that any other form of review.

B. Comparative Police Review Systems

Since the **Wickersham Commission** of the early 1930s, the idea of having someone other than the police review allegations of police misconduct has been a controversial topic. First attempted in just a few places, and not with much staying power, civilian review boards have now been put into place in a substantial number of locations across America. The central debate in this field is that between the champions of civilian review and the defenders of IA systems. The overwhelming majority of allegations of police misconduct are allegations of ineptitude and they are invariably dealt with by police leaders at the immediate supervisory level. But often enough, allegations of police misconduct come from citizens. And the study of police review systems is about analyzing who should deal with such citizens' complaints.

There are three main types of review systems. There are internal police-operated review mechanisms, civilian review boards, and hybrid systems that include elements of both the police and civilian systems. Let us consider them each briefly here.

Internal Affairs. *Internal affairs* is a generic term that refers to all review systems operated by sworn police personnel. The law in most states requires that police departments have in place a system for the acceptance and investigation of citizens' complaints. But most police organizations receive so few complaints of police misconduct that their case load of complaints is very small. Thus, most police organizations investigate citizen allegations of misconduct on an ad hoc basis. Such investigations are usually assigned by the chief of police to a trusted middle manager—typically a lieutenant. In only a few, very large departments are there enough complaints to warrant having a separate body called IA.

IA processes are completely in-house. Allegations are accepted at police headquarters, statements are given to police investigators, investigations are done by the police, outcomes are decided by IA personnel, and sanctions are handed out by the chief when officers are found guilty. Everything is done by sworn police officers. These investigations are done in secret and the results are kept from the public, even from complaining citizens.

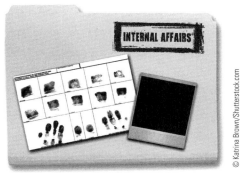

Internal affairs conducts investigations into misconduct that are in most places thorough and professional; the problem is that most people outside of police circles do not believe this.

There are good, solid rationalizations behind allowing the police to conduct such investigations. First, it is assumed that because of their expertise, police officers will do the most thorough and effective job possible of investigating. Second, it is assumed that police investigators and leaders are driven to maintain the cleanest organization possible. Not only with regard to individual cases, but with respect to keeping the image of the police department clean and professional, the idea is that the police are the best people to conduct such inquiries.

Third, it is assumed that no one from outside the police organization will be familiar enough with the multiple standards of conduct to which the police must be held. Only police officers will know the combination of the law, general police practices, and specific regulations well enough to hold other police officers accountable. Fourth, it is argued that no one outside a given police department will understand enough about the specific operational reality of how beats, high crime areas, and personnel issues are handled within that department. Thus, no one outside the department will know how and why operations are carried out the way they are.

Civilian Review Boards.   Initially just an idea that was considered by those who distrusted the police, the concept of civilian review has grown pronouncedly in the past few years. Today, there are approximately 70 civilian review boards or hybrid review systems that investigate citizen complaints against the police. Civilian review is evolving quickly. As the name implies, **civilian review boards** are populated by non-police people who accept, investigate, and adjudicate citizens' complaints.

There are a number of solid, logical reasons for civilian review boards. They offer the complaining citizen an alternate, civilian-run location for making their initial complaint. This is done because it is assumed that some citizens are intimidated by being required to go to police headquarters in order to file a complaint. Second, investigations are conducted by civilian, non-police personnel. It is assumed by proponents of this type of review that civilian investigators will bring more objectivity to the process. Third, the process is more open. Not only are investigative files made available to the public in most places but public hearings are often conducted. These are semi-judicialized hearings that include participants from both sides of the investigation. So the process of civilian review is accomplished in the open and by non-police personnel.

Hybrid Systems.   There are important strengths in each of these processes, but each also has its drawbacks. So in some jurisdictions, systems have been developed that are **hybrid review systems.** They attempt to take advantage of the strengths of both internal affairs and civilian review boards, without sacrificing the integrity of the process. One such system operates as the Office of Citizen's Complaints (OCC) in Kansas City, Missouri, and it is this system that we will discuss briefly here.

At the OCC, citizens may make complaints either at a police station or at the OCC office. Civilians interview complainants, outline allegations, and initiate complaint cases. Then the complaints are handed over to the police department's IA for investigation. The OCC monitors these investigations. OCC civilians can suggest investigative strategies at the outset and then audit the investigations. Finalized investigative reports are open to the public, unlike in the IA system.

Police officer guilt or innocence is determined by the director of the OCC. The director then advises the chief of police about this decision. On those rare occasions where the director and the chief do not agree, the two get together and review the investigation and come to a mutual agreement. Thus, the OCC system is partly civilianized and partly operated by the police.

C. Analysis

Before we move to compare these systems to each other directly, it is important to note several non-intuitive research findings relating to police review systems. First, comparing systems operating in parallel, it turns out that IA tends to find police officers guilty of misconduct slightly *more* often than does civilian review. Such findings have been reported in several jurisdictions. Second, it has been found that a large majority of police officers that work in jurisdictions that *do not* have civilian review are against the idea. However, when officers are surveyed who work in jurisdictions that *do* have civilian review, they believe it to be a good idea—and by a large margin. With these rather counterintuitive findings in mind, let us turn to make a direct comparison of these systems.

The major strengths of the IA system are several. First, professional, experienced police investigators conduct the inquiries. They are conversant with the law, the substance of how the police are trained, and the pragmatic operations of the local department—including beat differentiation, shift assignments, crime patterns, and so forth. So the systems have integrity. Second, today's internal police investigators tend to take their responsibility very seriously; they see themselves as the guardians of the police image and of police professionalism. Rank and file officers take internal review seriously too, because it represents review by their peers. Internal systems thus possess legitimacy—in the eyes of the police. Investigated officers tend to learn from their mistakes if they are found to be at fault by other police officers. The weaknesses of IA review are: (1) it operates completely in secret, (2) it suffers from the perception—externally—that it is unfair to citizens, and (3) it may conduct investigations with an inappropriate deference to subcultural values.

The strengths of the civilian review system are also several. First, it is much more open to the public than internal review. Second, its investigatory findings are open to the public. Third, the decision-making phase includes open hearings, which avail not only complaining parties but the public in general an opportunity to witness the process. Both of these dynamics suggest that the civilian system possesses legitimacy—in the minds of the citizenry. The weaknesses of civilian review are: (1) sometimes its investigators are not conversant with police practices and with local police operations, (2) police officers tend to ignore its dictates, considering them to be irrelevant to their profession, and (3) it is expensive.

The reason that civilian review is expensive is that where it operates in a genuinely independent way, completely removed from the police departmental apparatus, it usually operates in parallel with internal systems. Because the law requires the police to do their own investigations, there are two systems operational—the internal one and the external one. And the taxpaying public must foot the bill for both.

Which system is best? The answer seems to be that the balance between civilian review and internal review presented by the hybrid system is best. It enjoys several of the advantages of the internal system: (1) investigations are done by police officers, (2) rank and file officers who are sanctioned must respect the fact that experienced police officers have found them to be culpable, and (3) it leaves the disciplining to the chief and to the chain of command. It thus possesses integrity. Research indicates that it is accepted and respected by police officers too, possessing legitimacy among the police.

On the other hand, the hybrid system enjoys several of the advantages of the civilian system: (1) it is more accessible to receiving complaints at the input stage of the process, (2) it is much more open than the internal system, allowing the public access to its findings, (3) it is largely run by civilians with a civilian administrator making final decisions in concert with the chief, and (4) because there are not two systems operating in parallel, the hybrid system is not expensive. It costs about as much to run the hybrid system as it does to run the IA process. Finally, (5) the externally perceived legitimacy—what citizens think about it—of the hybrid system is greater than that of the IA process. So the hybrid system seems to work to utilize the strengths of each of the other forms of police review and does so in a fiscally responsible way.

BOX 13.6

 CIVILIAN REVIEW: SOME SURPRISING FINDINGS

The extensive research reported in Perez's 1994 book *Common Sense about Police Review* included several counterintuitive findings with regard to the review of police conduct by civilian boards. To wit:

- Civilian review boards are actually slightly *less* prone to find the police guilty of misconduct than are internal affairs systems.
- While police officers who have no experience with civilian review are almost universally against it—feeling that it will be biased and unfair to police officers—those officers who *do* have experience with civilian review are not against it.
- Minority police officers—whether or not they have experience with civilian review—tend to support the idea of civilian review, and by a wide margin.

Douglas W. Perez, *Common Sense about Police Review*
(Philadelphia: Temple University Press, 1994)

D. The Ideal Process?

After all of this comparative analysis it behooves us to take a moment and reflect upon what sort of police review process might very well be optimum. What would that look like? What would be prioritized?

Informality.   First, such a system would take cognizance of the importance of handling as many minor instances of misconduct as possible in an informal manner. The overwhelming majority of instances of police misconduct, and even of citizens' complaints, involve minor, non-threatening sorts of misbehavior. These are little offenses that are not the sort for which an officer might be terminated. They should be handled informally because such a process is most likely to create not only positive relations between the police and their community, but positive behavioral change on the part of errant police officers.

Union Cooperation.   Police unions defend errant officers universally, no matter *what* they might have done. Is it possible that at some point in the future police professional organizations might consider accountability to be a concern of theirs? Might police organizations treat errant behavior in the same way as do the American Medical Association or the American Bar Association and create peer groups that look into allegations of misconduct? For as much as this sounds far-fetched, it would be an extremely important step—one that would significantly encourage the acceleration of the process of professionalization.

Review Boards. Currently operational only in Toronto, Canada, the optimum hearing board is one that includes the perspectives of the citizenry, the legal profession, and the police. When the Toronto board sits openly in judgment over a case, there is a three-member panel that includes a police officer, a lawyer, and a citizen. Thus, three varying perspectives are brought into play at the moment that decisions about police officer culpability are made.

No-Fault Discipline. Finally, a growing dynamic throughout America, and unfortunately not often utilized in the world of policing, is the idea of **no-fault discipline.** First envisioned more than three decades ago in the business world, no-fault discipline is utilized when employees have transgressed some rule, but have not done anything that would warrant termination. This form of discipline is particularly utilitarian because it does not tend to create the type of diffidence that traditional systems do.

Most police officers tend to believe that civilian review boards will be unfair to the police; most civilians believe that they will be more objective than internal affairs.

Having analyzed in a comparative way the several forms which police review takes, we now turn to engage two final ideas about accountability strategies.

13-4 ● WHAT CAN ONE OFFICER DO?

In police organizations where personal gain–type misconduct is not the norm, it is easy enough to avoid it. The personal commitment to behave ethically made by an individual of good character is sustained in such organizations by a subculture-wide understanding. However, in organizations that have a history of such corrupt behavior and that still maintain the blue code of silence, the road of the individual officer who wishes to avoid it may be much harder. As the story of Frank Serpico shows (see Box 13.7), it can be a long, lonely, uphill fight to avoid such temptations and to behave in a professional manner.

BOX 13.7

THE STORY OF FRANK SERPICO

Frank Serpico was a young man in New York who had always wanted to be a police officer. His dramatic story has been told in several books and in a popular Hollywood movie. Serpico was sworn in as a New York police officer in the 1960s. Surrounded by corruption, both on the part of uniformed officers and detectives, Serpico vowed never to take graft and to do his job honestly. Initially, he was left alone by corrupt officers and seen as a sort of comic figure in the department.

But when he worked his way up the assignment ladder and became a detective, this changed. Serpico began to receive threats relating to the corruption he was avoiding. The corruption he witnessed was so rampant and offended his sense of ethics so profoundly that he began to participate in internal investigations into corruption. This participation amplified the threats to the extent that he feared for his life. He feared corrupt police officers would kill him to cover up their misdeeds.

Eventually he was shot on duty, attempting a drug bust, under circumstances that suggested he was left without cover by his fellow (corrupt) cops. Frank Serpico had to retire at a very young age from his beloved profession because of the bullet that remained lodged in his head and because both he and the department understood that his safety could never effectively be guaranteed.

But that is no excuse for going along with behavior that is unethical. No good fathers or mothers would accept the "everybody's doing it" excuse from their children, and professional police officers cannot be any different. Finding those officers within the organization who are committed to genuine professionalism can help. Keeping in contact with them—professionals outside of a deviant subculture—will avail the ethical officer of much-needed support.

In the long run, only the character of the individual can work toward professional competence and against such odds. We are left with the old adage, "It is better to light one candle than to curse the darkness." Who you are and what you are made of is what avoiding these temptations is all about. The officer of good character will find within himself or herself the sustenance to do the job honestly, effectively, and ethically without reference to rationalizations and excuses about what others are doing.

13-5 ● CHARACTER REVISITED

We cannot finish this discussion without referring back to our discussions about character. In a real sense, everything police officers do at any time in their lives indicates what kind of people they are and thus paints a picture of their character. Nothing—no matter how private or personal—can be left out of our analysis of a person's (or police officer's) character.

As surely as character determines one's competence as a professional, it is fashioned and exhibited in everything we do every day. Thus, we might suggest that nothing in the life of a powerful agent of the state (police officer) is personal and private. That, of course, is an unacceptable idea to us as Americans accustomed to constitutional protections regarding privacy. But it does give us food for thought regarding how the competent professional must approach this issue of personal misconduct. The professional police officer must be constantly vigilant with regard to his or her own personal behavior. We are our own consciences, and nothing and no one outside of our own souls should be remotely as important to us as our own evaluations of who we are and how we ought to act.

13-6 ◉ SUMMARY

This chapter has run the gamut from discussing the power of police leadership for creating ethical standards of conduct to considering the utility of informal accountability mechanisms to engaging the controversial debate between internal and external review systems. Along the way, we have seen that when any sort of misconduct occurs that is not the type for which termination might be apposite, informal systems are best. This is a universal principle.

It is now time for our discussion to turn in the direction of our final set of chapters, those that suggest future directions in the field.

13-7 ◉ TOPICS FOR DISCUSSION

1. Consider the multiple roles of the sergeant, as teacher, mentor, and coach. When is the sergeant a coach? When, in fact, is the coaching metaphor not a good one?

2. Discuss the lack of training in ethics at the traditional police academy. Why is this unacceptable? What sorts of changes do you favor? Do you think that the discussions included in this book should be included in an academy curriculum?

3. Make an argument that the only reasonable way to investigate allegations of police misconduct is to trust them to people outside of the police culture. Then make the opposite argument—that only police officers are knowledgeable enough to accomplish this job effectively.

4. Given your knowledge of the politics of police unions, do you think they will ever change and take police accountability to heart? Why or why not?

13-8 ⊙ ETHICAL SCENARIO

Internal affairs schedules an interview with a police officer. After some initial angst, the officer relaxes a bit when he realizes that he is not the subject under investigation. It is another officer who works on the same watch. As the questioning progresses, the officer being interviewed realizes that what is at issue is a Dirty Harry–like piece of alleged misconduct. The officer being investigated has been accused by the local gang leader and drug dealer of lying in court. What should the officer being questioned do? It is one thing to cooperate with an investigation focusing on officers who might be taking money from a drug dealer in exchange for not arresting him. It is quite another thing to cooperate with an investigation into the behavior of an officer who was only trying to get the gang leader/drug dealer off of the streets. Again, what should the officer do? What *will* the officer do? What would you do?

13-9 ⊙ WRITING EXERCISE

Review Box 13.6. Construct an essay engaging the counterintuitive findings in this box. Such an essay should not only focus on the specific points mentioned but also on how important it is for today's contemporary officers to understand them. Civilian review is a movement that is growing rapidly. The police just about everywhere will have to deal with it at some point in the near future. Why is it important that they understand what this box suggests about the civilianization of police review?

13-10 ⊙ KEY TERMS

civilian review boards: Police review systems that are operated entirely by non-police civilians.

duck hunting ponds: Locations where police officers can write tickets easily due to the numbers of speeding motorists.

facilitators: Role that middle managers (usually lieutenants and captains) play in today's police world of COP.

field training officer (FTO): Experienced officer who teaches rookie police officers out on the street after they have attended the police academy, but before they are allowed to police on their own.

hybrid review systems: Police review systems made up partly of civilians and partly of sworn police officers, such as the OCC in Kansas City, Missouri.

integrity: Concept involved in evaluating police review systems having to do with the openness of the process, its investigatory thoroughness, and the objectivity of its outcomes.

learning: Concept involved in evaluating police review systems having to do with whether or not the system generates change in errant police officer behavior.

legitimacy: Concept involved in evaluating police review systems having to do with how the integrity of the systems is perceived externally.

middle manager: Police supervisor between sergeant and upper level management; usually a lieutenant or captain.

no-fault discipline: System that sanctions errant behavior using positive counseling and training.

police officer review boards: Internal boards used by police departments to review the use of firearms and/or force.

teaching democracy and legality: Paradoxical reality for chiefs of police who must balance doing both at once, even though they often conflict with each other.

Wickersham Commission: The first major commission looking into the operations of the American criminal justice system and the police in particular; met in 1932.

PART IV

Implications

In Part IV, we will use all that we have discussed to accomplish two tasks. First, in Chapter 14 ("The Law Enforcement Code of Ethics") we will relate our ethic to the code of ethics that has underwritten the practice of police work for many years. We will find that while it has its critics, it is a thoughtful, educated, and professional code of conduct that is of practical utility for those in police service on the street every day.

Second, in Chapter 15 ("Being a Good Officer") we will engage in a discussion of how the contemporary professional officer can actively work at developing an ethics-based competence to be effective as a proactive member of today's police force. These will be critical discussions for the thoughtful reader.

CHAPTER 14

The Law Enforcement Code of Ethics

Chapter Outline

"Any officer who takes this [Law Enforcement Code of Ethics] seriously will quickly learn that he cannot do what the code seems to require. He will then either have to quit the force or consign its mandates to Code Heaven."

—Michael Davis, criminologist

Most professions have a code of ethics, and police work is no exception. This chapter will analyze the Law Enforcement Code of Ethics (see Box 14.1) and apply our ethical perspectives to its tenets. We will see that various schools of thought regarding what it means to be a good person, a good police officer, and to do good works in life are all included in the ideas and ideals embodied in the code. Along the way, we will discuss some criticisms of the

BOX 14.1

THE LAW ENFORCEMENT CODE OF ETHICS

As a Law Enforcement Officer my fundamental duty is to serve mankind; to safeguard lives and property; to protect the innocent against deception, the weak against oppression or intimidation, and the peaceful against violence of disorder; and to respect the Constitutional Rights of all men to liberty, equality, and justice.

I will keep my private life unsullied as an example to all; maintain courageous calm in the face of danger, scorn, or ridicule; develop self-restraint, and be constantly mindful of the welfare of others. Honest in thought and deed in both my personal and official life, I will be exemplary in obeying the laws of the land and the regulations of my department. Whatever I see or hear of a confidential nature or that is confided to me in my official capacity will be kept ever secret unless revelation is necessary in the performance of my duty.

I will never act officiously or permit personal feelings, prejudices, animosities, or friendship to influence my decision. With no compromise for crime and with relentless prosecution of criminals, I will enforce the law courteously and appropriately without fear or favor, malice or ill will, never employing unnecessary force or violence and never accepting gratuities.

I recognize the badge of my office as a symbol of public faith, and I accept it as a public trust to be held so long as I am true to the ethics of the police service. I will constantly strive to achieve these objectives and ideals, dedicating myself before God to my chosen profession . . . law enforcement.

code that suggest it is unrealistic and, therefore, might do more harm than good. Finally, we will argue that the code, with its somewhat vague, general, and idealistic construction, is an important focal point for any serious police officer who seeks to become the consummate professional.

In the tradition of jadedness that often is associated with the police, some officers criticize the Law Enforcement Code of Ethics because of its vagueness. Police officers are often known to consider that their world (community, department, job, etc.) is "going to hell in a hand basket." To some extent, criticisms of the code are understandable as emblematic of this propensity. We have noted along the way here that criminal statutes that are vague can be declared unconstitutional for the very logical reason that they are difficult to understand. Laws are considered to be unfair to citizens if they are so vague as to be unclear or indiscernible. Equally, some critics consider that the code is unfair to police officers for the same reasons.

However, such a criticism is out of place when discussing codes of ethics. Such codes are *meant* to be broad, general, and universal. If they are to accomplish their task, professional codes of ethics need to be vague and general, perhaps even nebulous. By its very nature, a code of ethics will only be useful if it avoids any propensity to be too focused or specific. To some extent, the most important function of a code of ethics is to be broad enough to encompass many aspects of the professional's duties and responsibilities. As such, a code is *supposed* to be vague, in the sense that it is meant to be a general statement of philosophy.

14-1 ● CODES OF ETHICS

The function of professional **codes of ethics** is often misunderstood. This is not only because people sometimes believe them to be too vague, as noted above, but also because they are presumed to be unrealistic. A common criticism of an ethical code is that it is driven by **platitudes.** This criticism is often unfounded and indicates a profound misunderstanding of the function of such codes. Only if a code is meaningless or genuinely silly is it subject to the critique that it is platitudinous.

A. A Code Typology

There are several different types of codes of ethics, ranging from the specific to the general in their approaches to defining appropriate conduct for professionals. At the most specific or practical level, some codes are like police departmental general order manuals. That is, they provide mandatory sets of rules, usually very long and complicated, which serve as the basis upon which discipline is meted out when professionals misbehave. Such codes are practical in the sense that they attempt to present specific, how-to-do-it type rules for day-to-day professional life. They are impractical, however, due to their unwieldy, complicated, voluminous nature. They are "just too big to handle."

The second type of code provides general statements of principles or guidelines that present values for an organization. Many police departments and organizations of all kinds, private and public, have these sets of guidelines. Some of these codes are elaborate, expanded **mission statements.** They are attempts to give organizations long-range rather than immediate, short-term goals at which to aim. They are less specific than general orders but more task-oriented.

Perhaps the ultimate "aspirational code" in our world is the Ten Commandments. This code makes up part of the ethical canons of the Jewish, Christian, and Islamic religions.

The third type of code of ethics is the **aspirational code.** This type constructs an ideal model of what the profession should be like and how the professional should behave. The Law Enforcement Code of Ethics is such a code. It has its critics precisely because it is not specific and is, instead, idealistic and general. Yet its strength lies in just this idealism. The specifics of how one behaves as a police officer and handles various types of details are so complicated and variable that any attempt to categorize them is doomed to failure. As is usually the case with general order manuals, lists for police officers consisting of what to do and what not to do are so voluminous they are almost worthless. No one could read, study, understand, and completely memorize them. Thus, general order manuals are voluminous and impossible to discern, and are used as shields behind which administrators hide if and when officers break a rule of any kind.

B. The Tone of the Law Enforcement Code

As an aspirational code, the Law Enforcement Code of Ethics aims to construct an idealized vision of how the competent and ethical professional should be and behave. It sets general guidelines and presents ethical tenets toward which the professional should aim. Understanding that no one is a saint under the pressure of life on the street as a cop, the code suggests an ideal at which all competence-seeking, professional police officers ought to aim in both their private and professional lives.

One more point is apposite before we begin a specific analysis of the code. The tone that the code takes is a purposeful one. It sounds idealistic and **utopian.** It presents a vision of the consummate professional's approach. It is philosophical. It sounds like an oath. This is all done on purpose. It is neither a general order manual nor a mission statement. It is neither too protracted and inclusive nor too terse and amorphous. It is aimed at a middle ground in between the two extremes. Its tone is idealized but thoughtful, generalized but useful. It aims at perfection yet avoids being too romantic.

Let us consider the specifics of the code and analyze how what it suggests parallels several ethical perspectives.

14-2 ● THE CODE

One of the complications and paradoxes of police work is that no one set of classical, ethical principles is always applicable to every situation and to every moment's challenges. Our discussion has included three ethical perspectives. We have treated Kant's ethical formalism, Mill's utilitarianism, and our own ethic to live by, which is a combination of the other two. We will discuss all three of them here.

A. Ethical Formalism

The Law Enforcement Code of Ethics presents numerous principles that logically fit into the perspective of ethical formalism. In a Kantian sense, the code suggests that some principles by which police officers ought to live are absolute. No amount of rationalization, before or after the fact, can (or should) be used to explain away or to make excuses about police officer behavior that transgresses these principles. Examples of these absolute principles are included in Box 14.2.

It behooves us to consider an example from these principles to illustrate what we mean when we say they represent absolute rules of conduct. In Chapter 11, we discussed Kania's idea that the acceptance of small gratuities by police officers might be a good thing. The familiar and friendly relationship that might develop between police officer and gift giver would be good for

BOX 14.2

ETHICAL FORMALISM: ABSOLUTE RULES OF POLICE CONDUCT

The code includes several elements or principles that can be considered absolutist in their content:

- I will be exemplary in obeying the laws of the land and the regulations of my department.
- I will never act officiously or permit personal feelings, prejudices, animosities, or friendship to influence my decisions.
- I will enforce the law courteously and appropriately without fear or favor, malice or ill will.
- I will never accept gratuities.

developing the type of bonds between police and citizens that community-based policing is all about. This is, at any rate, Kania's suggestion. What could possibly be wrong with such an idealized recommendation?

In asking the police officer to vow to avoid taking any gratuities whatsoever, the code asserts that the acceptance of any gifts involves a dereliction of the officer's duty. No matter how small the gift might be, the code suggests that—in a Kantian, absolutist sense—when an officer accepts any gratuity, he or she makes a moral judgment that sacrifices the authority of the badge in the name of favoritism. While it is seldom stated, there is an implicit **quid pro quo** in such citizen–police interactions. If the gift-accepting officer meets the gift giver on the street in a citizen–police encounter, it is always assumed that something other than an anonymous interaction will proceed. The chef who drives drunk on the way home from the restaurant, the waitress who slips through a stop sign without coming to a complete stop, the tire salesman who squeezes the speed limit—all of these people present ethical problems to police officers if they have allowed themselves to be the recipients of chef or waitress or tire salesman gratitude in the form of gifts, deals, or discounts.

The absolute statement against taking gratuities rejects utilitarianism. It reminds us about the slippery slope idea that small gratuities can lead to larger ones, that grass eating leads to meat eating. The code rejects Kania's suggestion that some small gratuities should be ignored and accepts the argument that any gift carries with it the assumption of future, reciprocal favors. If free coffee is given to a police officer merely because the coffee-giver is in a good mood and feels a sense of community, and not because the coffee-giver expects any future potential favor, then why is free coffee not given out to everyone? Free cups of coffee mean something, the code suggests. And no matter what they do or do not mean to the coffee-giver, they cannot be accepted by the police officer.

The code's logic here may seem too rigid and judgmental to some. In fact, a discussion about just this type of police–citizen interaction is often conducted at police academies. And historically, police officers, even when they are "mere" cadets, have tended to rail against the suggestion that "just" a free cup of coffee is unacceptable. But this is precisely

© tom carter/Alamy

A Prince George's County police graduate is sworn in at the graduation of 59 new recruits. Police officers are sworn in so often that they sometimes forget the importance of taking oaths . . . particularly their oath to uphold the Law Enforcement Code.

the strength of the Kantian approach. It presents duties and responsibilities that are absolute and not open to debate. It thus creates a code of behavior that is unassailable, not subject to interpretation, not open to be manipulated in light of what someone (or anyone) considers the practical realities of particular circumstances. Ethical formalism is thus the friend of the rule of law. We know from earlier discussions that deviants use any number of ways to rationalize misbehavior. Ethical formalism suggests an absolute set of principles from which there is no escaping into the world of rationalization and excuse making.

Now, applying our ethic to live by, we suggest that the code is correct here and that Kantians, equally, are correct. To accept any gratuity is to create a future situation that involves favoritism. This flies in the face of our principle of applying justice equitably. Even a simple free cup of coffee can create in the police officer/citizen interaction of the future a dynamic that is troublesome (see Box 14.3). With regard to free coffee or half-priced food in particular, why do it? Why create such a problem in the first place?

BOX 14.3

THE TROUBLE WITH LITTLE GRATUITIES

A restaurant in a violent and crime-ridden area provided local police officers with free cups of coffee and half-priced food whenever they showed up. This, the owners and operators reasoned, kept the police around and was good insurance against being robbed. Indeed, the establishment sat in the middle of the highest crime area in the county and was never robbed or burgled.

One night after closing, the cook of the restaurant was stopped on his way home by several of the officers who benefited from this practice. The cook was drunk, very drunk, driving all over the road in an extremely dangerous manner. What were the officers to do? This man was a sort of patron to the officers, having given them substantial gifts over the years. They were in an awkward situation. While the man was not arrested, the two officers involved resolved never to go to the restaurant again and never to take free food or coffee again because of the situation in which they had been placed.

In making this decision, these officers were showing the good character that it takes to question one's perspective and behavior. They were acting as competent professionals, completely in tune with our ethic to live by. And they were rejecting Kania's suggestion that accepting small gratuities can benefit the police–community relationship.

B. Utilitarianism

The rest of the examples of elements of the code highlighted in Box 14.2 are equally absolutist in their content. But there is more in the code. Its pronouncements also include principles that are clearly utilitarian. (Both act utilitarianism and rule utilitarianism are in evidence in the code.) With regard to our ethic to live by, these tenets of the code ask the professional officer to think about the principle of beneficence. Specifically, they are about doing good and preventing or eliminating evil.

Box 14.4 exhibits examples of the code's utilitarianism relating to specific situations—asking officers to focus on those citizens immediately involved in details on the street. Clearly, one of the most important charges all police officers must undertake is to "protect the peaceful against violence or disorder." But what this principle means and how one might go about attempting to attain it on the street present the police officer with a complicated, variable set of concerns and tactics.

Who are "the peaceful"? This is not always clear. Are "the peaceful" those citizens who want quiet to prevail on a Saturday night in their neighborhoods? If so, then are partygoers in some sense criminals or, at the very least, people who mean to do harm and create disorder? In celebration of the turn of the year, are not New Year's Eve revelers decent, law-abiding citizens? Do they not have the right, on such an occasion, to make some noise, dance and play, drink and cavort, and so on? How about students celebrating the victory of their school's national championship hockey team? How about the revelers on election night in 2008, discussed in Box 14.6?

In considering what do about such a loud party call on New Year's Eve, officers must strike a balance. Utilitarianism tells us these balances will not

BOX 14.4

UTILITARIANISM: RESPONDING TO SPECIFIC SITUATIONS

The Law Enforcement Code of Ethics includes the following principles that should be considered variable in that they require police officers to take into account the numerous ramifications of taking action in specific cases. Police officers should always attempt to calculate the consequences of different potential solutions to everyday problems as they seek to:

- Safeguard lives and property
- Protect the innocent against deception
- Protect the weak against oppression or intimidation
- Protect the peaceful against violence or disorder
- Maintain courage in the face of danger, scorn, or ridicule

always look the same and the appropriate police actions to be taken will not always take the same form. If called to suppress the noise of a New Year's party, police officers may very well tend to leave the partiers alone and even to explain to the complaining citizen that "this is one of those times when making noise and partying is appropriate." Equally applicable, if a loud party is occurring in a college town on the night of the big football victory, the police may be understandably reluctant to challenge the rights of the Saturday night noisemakers.

But if a loud party takes place on a Tuesday night—a school night and a work night—doesn't the formula change? Isn't it true that the same people making exactly the same amount of noise in exactly the same place might be guilty of disturbing the peace on a Tuesday night when they were not guilty of it on a Saturday night? Common sense and utilitarian logic say these are two completely different situations. The competent, professional police officer needs to understand this, act accordingly, and be comfortable with the fact that there is no single appropriate, legal, ethical rule for dealing with loud parties that fits all conditions and all occasions.

Focusing on the specific circumstances of the individual incident, police officers, operating as utilitarians, have to acknowledge that what is fair, just, and (even) legal in dealing with such details will never be quite the same. This is true even though their charge to "protect the peaceful from violence and disorder" must always be taken seriously and acted upon. Our ethic to live by, which includes this utilitarian idea, suggests that on such occasions genuine "harm" is not at issue. But "doing good" is. It is one of the multiple roles of the police to help people to pursue good in their lives and to allow them, whenever possible, the individual responsibility to make choices. When merely loud noise is at issue, such a situation is present.

In Chapter 8, we differentiated between two types of utilitarianism. The Law Enforcement Code of Ethics includes both. Recall that rule utilitarianism involves variable tactics and outcomes that are not as closely related to the specific incidents presented to the police officer as act utilitarianism is. That is, while rule utilitarianism shares with act utilitarianism a lack of absolutism, it nevertheless is different because it focuses on the long-term implications of police decision making. When police officers conduct themselves as rule utilitarians, they make decisions—which may differ from time to time, place to place, and circumstance to circumstance—that focus on the importance of the consequences for society if all police officers behaved in the same way all of the time.

Box 14.5 exhibits examples of principles included in the code that exhort individual officers to consider the larger and long-term significance of their decisions on the street.

While not setting absolute principles of determining right conduct (as ethical formalism does), utilitarianism sees police behavior in a broader context. Certainly, no one could argue with the assertion that the police officer has a "fundamental duty to serve mankind." This principle is basic to the police service and is central to our ethic to live by. Anyone who enters police

BOX 14.5

UTILITARIANISM: THE LONG-TERM IMPORTANCE OF INDIVIDUAL DETAILS

The Law Enforcement Code of Ethics contains several utilitarian principles that require the police officer to take a broad view of the best interests of the community and of justice in the long run. When making individual decisions regarding choices of action, police officers must remember that:

- My fundamental duty is to serve mankind.
- I must keep my private life unsullied as an example to all.
- I must be honest in thought and deed in both my personal and official lives.
- I recognize the badge of my office as a symbol of public faith, and I accept it as a public trust to be held so long as I am true to the ethics of the police service.

work without this in mind, without this underwriting principle as the central reason for his or her professional commitment, is in the wrong business and should get out. The trials and tribulations of the workaday experience, the personal stresses and sacrifices involved, the tests and challenges of police work, all of these are prices not worth paying unless they are underwritten by a commitment to serve humanity, to help people.

But what does such a fundamental duty involve? What does it mean to serve mankind? Police officers make so many decisions that affect people's lives directly that they are consistently challenged to take the broader, long-term interests of people, communities, and justice into account. As we have taken great pains to point out, balances must be struck between the interests of individual citizens. Exactly when, if ever, do the interests of society outweigh those of the individual?

For example, one of the classic questions used (usually by oral board examiners) to confront police officer candidates is, "What would you do if you stopped a drunk driver and found that it was a friend of yours?" This question presents the would-be police officer with an ethical dilemma of the tallest order. While it doesn't happen very often on the street, being confronted with the criminal behavior of a friend or acquaintance does occur. What to do?

Utilitarianism (like our ethic to live by) suggests that in deciding whether or not to make an arrest, officers must consider the long-term interests of justice. If friends are let go, then utilitarianism suggests everyone should be let go. Given the impact drunk driving has on our society (thousands of deaths every year are caused by it), how could an ethical officer live with letting a friend go? The answer is that the ethical officer cannot. Such a decision (to let a drunk driver continue driving) would not only constitute a failure to remove harm (the principle of beneficence), but it would also interfere with the principle that justice ought to be applied equally to all.

So included in our ethic to live by is the utilitarian logic that the long-term implications of making a rule for everyone must be taken into account in a way that protects the interests of all. In the drunk-driving example, the ethical officer must either make an arrest or, if time and situation permit, hand the detail over to another officer. In doing this, the officer would be ensuring that the law is applied objectively and in an evenhanded manner to all.

The vagueness of the Law Enforcement Code of Ethics is so pronounced that there are critics who consider it to be a waste of time. It is toward this discussion of the criticisms of the code that we now turn.

14-3 ● THE CODE AS A "TARGET"

Even though the Law Enforcement Code of Ethics is widely accepted as a meaningful set of principles upon which to focus the police officer's career, it has its critics. As criminal ethicist Joycelyn Pollock states, "One argument is that the code specifies such perfect behavior that it is irrelevant to the realities of most officers. The wide disparity between the code and actual behavior is detrimental to the validity and credibility of the code."

Aside from this argument—that it is impossible and impractical to live up to the code—is another that states the code is simply too vague and confusing. It is not specific enough as a how-to-do-it guide, critics say, and merely adds confusion to the problem of the multiple, conflicting, and vague police roles that create some of the central frustrations of police work.

Is this criticism valid? Are we asking too much of police officers that they live by the code's ideals? Is it a waste of time, in the real world, to ask people to do things that are if not impossible at least extremely difficult? How do we answer these critics?

From our perspective, these critics miss the point of this or any other code of conduct. Certainly, it is extremely troublesome to expect people operating under the stresses of everyday police work to live up to the code's dictates every day. Even so, why is it a waste of time to ask people to do their best to attempt to live up to such ideals? Isn't it the height of cynicism to give up on trying to behave in an ideal way? Are we saying that because people cannot always be perfect, because they have character flaws, we should avoid asking them to try to be so? Furthermore, isn't it genuinely dangerous to build excuses into the minds of such powerful individuals as police officers? Are we not creating the excuse that because police officers cannot live up to such ideals all of the time it is acceptable for them

BOX 14.6

AN EXAMPLE OF DOING GOOD

On the night that Barack Obama was elected president of the United States, thousands of college students, at hundreds of colleges and universities across the country, erupted into spontaneous demonstrations. They came out into the streets, honked horns, sang and danced, and in many place held impromptu parades. This all occurred in the middle of the night.

Now, this was a Tuesday night. (Actually, it was very early on a Wednesday morning.) And thus it was a workday night and a school night. In many locations, the revelers were left alone by the police to party, to make noise, and—in essence—to "disturb the peace." In many places, the police blocked off side streets and took care to guide the students through their cities, making sure that nothing unsafe occurred.

The police avoided invoking the absolute dictates of the law that night, because they prioritized the job of doing good (or, in this case, allowing good) to be done in their communities.

to behave in whatever fashion they can rationalize—due to the stresses of the job?

What are the implications of giving up on such a code? We believe the long-term ramifications of this type of thinking are devastating for police officers, for citizens, for society, and for justice. For example, because many people find it impossible to avoid driving while drunk, are we to give up on applying that law? Because people cheat on their spouses, are we to give up on the institution of marriage? Because children and adults fail to learn what they should in school, are we to give up on education? And in the grandest scheme

Positive, upbeat crowd situations can sometimes provide police with an opportunity to avoid applying the law as written and, instead, do positive good.

of things, because people regularly transgress against all sorts of rules, laws, moral tenets, and ethical principles in life, are we to say that having norms and values of any kind is a waste of time?

Simply because police officers, like all people, are flawed human beings, and because it is impossible to live up to the tenets of the Law Enforcement Code of Ethics all of the time does not give us the go-ahead to abandon the attempt to do so. The reason there are rules, regulations, laws, courts, and prisons is that people fail to behave themselves when left on their own in the first place. If we say to police officers, to ourselves, that we may use the excuse that we are imperfect human beings to rationalize not even trying to be moral individuals, then more than the ethics of police officers are at stake. Such a cynical approach to ethics allows that setting up standards of conduct, being impossible to live by all of the time as they are, is an exercise in futility. If this were the case, then society and all human institutions are complete wastes of time. The law itself is a waste of time.

The Law Enforcement Code of Ethics encompasses an important set of principles, defines an ideal conceptualization of what a police officer ought to be, and sets up a goal toward which all honest, hardworking, dedicated professionals can aim. As such, it is or ought to be a critical part of the life of every police officer everywhere.

14-4 ◉ SUMMARY

In this chapter, we have gone back to our two classical schools of thought about ethics and shown how they are included in our ethic to live by. We have taken the Law Enforcement Code of Ethics apart, to some extent, and discussed how our composite ethic, an ethic to live by, applies to different sorts of ethical questions faced by police officers on a regular basis. Our examples are commonplace and not obscure by any means. In working through this process, we have attempted to indicate that the ethic to live by (see Chapter 9) is an appropriate, measured, logical way to approach ethical decision making in police work.

Equally, we have dissected the Law Enforcement Code of Ethics and shown that it is a well constructed, although vague, set of principles that translates the two principles of the ethic to live by into a larger set of general tenets. Finally, we have discussed criticisms of the code and suggested that critics miss the point, the strength of the code. We grant that it is vague and not full of specific "rules of the road," but given the multiple, conflicting, and vague roles the police have to play on the street, the code is a good attempt at presenting our ethic to live by in more concrete terms.

No one dealing with the stresses and dilemmas of police work will be able to live up to its tenets completely all of the time. But the Law Enforcement Code of Ethics is an important target at which all competent professionals can direct their efforts to live up to the principles of beneficence and justice.

14-5 ⦿ TOPICS FOR DISCUSSION

1. Read and discuss the Law Enforcement Code of Ethics, taking particular note of how vague its pronouncements are. What does it tell us about how to act as police officers and what does it leave to our own imaginations and ethical perspectives?

2. Discuss the text's example of confronting a drunk-driving friend while on duty. What would you do? What should you do? Apply Kant, Mill, and our ethic to live by to the dilemma presented to you by the competing duties to stick by a friend and to apply the law justly.

3. Critics point out that the differences between the code's dictates and the real world of police work are great. Discuss both the strengths and the weaknesses of the code's lack of realism.

4. Consider once again the criticism that the code is too vague. What sorts of pronouncements might you include in such a code if you were to make it more specific? Would that make for a better code? What utility would such a code have that the existing code lacks?

14-6 ⦿ ETHICAL SCENARIO

Sometimes police officers are offered free coffee or food when they are on or even off duty. Kania calls this "a little bit of graft," and sees it as a positive police–community relations tool. What about this? Is he correct? Is there a large difference between taking a free meal and taking money from a suspect? Does the amount of money matter? Does the value of the food matter? Should the police in fact take care not to fall into *any* type, level, or degree of graft or corruption? Or is Kania's idea of "keeping it in perspective" the way to go? What do you think and why?

14-7 ⦿ WRITING EXERCISE

Write an essay engaging this topic: Some say that the Law Enforcement Code of Ethics is a classic example of utopian platitudes. We often hear from "the good ol' boys" that today's advanced education of police officers and this code too are unrealistic exercises that waste the time of the police. Worse, some of the good ol' boys suggest that taking such "book learning" seriously can actually be dangerous. What do they mean? Do you agree or disagree? Why? What might you say to a good ol' boy if you could discuss this with him? (Instructors: Have your class bring their essays for reflection and analysis and then lead them in a discussion and/or debate about this classic contemporary argument.)

14-8 ◉ KEY TERMS

aspirational code: The type of professional code that suggests optimum conduct and ethics; posits behavior for the professional that is of a desirous nature.

codes of ethics: Sets of professional principles that comprise written explications of the internalized codes of ethics that are emblematic of the professions.

mission statements: Pronouncements of the principles and goals of organizations, institutions, businesses, and, in recent years, even individuals; in vogue for the past three decades, these composite manifestos explicate directions and foci of varying specificity.

platitudes: A flat, trite, or weak utterance; a dull or stale truism; a commonplace remark.

quid pro quo: One thing for, or in place of, another; tit for tat.

utopian: Refers to *Utopia*, a book about an ideal city and society written by Thomas More; also the name of the ideal city.

CHAPTER 15

Being a Good Officer

Chapter Outline

"Police work is just common sense. Any good person can become a good police officer."

—Skip Stevens, retired police officer

As our introductory quote from an experienced police officer indicates, there is nothing magical about becoming a good police officer. Good officers are not in any sense born into this world. Any good, hard-working, honest person with the requisite physical abilities and intelligence can become a competent professional if he or she is willing to work at it. This final chapter discusses how a person might approach that task—the job of becoming a competent professional—in the face of all of the stresses, opportunities for failure, and ethical dilemmas presented by life on the street in uniform.

In this chapter, we will tackle several sets of ideas that provide strategies for such an endeavor. We will talk at length about the educational experience that informs the modern police officer's professional preparation. The call for police officers with higher education was heard often during the tumultuous 1960s. Numerous **riot commissions** at that time reflected upon how the police handled—or to be more accurate, mishandled—both inner-city riots and college campus antiwar demonstrations. While the cause of some riots were localized and multiple, one factor was constant: Each and every commission that looked into the disorders of that decade decried the inability of the police to handle such situations in a reasonable manner. Not only were the police poorly trained, but their general demeanor and attitude indicated to riot commissions that they were completely unable to fathom what was going on in front of them. Driven by lower-middle-class **white rage,** the police of the '60s were not only disorganized and unprofessional. They were driven by racially focused hatred and an unsophisticated anger focused against middle-class college students whom they clearly misunderstood in profound ways.

Aside from discussing what college can do, and is doing, for the creation of ethical, professional police officers, we will also reflect upon the work of Lawrence Kohlberg, who studied how people learn morality. Finally, we will once again visit William Muir and focus on his reflections regarding the development of competent, ethical police officers.

Associated Press

In the 1960s, there were numerous "police riots" wherein the police lost their composure, forgot their training—for example, swinging their batons over their heads rather than using them the way there were trained to do—and essentially ran wild.

15-1 ● EDUCATION: THE IMPORTANCE OF THE LIBERAL ARTS

Studying the **liberal arts** involves experiencing a curriculum that avails college students of general knowledge in the fields of literature, language, philosophy, government, history, mathematics, and science. Aside from this substantive focus, the liberal arts education also focuses on developing the student's capabilities of rational thought, cogent analysis, and writing or communication abilities. So there are two sets of reasons why a college experience is important for the competent professional; they are process-oriented and substance-oriented.

A. The Substance of College

Modern college programs in **criminal justice studies** expose students to practical knowledge that is of great importance. Some topics have direct, day-to-day relevance for the police officer's participation in the criminal justice system. Classes on forensics, interrogation, search and seizure, and law are but a few examples of practical areas of expertise that can be expanded in the classroom. The competence of the police professional can be greatly enhanced by continuous exposure to cutting-edge theory and practice in these important police-related fields.

But exposure to the liberal arts includes far more than such practical courses. To become a competent officer, the individual can benefit from any number of courses of study that might appear at first glance to be only remotely related to the job of policing the streets. Developing a well-rounded, broad-based understanding of history, psychology, sociology, and political science—to name but a few subject areas—is of critical importance to creating a genuinely educated and integrated individual (See Box 15.1.).

It makes good sense to understand the broad sweep of American history, beginning with the colonial experience and the struggle for independence. Understanding how and why the Revolutionary War was fought gives the officer a feeling for the central ideals of America, such as limited government and individual rights, that are underwritten by our institutions and our treasured historical documents. The Declaration of Independence, the Constitution, the Bill of Rights, and the **Gettysburg Address** all speak about American ideals that offer important insights into being a police officer.

Understanding the history of slavery and the Civil War, the two World Wars, the labor movement, the civil rights movement, and even more recent events, such as the feminist and gay rights movements, will give officers an important perspective. This perspective helps them understand the concerns of any number of different types of citizens they regularly encounter on the street. The study of the history of policing undertaken in most criminal justice programs can help a contemporary officer understand just what COP is all about. This in turn helps officers deal with the changing expectations with which people confront police officers today.

BOX 15.1

THE SUBJECT MATTER

A liberal arts education is meant to afford the student a broad-based experience that includes study in a multiplicity of fields. A partial list of particularly important subjects might be:

- **Philosophy:** To inform the professional experience with a base-level understanding of the ethical component of competence

- **Political science:** To inform the student about the basic structure of American governmental institutions and electoral processes

- **History:** To understand the development of Western liberalism and American history in a way that draws the student into focused discussion about slavery, the civil rights movement, the antiwar movement of the '60s, and the Industrial Revolution

- **Psychology:** To deal with the basics of personality formation, criminality, adolescent psychology, and deviant behavior

- **Sociology:** To understand the creation and maintenance of social norms, values, and institutions with specific reference to gang theory, subcultural dynamics, and informal norm maintenance

- **Science:** To develop a basic understanding that informs forensics

- **Composition:** To develop an expertise in communication skills

Psychology courses on abnormal psychology, personality development and disorders, **adolescent psychology,** and individual techniques for rationalizing deviance all help create a broad understanding of the human experience. In sociology, students learn about the creation of norms and values, about the dynamics of subcultures, about diverse cultural experiences and expectations, and about deviance in particular. All of this is good because it expands an officer's ability to be competent in dealing with diverse people and with the complicated dynamics that create both deviance and normality in the world.

In political science, students learn about American institutions, how change occurs in the law, and the place of the courts, legislatures, and the police in our complicated system of governance. The multiple stresses and conflicting goals and roles of the American police can create frustration in the modern officer who does not possess an understanding of these subjects. Ignorance of these topics can make an officer prone toward Dirty Harry–type cynicism. This in turn can make effective policing impossible.

This is a partial list, of course. When college students take **general education** courses or what used to be called **breadth requirements**, they are expanding their general knowledge of people, the world, their own society, other societies, and the place of people in both the world and society. Since there are a multiplicity of other courses that might add to general knowledge, the liberal arts education is about obtaining the most broad-based academic experience a person can get.

B. The Process of College

But there is certainly more involved in the experience than engaging in study and discussion of these particular subjects. The college endeavor involves opening up oneself to all sorts of experiences and points of view that a person does not otherwise tend to engage in life. (See Box 15.2.)

Some people joke about this, due to their own lack of perspective (to be honest), but at college one hears about poverty, racism, ignorance, disease, war, and pestilence. One hears discussions about **communism, socialism, fascism, totalitarianism, capitalism,** and so forth. One interacts with people of different races, religions, ethnic backgrounds, and personal and national histories.

In essence, what this is about is questioning. That's what the word *liberal* refers to. In one's college years, one is in the business of "questioning what you think you know." This is because, due to false media images, dishonest politicos or corporate executives, and incompetent teaching at lower levels, most people enter into college with a substantial amount of misinformation stored in their brains. The college experience is about questioning and seeking answers—not just to the obvious questions, relating to what one knows one does not understand, but with regard to other questions about myths and falsehoods that one buys into when one lives in a world where people do not regularly question authority figures or official information peddlers.

BOX 15.2

REASONS FOR POLICE OFFICERS TO GO TO COLLEGE

- To experience interactions with different types of people, points of view, ideas, and ideals, and to practice questioning one's own perspective
- To learn specific subject matter related directly to police work and related in general to the development of an understanding of culture and American institutions
- To expose officers to perspectives on life other than those found in the police subculture

All of this is what college entails. The better the college, the more questioning goes on. And the more questioning that goes on, the more educated (in a general sense) a college student becomes.

15-2 ● KOHLBERG: DEVELOPING MORALITY

Psychologist Lawrence Kohlberg studied the development over time of morals and ethical thinking. He found that people go through certain stages in putting together an increasingly sophisticated understanding of morals. After several decades of studying moral development, Kohlberg made some specific suggestions about how ethical thinking could be encouraged.

When looking at the list in Box 15.3, it seems to be an argument supporting the utility of a broad-based college education. While Kohlberg didn't specifically refer either to college or to police officers, for the purposes of our discussion the idea that a liberal arts education is important for development of police professionalism is central.

The experience of taking college classes, whether or not one goes to college with the intention of obtaining a degree, is good for police officers for two reasons. The first flows directly from Kohlberg's list. It has to do with the historical rationale for obtaining a broad-based, liberal arts education in general. As Kohlberg seems to be telling us, the process-oriented reasons for including the college experience in the life of the professional police officer have to do with engendering an appreciation for moral thinking. Kohlberg's list suggests it is good to have practice in hearing other people's points of view, confronting ethical dilemmas, questioning one's own ways of thinking, arguing logically, and so on. What these experiences amount to are in a procedural sense what the college experience is all about. Going to lectures, taking notes, studying them, reading books with varying points of view, getting into debates in the classroom and over coffee, writing papers wherein you take a stance and defend it logically—all of these things are what

Time & Life Pictures/Getty Photos

In contemporary times, it is a good sign that so many police officers feel free to behave as caring, empathetic people, especially when they are dealing with adolescents, who are going through the most challenging and awkward phase of their lives.

BOX 15.3

KOHLBERG'S IDEAS FOR ENCOURAGING MORAL GROWTH

Psychologist Lawrence Kohlberg described the following criteria as being necessary for moral growth. Being exposed to these types of experiences expands the individual's ethical understanding and thus helps to engender professionalism:

- Being in situations where seeing things from other points of view is encouraged
- Engaging in logical thinking
- Having the responsibility to make moral decisions and to influence one's own moral world
- Being exposed to moral controversy and thus to ambiguity
- Being exposed to the reasoning of an individual whose moral thinking is more sophisticated than one's own
- Participating in creating and maintaining a just community

college is about. People who experience them are participating in the ongoing creation of their own increasingly sophisticated points of view, the expansion of their perspectives on life, and the enhancement of their personal ethical frames of reference. This is one way in which people improve their character.

Wrestling with other people's points of view is something police officers do every day on the street. Facing up to ethical dilemmas and making the right choices are skills that can be improved with practice. Understanding that life on the street is full of ambiguities and being comfortable living with them are equally life-process-oriented skills that can be enhanced in any individual. Participating in democratic and semi-democratic community development is the essence of the modern community-based policing officer's role. Kohlberg's entire list of experiences involves practicing skills and honing abilities that are directly relevant to the process involved in successfully policing a beat in a competent and professional manner.

A critical part of developing professionalism is going through the kind of intellectual experience college involves. But the college experience involves more than merely being around and intermingling with people who hold other points of view and who have different experiences in life. There is a great deal of substantive learning college can bring to any individual that helps to engender professional competence in the police officer. This is the substance-oriented reason for going to college.

Kohlberg asks us to engage the central reason for obtaining an education—that the learned individual possesses a certain wide-ranging understanding of life, the human experience, their society, and its institutions

Time & Life Pictures/Getty Photos

and history. This learning creates in the individual the ability to go about the job of policing, of moralizing for others, and of making life-changing decisions for them using a foundation that integrates intelligence, problem-solving abilities, substantive learning, knowledge about the real world, and insightful intuition.

Lawrence Kohlberg is the most famous of the psychologists who have studied how we obtain our conceptualizations of right and wrong or how we obtain our views of morality.

This laundry list of reasons for experiencing at least some college courses is powerful enough in itself. But there is one more important reason for officers to be involved in ongoing educational experiences throughout the course of their lives in uniform. As we have discussed in several places, the police subculture is a powerful entity that can give an officer support and a sense of belonging. But membership in such a subculture can also have its drawbacks.

Spending most if not all of one's time with members of a single-minded group can make any individual narrow, limited, and stilted in his or her view of life and approach to problem solving. Such experience can convince a person that there is only one way to see the world, to think about life, to live and enjoy life, and to define the good in life. Because it is a basic principle of our diverse American culture that none of these things is true, spending time in such an exclusive club can have terrible consequences for the interests of justice on the street, given that "the police are the law."

Continued experiences in the world of ideas and the give and take of intellectual life, coupled with ongoing interactions with people who are not members of the police subculture, can have a positive impact on any officer's perspective. And that impact will, in turn, impact the competence of the officer and his or her ability to do the job effectively. This then has its effect upon the lives of citizens on the street in the form of engendering a feeling for justice and the rule of law that is not compartmentalized into any one school of thought about what the good in life is.

15-3 ● MUIR AND CAUSING PROFESSIONALISM

Aside from "being educated" in this general sense, Muir had some important thoughts about police professionalism. He studied a group of young police officers and reflected on how it was possible to engender or create professionalism in the young officer in particular. As adults we are already formed in some sense and already possess, when we enter the police service, our own individual sets of values, expectations of life, understandings of right and wrong, and personality structures. In other words, we have our character in place. Yet change is possible. Muir talked about how conscious work toward expanding one's practical knowledge and intellectual horizons can enhance one's ability to deal with the moral dilemmas of police work.

Muir talked about three ways in which professionalism could be nurtured: language, learning, and leadership. (See Box 15.4.) When discussing language, Muir focused on the need for police officers to be gregarious or talkative. He suggested that enjoying "chewing the fat" is integral to the job of relating to people and to both understanding and motivating them. Talking and listening to people are a part of the give and take of communicating via language. Such communication teaches the intelligent police officer about specific people, about groups of people, about the social atmosphere on a given beat, about people's expectations of the police, and about people's understanding of the good in life.

BOX 15.4

MUIR'S METHODS FOR CAUSING PROFESSIONALISM

Three factors were emphasized by Muir, not because they are the only ways in which professionalism develops, but because they are clearly factors the police themselves can control. Thus, on the job—after being hired and completing initial academy training—individual officers and police supervisors can work together to engender professionalism by focusing on these factors:

- **Language** Professional police work requires gregariousness, eloquence, and in general the enjoyment of talk.

- **Learning** Encouraged by the professional sergeant, police officers need to consistently focus on learning. On the job and in the classroom, they must expand their understanding of human nature, the law, and alternative methods of dealing with the problems of their communities and of individual people.

- **Leadership** Encouraged by the professional chief and/or upper-level managers, police officers can work in an environment that is safe from outside political influence and is permeated by the understanding that being a competent professional will bring great rewards. On the other hand, incompetence in its many forms will not be tolerated.

Experiencing this sort of interaction on a regular basis engenders professionalism by keeping the police in touch with the citizens they serve. But there is more to what Muir is saying. Muir suggests that talking to people involves teaching and persuading them about how to live a good life. Young people in particular are prone to respond to intelligent, caring, honest police officers who teach them there is a great deal to be gained by playing by the rules in life. As teachers in a curbside classroom, professional police officers could do more to generate peace and respect for the law and to change the lives of individuals under certain circumstances than all the rest of society's institutions combined.

Thus, understanding language and using it for good purposes is one way for the professional to get the job done on the street. Of Muir's three points, this is the most critical for our discussion because it is most directly in the hands of each individual police officer.

Muir's other two points deal with a type of learning about competence on the job that is related to the teaching of cops by their sergeants and the leadership of the chief. The learning that stems from the sergeant and the leadership that comes from the chief are important later in the careers of young officers, when they themselves become sergeants and chiefs and their own abilities to engender professionalism, as Muir suggests, are directly related to their abilities as police leaders.

15-4 • BEING A GOOD PERSON

We have come full circle in this book, back to the idea we suggested in its first pages: To be a competent, professional police officer is to cultivate the moral habits that are necessary to be a good person. There is no divorcing the police role from the individual's role as a person. There is no dividing line that separates the private life from the professional one. A person is not one human being at home and another on the job. He or she is integrated into a whole that the thoughtful, competent professional consciously cultivates.

In seeking to put together the competence necessary to be an effective street cop, the individual officer must possess a large amount of procedural expertise about how to be a cop in the practical sense. Then, too, substantive knowledge about the law, crime causation, and the criminal justice system's process is indispensable. Finally, a practical, working understanding of how a given police department works and of the expectations of a given community and its neighborhoods must round out the tremendous volume of information and skills possessed by the competent officer.

The glue that holds all of this together is the police officer's personal ethical perspective. Police work is all about character. Without an understanding of the ethical implications of the job, and without possessing the ability to solve ethical dilemmas for others, the police officer is lost in a sea of bits and pieces of knowledge that lack integration. To put it all together and become today's competent, professional officer is to possess this body of knowledge and to integrate it with an understanding of what it means to be a good person, to live a good life, and to be an ethical officer. These two entities—the body of knowledge and the ethical perspective—are worthless without each other.

15-5 • FINAL MESSAGES

In this chapter, we have discussed several ideas about how intelligent, professional officers can and must work at continually reinventing themselves. We are back to Chapter 7's ideas about working on character. Questioning, adapting, re-evaluating, and learning are at the heart of this effort. To be stagnant, to think that "I have it figured out," is to make a fatal error. No police officer has all the answers and knows exactly how to do it all. No police officer is so intelligent and so experienced that professional growth can cease. This reality defines both the best and the worst dynamics of police work.

One can never stop working on his or her professional body of knowledge and upon his or her craftsmanship. No one is ever "done" with inventing himself or herself as a police officer. This can appear to be a stressful reality because it means there is no slacking off, no time to waste on self-congratulation, no vacations from doing the hard work of self-improvement. On the positive side, it makes police work exciting and dynamic. If you are never done learning and reinventing yourself, then you are involved in a job that is never quite the same from day to day.

So here, at the end of our book, one message for readers to take with them is this: Police work is a challenging profession that provides a never-ending sequence of stimulating experiences. Officers who seek to be the best they can be must continuously strive to challenge themselves. No amount of external motivation will substitute for the personal commitment to grow and to enhance knowledge, skills, and character.

A second message woven throughout the book is that the most appropriate focal point for this growth is our ethic to live by. In embracing a consistent, relentless awareness of the requirements of the principles of beneficence

BOX 15.5

REVIEW: OUR ETHIC TO LIVE BY

- Beneficence: The *prima facie* obligation to "do good"
  - Always do good/never do harm
  - Prevent harm/remove harm
- Justice: The obligation to make "equal distribution"
  - Equality of substantive treatment
  - Equality before the law (equality of opportunity)

and distributive justice, police officers not only do good for their communities but also participate in creating dynamic lives for themselves. Cutting through all of the multiple, conflicting, and vague roles required of police officers, these principles provide a beacon toward which police officers can aim all of their efforts and from which they will, in turn, receive direction and sustenance.

This book does not attempt to create lists of dos and don'ts. Police officers do that for themselves. They always have. No matter what amount of academic training or level of experience they may possess, police officers have always made up their own guidelines and practical rules of thumb for handling different types of details. This is perfectly appropriate as long as such self-generated guidelines are never considered to be finished and as long as police officers attempt to focus their ever-changing practical rules on our two over-riding principles: beneficence and justice.

15-6 ◉ TOPICS FOR DISCUSSION

1. Consider the authors' argument that a college education is important for all police officers. Discuss how the theory of the classroom can be applied to the practical realities of life on the street. What do you think of the axiom that a college education is not necessary because "you can't learn police work from a book"?

2. Consider Kohlberg's ideas about how people obtain their understanding of morality. What do you think is missing? Is it remarkable (something about which an intelligent person should "remark") that his list is so secular, and doesn't even imply that religion, for example, is important? What do you think? Does religion actually fit in (on) this list, and Kohlberg just doesn't label it as being divorced from other experiences that develop a moral sense?

3. Refer to Box 15.4 and Muir's reflections on how to make a competent, professional officer. When discussing language, he wrote that teaching and persuading people was a big part of the job. Discuss how being the "strong, silent type" of police officer is a mistake as it alienates the officer from people and from life on the beat.

4. Other than taking some college classes, what types of non-police-related experiences, hobbies, and avocations might help to make a police officer develop, grow, and become more competent? Discuss why it is so important to stay in touch with ways of thinking outside the police subculture and to cultivate civilians as friends.

5. In your mind, for a moment, put together Kohlberg's ideas about how people obtain their conceptualizations about ethics with Muir's ideas of the three types of power. If all other things are equal on any given detail, shouldn't you expect to use coercion on younger citizens, reciprocity on

older ones, and finally, exhortation on adults? (This would be because people's notions about morality gain sophistication as they grow older, of course.) What are the implications for a police officer? Is it more ethically acceptable to treat a teenager with threats than it is to do so with an older person? Isn't that counterintuitive? How would you conceptualize this problem and solve it for yourself.

15-7 ◉ ETHICAL SCENARIO

An officer receives a complaint about sexual harassment. A tourist in San Diego wants a Mexican man arrested for "disturbing the peace" for making sexually suggestive comments about her as she strolled through the Old Town tourist area. Upon arrival, the officer finds that the man was himself enjoying the walk with several Mexican male friends. He is not belligerent and, in fact, is both compliant and confused. Because she has taken a college course on Mexican culture, the officer knows that this type of behavior is normal for the Mexican man and, in fact, is considered to be complimentary toward the woman. And too, she understands that the man was behaving in a way that substantiated his "machismo" in front of his friends.

What should be done? California law does indeed make it a crime to use lewd or suggestive language in public. But the officer believes that this detail involves nothing more than a misunderstanding between clashing cultures. What should the officer do?

15-8 ◉ WRITING EXERCISE

For the last writing assignment of the book, construct an essay that engages two questions. First, discuss what "good character" is for a police officer. Given what Aristotle, Kant, Mill, Muir, and Kohlberg have written, what are your conclusions with regard to what makes a good officer? Second, how do you now respond to the idea from the beginning of our discussions that competence and ethical behavior are directly linked with each other? Explain what is meant by the central thesis of the book: that it is impossible to be a good police officer without being an ethical one.

15-9 ◉ KEY TERMS

adolescent psychology: The study of the teenaged personality with specific reference to the trials and tribulations of going through the process of change from girl/boy to woman/man.

breadth requirements: Educational requirements at colleges and universities demanding that students take a broad-based set of courses, and not focus strictly upon their major fields of study; general education requirements.

capitalism: Merit-based economic system common to most industrialized democracies involving free market competition between business corporations and individuals.

communism: System of egalitarian economics envisioned by Karl Marx in the mid-19th century involving common ownership of all property and a "dictatorship of the proletariat."

criminal justice studies: The fastest growing major in American education, involving the study of crime causation, criminal law, and the criminal justice system.

fascism: A severe and autocratic governmental system that exercises rigid censorship and forcible suppression of its citizenry.

general education: Educational requirement at colleges and universities demanding that students take a broad-based set of courses, and not focus strictly upon their major fields of study; breadth requirements.

Gettysburg Address: Speech delivered at the dedication of the National Cemetery in Gettysburg, Pennsylvania, by President Abraham Lincoln that refocused the American ideal and reinvented the definition of our country.

liberal arts: Field of study at colleges and universities involving a broad-based series of courses aimed at providing students with a far-reaching education.

riot commissions: Ad hoc committees of prominent citizens and academics created in the 1960s to investigate inner-city riots, disturbances on college campuses, and police riots.

socialism: Economic system involving collective ownership or regulation of major industries, but individual ownership of houses and chattels; the dominant form of economy in the industrialized world.

totalitarianism: System of government involving total control over people's lives, from their individual liberties to their economic futures; examples include the former Soviet Union (a communist form) or Nazi Germany (a fascistic form).

white rage: Outrage of a significant number of white people in America during the 1960s when they believed that minorities were obtaining benefits and services without earning them.

BIBLIOGRAPHICAL ESSAY

• •

This essay is presented for the reader interested in following up on the various topics in our text. It briefly outlines some important books written in the fields through which we have traveled. We divide this piece into four areas of interest. First, we will talk about books written by sociologists and political scientists about the police in general. Second, we will list introductory texts that might be used to pursue an interest in the causes and common forms of police deviance. Third, we cite a number of studies and theoretical works about the problem of holding the police accountable for their misbehavior when it occurs. Finally, the field of criminal justice ethics and police ethics in particular will be discussed.

● POLICE WORK GENERALLY

A good reference book about the police, one which has been updated several times since its original publication in 1967, is Jerome Skolnick's *Justice Without Trial*, 3rd Ed. (New York: John C. Wiley and Sons, 1994). This work will give the reader a feel for how earlier sociologists viewed the study of the police. A good textbook on the police and police systems, one of the most widely used in America, is Samuel Walker's *The Police in America*, 3rd Ed. (New York: Wadsworth, 2010). Both of these classic works will ground the reader in an understanding of how the police are viewed and analyzed by academics.

In this text, we have often referred to William K. Muir, Jr.'s work, *Police: Streetcorner Politicians* (Chicago: University of Chicago Press, 1977). The reader may very well want to go to the original source to experience Muir's ideas directly. This book, one of the most insightful works ever done on the police, in our opinion, explains Muir's ideas about coercive power, professionalism, and developing character. It is so central to our themes here that we recommend it without reservation as the most important book for anyone seeking additional insights into all of these subjects.

Carl Klockars, again someone whom we have cited several times in this work, wrote *The Idea of Police* (Newbury Park, CA: Sage Publications, 1985) in an effort to produce a short work for students in the field. This book discusses the role and functions of the police. For an analysis of the police subculture, a central topic for those interested in this field, see John Crank's *Understanding Police Culture* (Cincinnati: Anderson, 2004). It is not only an important work in itself, it exposes the reader to the entire field of study today—citing many authors, theories, and pieces of research. Also in this regard, Perez's *The Paradoxes of Police Work* (Clifton Park, NY: Cengage, 2010) engages in extended discussion of the paradoxes engaged in Chapter 3 and elsewhere herein, and in addition focuses on the police subculture in particular.

275

A good collection of essays on various topics relating to police work—including James Q. Wilson and George Kelling's famous "Broken Windows," one of the works that spawned the community oriented policing (COP) movement—is Steven Brandl and David Barlow's *Classics in Policing* (Cincinnati: Anderson, 1996). The reader interested in the roots of COP should also read Herman Goldstein's *Problem-Oriented Policing* (Philadelphia: Temple University Press, 1990), a book that is largely given co-credit along with the work of Wilson and Kelling for the ideas and ideals behind COP.

With regard to police leadership, a classic, authoritative textbook in the field is William Geller's *Police Leadership in America: Crisis and Opportunity* (New York: Praeger, 1985). A more contemporary treatment of leadership, referring often to the ethical component of police supervision, and building upon the idea that traditional leadership is outdated, is P. J. Ortmeier and Edwin Meese's *Leadership, Ethics, and Police: Challenges for the 21st Century*, 2nd Ed. (Englewood Cliffs, NJ: Prentice Hall, 2009). Putting together both the concepts of the paradoxes of police work and a focus on leadership that eschews the command and control model, is Douglas Perez and Michael Barkhurst's *The Paradoxes of Leadership in Police Management* (Clifton Park, NY: Cengage, 2011).

II ● POLICE DEVIANCE

Victor Kappeler, Richard Sluder, and Geoffrey Alpert wrote *Forces of Deviance* (Prospect Heights, IL: Waveland, 1998), which discusses police deviance in depth. This book includes within its arguments a discussion of the work of Gary Sykes and David Matza on deviance in general, something we alluded to in Chapter 12. John Crank and Michael Caldero's work *Police Ethics: The Corruption of Noble Cause* (Cincinnati: Anderson, 2010) is an important, in-depth treatment of one type of police misconduct: the Dirty Harry problem to which we have often alluded.

Police Deviance, by Thomas Barker and David L. Carter (Cincinnati: Anderson, 1993) has become one of the essential works in the field. Its discussion of the causal factors leading to police misconduct is focused and cogent. It is cited by virtually everyone writing on the topic since its publication. *Police Corruption: Exploring Police Deviance and Crime* is a similar piece, albeit a bit more up to the minute. It is by Maurice Punch (London: Willan, 2009).

A specific treatment of what is always the most controversial of all topics with regard to policing is *Race and Police Brutality: Roots of an Urban Dilemma* (Albany: State University of New York, 2008), by Malcolm D. Holmes. While a multiplicity of work has been done in the field, this is a good, up-to-date compilation and overview.

III ● POLICE ACCOUNTABILITY

A compilation of the arguments on either side of the debate about police review systems can be found in Douglas Perez's comparative consideration of internal affairs and civilian review options (Philadelphia: Temple University

Press, 1994). An alternative take on the same balancing act can be obtained in *Managing Accountability Systems for Police Conduct: Internal Affairs and External Oversights* (Prospect Heights, IL: Waveland Press, 2008), by Jeffrey J. Noble and Geoffrey P. Alpert.

For a view from the pro-civilian review side, see Samuel Walker's *The Role of Citizen Oversight* (New York: Thomson, 2006). Also by Walker, and squarely supporting the civilian review side of the argument, is *The New World of Police Accountability* (Newbury Park, CA: Sage Publications, 2004). Walker's work is the quintessential compilation of the civilian review arguments, going back to the early 1930s when the Wickersham Commission first called for an alternative to internal review. An even more up-to-date work on the same topic is *Enforcing Police Accountability through Civilian Oversight* (Newbury Park, CA: Sage Publications, 2010) by Sander Sen.

IV • POLICE ETHICS

Joycelyn Pollock wrote *Ethics in Crime and Justice* (Belmont, CA: Wadsworth, 2011), to which we have made reference in several places. This work discusses in greater detail the philosophical perspectives to which we have referred. It also includes numerous other schools of thought, such as those of natural law, religion, and the ethics of care in a way our short work has not. Pollock sets up her philosophical perspectives and then applies them in a step-by-step manner to all areas of the criminal justice field, not just to the police.

Other good treatments of ethics in the criminal justice field in general are *Criminal Justice Ethics*, by Paul Leighton and Jeffrey Reiman (Englewood Cliffs, NJ: Prentice Hall, 2000) and *Professional Ethics in Criminal Justice: Being Ethical When No One Is Looking*, 2nd Ed., by Jay S. Albanese (Boston: Allyn & Bacon, 2007). This is a growing field, but these three works approach the topic from our positivist, from-the-ground-up perspective by beginning with some significant discussion of ethics from an historic, philosophical perspective.

We do not wish to imply that it is lacking in utilitarian value, but *Enforcing Ethics: A Scenario-Based Workbook for Police and Corrections Recruits and Officers,* 3rd Ed. (Englewood Cliffs, NJ: Prentice Hall, 2007), by Debbie J. Goodman is an example of the sort of "how not to screw up" approach that we have pointed out at the onset of our discussion here. Also in the field are *Ethics in Policing: Misconduct and Integrity*, by Julie B. Raines (New York: Jones and Bartlett, 2009), and *Ethics in Policing*, by Edwin J. Delattre (New York: AEI Press, 2006). Delattre's work in particular has become respected in this arena. Even so, neither of these works consider the philosophical underpinnings of ethics generally before they move to discuss police ethics on the street.

INDEX